The AIA Construction Management Contracts

A CONCISE ANALYSIS OF THE 2019 REVISIONS

PETER W. HAHN
DAVID A. SCOTTI
KRISTIN E. PROTAS
ALLISON TALLER REICH

AMERICAN BAR ASSOCIATION
Forum on Construction Law

Cover design by Tahiti Spears

Printed in the United States of America.

24 23 22 21 20 5 4 3 2 1

A catalog record for this book is available from the Library of Congress.

Discounts are available for books ordered in bulk. Special consideration is given to state bars, CLE programs, and other bar-related organizations. Inquire at Book Publishing, ABA Publishing, American Bar Association, 321 N. Clark Street, Chicago, Illinois 60654-7598.

www.shopABA.org

Table of Contents

About the Editors and Authors

Editors

Peter W. Hahn is a partner in the construction law practice group of Benesch Friedlander Coplan and Aronoff in Columbus, Ohio. He advises owners and contractors on issues and liability avoidance at every phase of a construction project, from the drafting and negotiation of contracts through post-project issues and construction defect claims. He also regularly advises public authorities throughout Ohio and Kentucky on such topics as construction procurement, project delivery methods, contract terms, regulatory compliance, and claims. He has spoken at national meetings of the ABA Forum on Construction Law, was an editor of the Forum's 2017 A201 Deskbook, and is a member of the Steering Committee for Division 13 (Government Construction). He is the current chair of the Ohio State Bar Association's Construction Law Committee and a former chair of the Columbus Bar Association's Construction Law Committee. Peter has a B.A. degree from the College of Wooster and a J.D. from Washington University in St. Louis.

David A. Scotti is the founder and principal of Scotti Law Group, a boutique law firm in Pittsburgh, Pennsylvania, that focuses in construction law. Mr. Scotti concentrates his practice in advising contractors, owners, and design professionals in risk management from the earliest stages of conceptual design through project completion; prosecuting and defending a broad range of construction claims in state and federal courts and in domestic and international arbitration; negotiating and drafting construction and design contracts; and serving as an arbitrator and mediator. He has been recognized as a Pennsylvania Super Lawyer for Construction Litigation every year from 2013 through 2020. Mr. Scotti is currently in his fourth year of serving as the Chairman of the Publications Committee for the American Bar Association Forum on Construction Law. He previously served on the Forum's Governing Committee for three years and as Chairman of the Contract Documents Division. He has been an affiliate member of the Master Builders Association of Western Pennsylvania since 1989 and for more than 20 years has served as the sole lawyer on the Joint Committee of the Master Builders and the Pittsburgh Chapter of the American Institute of Architects. Mr. Scotti received his B.A. from Johns Hopkins University in 1977 and his J.D. from the University of Pittsburgh in 1980.

Authors

Kristin Protas has over 13 years of experience in contract negotiations, dispute resolution and proactive claim avoidance, and has been a trusted advisor to Gilbane Building Company's executive leadership over the last five years. She was hired in 2014 as senior legal counsel; then, in 2016, she was appointed Assistant Secretary for Gilbane Building Company. In 2018, she was promoted to vice president and in 2020, she was promoted to Assistant General Counsel. Kristin currently provides legal support to Gilbane's Mid-Atlantic division, Central Midwest division, and Human Resources department. She is a graduate of the University of Michigan with a B.A. in English Language and Literature and received her J.D. from Brooklyn Law School. She is a recipient of the Diversity Fellowship from the American Bar Association Forum on Construction Law and has spoken at the ABA Federal Procurement Institute, the ABA Forum on Construction Law, the Virginia State Bar's 36th Annual Construction Law and Public Contracts Seminar, the Virginia State Bar's Second Annual Federal Contracting Seminar for the Virginia State Bar and the Associated General Contractors of America.

Allison Taller Reich focuses on all aspects of construction law, from the very beginning of a project through completion and resolution of any claims. She represents owners and developers, construction managers, design-build contractors and general contractors, subcontractors, sureties, and other design and construction industry professionals. Allison immerses herself in the construction industry and is clients' first call for all types of issues including project delivery methods and contract forms, claim and change management, project close-out processes, and dispute resolution and litigation. She strives to obtain the best possible result for her clients at the earliest opportunity. Allison is committed to her clients and understands that the issues they face—large and small—can make or break for each client. Allison is also very involved in the community, including participating in the Cleveland Metropolitan Bar Association's 3Rs Program. She also serves on several nonprofit organization boards including the Boys and Girls Clubs of Cleveland's Bridge Board and the United Way of Greater Cleveland's Board of Directors. She is also involved in several legal and professional associations including the National Association of Women in Construction and the ABA Construction Forum as a member of Divisions 2, 3, 4, 12, and 13 and a member of the Technology Steering Committee. Allison is recognized on the Ohio Super Lawyers Rising Stars list.

Introduction

Every ten years or so, the American Institute of Architects updates its major families of construction contracts. In 2017, the AIA overhauled its design-bid-build documents anchored by the A201. In late 2019 and early 2020, the AIA released its revisions to its suite of construction management documents, last updated in 2009. This book summarizes and analyzes the major revisions in this latest release from the AIA.

Like other publishers of construction contracts, the AIA's construction management documents generally fall into two categories: documents for use when the construction manager serves as the owner's adviser, and documents for use when the construction manager serves as the constructor (or at-risk). The CM-as-Adviser documents have their own form of general conditions—the A232-2019—that integrates the role of the construction manager into the existing relationships among the owner, contractor, and architect. The CM-as-Adviser series also includes the C132-2019, which is the agreement between the owner and construction manager-as-adviser.

The CM-as-Constructor series uses the A201-2017 as the form of general conditions. Many of the changes to the CM-as-Constructor documents catch those documents up to the changes the AIA instituted in 2017, especially to the A201. In addition to bringing those documents into alignment with the A201-2017, the AIA's updates incorporate trends in the construction and insurance industries, as well as in general contract interpretation, over the last decade.

This book covers only the substantive changes to the AIA's major construction management documents published in 2019 and 2020. A more thorough analysis of these documents, as well as construction management documents published by other organizations, will be covered in the Forum on Construction Law's upcoming *Construction Management Law and Deskbook*.

PART I
Construction Manager as Adviser Series

This series concerns the use of construction managers as advisers ("CMa") as opposed to construction managers as constructors (also called construction managers-at-risk). Owners hire CMas to provide professional advice, consultation, and management services as a consultant to the owner during the entire duration of the project—often from preconstruction through final completion. CMas assume less risk on a project than CMcs since CMas do not construct or self-perform any work and do not enter into any contracts with contractors. Their only contract is with the owner. They act as a consultant to the owner, coordinate the flow of information to and from the owner with the architect and contractors retained by the owner, and provide coordination, management, and information to the other parties during the course of the project.

The revised AIA documents reviewed here are:

- C132–2019, Agreement Between Owner and Construction Manager as Adviser
- A132–2019, Agreement Between Owner and Contractor, Construction Manager as Adviser Edition
- A232–2019, General Conditions
- B132–2019, Agreement Between Owner and Architect, Construction Manager as Adviser Edition

C132–2019: Standard Form of Agreement between Owner and Construction Manager as Adviser

The C132 is the agreement between the owner and construction manager as advisor. It has undergone substantial revision since the 2009 edition.

ARTICLE 1 INITIAL INFORMATION

§ 1.1 This Agreement is based on the Initial Information set forth in this Section 1.1.

(~~Note the disposition for the following items by inserting the requested~~For each item in this section, insert the information or a statement such as "not applicable~~,~~ ~~"~~" or "unknown at time of execution~~" or "to be determined later by mutual agreement~~.")

§ 1.1.1 The Owner's program for the Project:

(~~Identify~~Insert the Owner's program, identify documentation that establishes the Owner's program, or state the manner in which the program will be developed.)

§ 1.1.2 The Project's physical characteristics:

(Identify or describe~~, if appropriate, size, location, dimensions, or other~~ pertinent information about the Project's physical characteristics, such as size; location; dimensions; geotechnical reports; site~~, boundary and~~ boundaries; topographic surveys; traffic and utility studies; availability of public and private utilities and services; legal description of the site~~;~~, etc.)

§ 1.1.3 The Owner's budget for the Cost of the Work, as defined in Section 6.1:

(Provide total and, if known, a line item breakdown.)

§ 1.1.4 The Owner's anticipated design and construction ~~schedule~~milestone dates:

- **.1** Design phase milestone dates, if any:
- **.2** ~~Commencement of construction~~ Construction commencement date:
- **.3** Substantial Completion date or dates:
- **.4** Other milestone dates:
- ~~**.4** Other:~~

§ 1.1.5 The Owner intends the following procurement method for the Project:

(Identify method such as competitive bid or negotiated ~~Contract or multiple Prime Contracts~~contract.)

§ 1.1.6 The Owner's requirements for accelerated or fast-track ~~scheduling~~design and construction, multiple bid packages, or phased construction are set forth below:

(~~List~~(Identify any requirements for fast-track scheduling or phased construction and, if applicable, list number and type of bid/procurement packages.)

§ 1.1.7 The Owner's anticipated Sustainable Objective for the Project:

(Identify and describe the Owner's Sustainable Objective for the Project, if any.)

§ 1.1.7.1 If the Owner identifies a Sustainable Objective, the Owner and Construction Manager shall complete and incorporate AIA Document E235™–2019, Sustainable Projects Exhibit, Construction Manager as Adviser Edition, into this Agreement to define the terms, conditions and services related to the Owner's Sustainable Objective. If E235–2019 is incorporated into this Agreement, the Owner and Construction Manager shall incorporate the completed E235–2019 into the agreements with the consultants and contractors performing services or Work in any way associated with the Sustainable Objective.

Most of the changes to Article 1 are minor, but substantive additions were made in Sections 1.1.7 and 1.1.7.1, which provide an opportunity to insert sustainable objectives and to use Exhibit E235–2019 for further refinement of those objectives. These additions reflect growing efforts within the construction industry to deliver more environmentally-friendly and sustainable projects.

§ 1.1.8 Other Project information:

(Identify special characteristics or needs of the Project not provided elsewhere~~, such as environmentally responsible design or historic preservation requirements~~.)

§ 1.1.~~8~~9 The Owner identifies the following representative in accordance with Section 5.5:

(List name, address, and other contact information.)

§ 1.1.~~9~~10 The persons or entities, in addition to the Owner's representative, who are required to review the Construction Manager's submittals to the Owner are as follows:

(List name, address, and other contact information.)

§ 1.1.11 ~~10~~ ~~Unless provided by the Construction Manager, the~~ The Owner ~~will~~shall retain the following consultants and ~~contractors~~Contractors:

(List name, legal status, address, and other contact information.)

- **.1** Land Surveyor:
- **.2** Geotechnical Engineer:
- **.3** Civil Engineer:
- **.4** Contractors, as defined in Section 1.4:
- **.5** Separate Contractors, as defined in Section 1.4:
- **.6** Other, if any:

(List any other consultants retained by the Owner~~, such as a Project or Program Manager, or construction contractor~~.)

Section 1.1.11 now includes separate sections for the identification of "Contractors" and "Separate Contractors," defined in Section 1.4.

§ 1.1.~~11~~12 The Construction Manager identifies the following representative in accordance with Section 2.~~4~~5:

(List name, address, and other contact information.)

§ 1.1.~~12~~13 The Construction Manager's staffing plan as required under Section 3.3.~~2~~3 shall include:

(List any specific requirements and personnel to be included in the staffing plan, if known.)

§ 1.1.~~13~~14 The Construction Manager's consultants retained under Basic Services, if any:

~~**.1** *Cost Estimator:*~~

(List name, legal status, address, and other contact information~~.)~~

~~**.2** *Other*~~ *of any* consultants~~:~~ *.)*

Changes to Section 1.1.14 eliminate examples or classifications of consultants retained by the construction manager and permit open-ended designation and description of such consultants.

> **§ 1.1.~~14~~15** The Construction Manager's consultants retained under ~~Additional~~Supplemental Services:

Similar to the B132, B133, and the 2017 owner-architect agreements, the change in Section 1.1.15 reflects the AIA's distinction between Supplemental Services (which are services beyond Basic Services on which the owner and architect agree at the time of contracting) and Additional Services (which are services beyond Basic Services that arise after contracting).

> **§ 1.2** The Owner and Construction Manager may rely on the Initial Information. Both parties, however, recognize that ~~such information~~the Initial Information may materially change and, in that event, the Owner and the Construction Manager shall appropriately adjust the ~~schedules,~~Construction Manager's services, schedule for the Construction Manager's services, and the Construction Manager's compensation. The Owner shall adjust the Owner's budget for the Cost of the Work and the Owner's anticipated design and construction milestones, as necessary, to accommodate material changes in the Initial Information.

Many of the substantive changes in the 2019 series of construction manager documents arise out of changes to the 2017 owner-contractor agreements, enhanced available technology, and changing expectations of parties (and particularly owners which have a strong interest in having projects completed faster to start generating revenue or meet tight schedules). As a result of those changes, design and construction phases occur concurrently more frequently on projects. One of the risks inherent with fast-tracking projects or beginning construction before design is fully complete is that changes to scope and budget can occur after construction has begun and will need to be accommodated and accounted for. Owners, therefore, may have to acknowledge and accept more changes to scope and cost than they did previously, and the revisions to the AIA agreements reflect that reality.

> **§ 1.3** The parties shall agree upon protocols governing the transmission and use of Instruments of Service or any other information or documentation in digital form. The parties will use AIA Document E203™–2013, Building Information Modeling and Digital Data Exhibit, to establish the protocols for the development, use, transmission, and exchange of digital data.

One of the fastest-growing technological developments in the industry is the use of Building Information Modeling (BIM), which requires its own set of protocols and processes for effective and efficient use. Section 1.3 of the C132 specifically provides for BIM and incorporates the E203–2013, which outlines the protocols, processes, and best practices to be implemented on the project to ensure effective use of that technology.

> **§ 1.3.1** Any use of, or reliance on, all or a portion of a building information model without agreement to protocols governing the use of, and reliance on, the information contained in the model and without having those protocols set forth in AIA Document E203™–2013, Building Information Modeling and Digital Data Exhibit, and the requisite AIA Document G202™–2013, Project Building Information Modeling Protocol Form, shall be at the using or relying party's sole risk and without liability to the other party and its contractors or consultants, the authors of, or contributors to, the building information model, and each of their agents and employees.

New Section 1.3.1 identifies the consequences for reliance on BIM without agreeing to protocols like those listed in the E203 and G202, placing the risk of that reliance on the using party.

> **§ 1.4** The term "Contractors" refers to persons or entities who perform Work under contracts with the Owner that are administered by the Construction Manager and Architect. The term "Contractors" is used to refer to such persons or entities, whether singular or plural. The term does not include the Owner's own forces, or Separate Contractors, which are persons or entities who perform construction under separate contracts with the Owner not administered by the Construction Manager and Architect.

New Section 1.4 distinguishes between Contractors (those contractors hired by the owner and administered by the construction manager) and Separate Contractors (those contractors hired by the owner but not administered by the construction manager).

ARTICLE 2 CONSTRUCTION MANAGER'S RESPONSIBILITIES

> **§ 2.4** The Construction Manager shall coordinate its services with those services provided by the Owner, the Architect, the Contractors, and the Owner's other consultants and Separate Contractors. The Construction Manager shall be entitled to rely on, and shall not be responsible for, the accuracy and completeness of services and information furnished by the Owner, the Architect, and the Owner's other consultants and Separate Contractors. The Construction Manager shall provide prompt written notice to the Owner if the Construction Manager becomes aware of any error, omission, or inconsistency in such services or information.

Section 2.4 is new and describes the construction manager's duties and obligations to coordinate its services with the other parties on the contract and permits the construction manager to rely on information provided by all parties except contractors, without liability for errors in that information or any duty to inspect or verify the information. The implication is that the construction manager is not entitled to rely on and is responsible for the accuracy and completeness of services and information provided by the contractors because the construction manager's scope of work includes the review and analysis of the contractors' submissions. If the construction manager becomes aware of any error, omission, or inconsistency in the services or information provided or performed by all the other parties, it must give prompt written notice to the owner.

~~§ 2.5~~**§ 2.6** The Construction Manager, as soon as practicable after execution of the Agreement, shall notify the Owner in writing of the names and qualifications of its proposed key staff members. Within 14 days of receipt of the names and qualifications of the Construction Manager's proposed key staff members, the Owner may reply to the Construction Manager in writing, stating (1) whether the Owner has reasonable objection to a proposed key staff member or (2) that the Owner requires additional time to review. Failure of the Owner to reply within the 14-day period shall constitute notice of no reasonable objection. The Construction Manager shall not staff any employees on the Project to whom the Owner has made reasonable and timely objection. The Construction Manager shall not change its key staff members without the Owner's consent, which shall not be unreasonably withheld or delayed.

New Section 2.6 requires the construction manager to give the owner notice of its proposed staff so that the owner can review and object to any of the proposed staff members.

§ 2.~~6~~8.1 ~~Comprehensive~~Commercial General Liability with policy limits of not less than ($) for each occurrence and ($) in the aggregate for bodily injury and property damage.

Changes to Section 2.8.1 replace "Comprehensive" General Liability insurance with "Commercial General Liability" insurance, which is a standard insurance policy that covers bodily injury, death, and damage to property up to the policy limits with many exceptions.

§ 2.~~6~~8.2 Automobile Liability covering vehicles owned, and ~~rented~~non-owned vehicles ~~operated~~used, by the Construction Manager with policy limits of not less than ___($___) ~~combined single limit and aggregate~~per accident for bodily injury, death of any person, and property damage arising out of the ownership, maintenance and use of those motor vehicles, along with any other statutorily required automobile coverage.

Changes to Section 2.8.2 mirror those in B132–2019 (Section 2.6.2) and establish the minimum automobile liability insurance that the construction manager is required to have on owned and non-owned vehicles used by the construction manager or any of its employees.

> **§ 2.68.3** The Construction Manager may ~~use umbrella or excess liability insurance to~~ achieve the required limits and coverage for ~~Comprehensive~~Commercial General Liability and Automobile Liability through a combination of primary and excess or umbrella liability insurance, provided ~~that~~ such primary and excess or umbrella ~~or excess~~liability insurance ~~results~~policies result in the same ~~type of~~or greater coverage as the coverages required ~~for the individual policies.~~ under Sections 2.68.1 and 2.8.2, and in no event shall any excess or umbrella liability insurance provide narrower coverage than the primary policy. The excess policy shall not require the exhaustion of the underlying limits only through the actual payment by the underlying insurers.

Similarly, changes to Section 2.8.3 mirror changes to Section 2.6.3 in the B132–2019, which permit the construction manager to achieve the required insurance minimums through a combination of primary, excess, and umbrella policies as long as the coverage and scope of the umbrella policy is not narrower than the primary policy's coverage and the umbrella policy does not require the primary policy's limits to be exhausted only by payment to the underlying insurers.

> ~~§ 2.6.6 The Construction Manager shall provide to the Owner~~**§ 2.8.6 Additional Insured Obligations.** To the fullest extent permitted by law, the Construction Manager shall cause the primary and excess or umbrella polices for Commercial General Liability and Automobile Liability to include the Owner as an additional insured for claims caused in whole or in part by the Construction Manager's negligent acts or omissions. The additional insured coverage shall be primary and non-contributory to any of the Owner's insurance policies and shall apply to both ongoing and completed operations.

New Section 2.8.6 also mirrors Section 2.6.7 of the B132–2019 and requires the construction manager to add the owner as an additional insured on the Commercial General Liability and Automobile Liability policies, whether those are single primary policies or primary policies coupled with excess or umbrella policies. These provisions permit the owner to enforce the insurance policies as if the owner were the primary insured. This flexibility is often desired by owners, but is not usually necessary to properly insure the project and can lead to higher premium costs.

> **§ 2.8.7** The Construction Manager shall provide certificates of insurance ~~evidencing~~to the Owner that evidence compliance with the requirements in this Section 2. 8~~6. The certificates will show the Owner as an additional insured on the Comprehensive General Liability, Automobile Liability, umbrella or excess policies.~~

Section 2.8.7 requires the construction manager to provide proof to the owner that it has obtained the required insurance policies for the required minimum limits and named the owner as an additional insured on all necessary policies. This mirrors the B132–2019's Section 2.6.8.

> **§ 2.9** The Construction Manager shall assist the Owner, Architect, and other Project participants in establishing building information modeling and digital data protocols for the Project using AIA Document E203™–2013, Building Information Modeling and Digital Data Exhibit, to establish the protocols for the development, use, transmission, and exchange of digital data.

New Section 2.9 requires the construction manager to assist the other parties using AIA Document E203–2013 to establish the processes and protocols for BIM, digital data, and other technology on the Project.

§ 2.10 A centralized electronic document management system will be used on the Project, and the Construction Manager shall be designated the Responsible Project Participant in section 3.5 of E203–2013, responsible for managing and maintaining the centralized electronic document management system. The centralized electronic document management system shall include all items listed in Article 3 of E203, and the following:

(List any items to be included that are not listed in Article 3 of E203–2013.)

New Section 2.10 requires the use of a centralized document management system for the project and designates the construction manager as the entity responsible for managing and maintaining that system. Although the E203 makes the use of a centralized document management system optional, this section makes it mandatory. This is the first time that the AIA has included this requirement in one of its construction contracts. The likely complexity of a project that uses a construction manager as an advisor led to making this a requirement. This Section also provides that the parties will use the E203 exhibit to establish the protocols for the development, use, transmission, and exchange of digital date.

§ 2.11 The Construction Manager shall retain all Project related documents and information it receives, and the Owner and Architect shall have access to the documents and information. The Construction Manager shall transmit the documents and information to the Owner at final completion.

New Section 2.11 requires the construction manager to maintain all project documents and information, provide the owner and architect access to all project documents and information, and transmit the project documents and information to the owner upon final completion of the project.

ARTICLE 3 SCOPE OF CONSTRUCTION MANAGER'S BASIC SERVICES

§ 3.1 Definition

The Construction Manager's Basic Services consist of those described in ~~Sections~~this Article 3~~.2 and 3.3~~, and include usual and customary ~~construction coordination~~Preconstruction and Construction Phase Services. Services not set forth in this Article 3 are Supplemental or Additional Services. The Owner, Construction Manager, and ~~scheduling, constructability review, cost estimating, and allocation of construction activities among the Multiple Prime~~ Contractors may agree, in consultation with the Architect, for the Construction Phase to commence prior to completion of the Preconstruction Phase, in which case, both phases will proceed concurrently.

Section 3.1 has been streamlined by using the more-encompassing defined terms "Preconstruction Phase Services" and "Construction Phase Services" instead of the specific list of activities expected of the construction manager in the 2009 version. All of those activities are encompassed within the defined terms. New language also expressly allows for construction to begin before design is completed.

> **§ 3.2.3** The Construction Manager shall prepare, and deliver to the Owner, for the Owner's approval, a written Construction Management Plan that includes, at a minimum, the following: (1) preliminary evaluations required in Section 3.2.2, (2) a Project schedule, (3) cost estimates, (4) recommendations for Project delivery method, and (5) Contractors' scopes of Work~~, if multiple Contractors or fast-track construction will be used.~~. The Construction Manager shall periodically update the Construction Management Plan, for the Owner's approval, over the course of the Project.

The only substantive changes to Section 3.2.3 clarify that the Construction Management Plan that the construction manager provides to the owner is for the owner's approval, not just review.

> **§ 3.2.4** The Construction Manager shall prepare and periodically update the Project schedule included in the Construction Management Plan for the Architect's review and the Owner's acceptance. The Construction Manager shall obtain the Architect's approval for the portion of the Project schedule relating to the performance of the Architect's services. The Project schedule shall coordinate and integrate the Construction Manager's services, the Architect's services, other Owner consultants' services, and the Owner's responsibilities and highlight items that affect the Project's timely completion.

Section 3.2.4 expands upon the construction manager's obligation to prepare a project schedule in Section 3.2.3.2 and requires the construction manager to obtain the architect's approval for any portion of the schedule related to the architect's performance and services. The overall project schedule still must be reviewed by the architect and approved by the owner.

> **§ 3.2.5** The Construction Manager shall update the Project schedule to include the components of the Work, including phasing of construction, times of commencement and completion required of each Contractor, ordering and delivery of products, including those that must be ordered in advance of construction, obtaining the required reviews and approvals of authorities having jurisdiction over the Project, and the occupancy requirements of the Owner.

New Section 3.2.5 has been relocated from Section 3.2.12. This Section defines and clarifies the information that should be included in the project schedule.

> **§ 3.~~4~~2.6** Based on the preliminary design and ~~other design criteria~~information prepared or provided by the Architect and other Owner consultants, the Construction Manager shall prepare, for the Architect's review and Owner's approval, preliminary estimates of the Cost of the Work or the cost of program requirements using area, volume or similar conceptual estimating techniques ~~for the Architect's review and Owner's approval. If the Architect suggests alternative materials and systems, the Construction Manager shall provide cost evaluations of those alternative materials and systems and may also provide its own suggestions~~, including the establishment of sufficient contingency to reasonably anticipate the development of the Project's design documents.

The primary substantive change to Section 3.2.6 is to clarify the construction manager's preliminary estimates of the cost of the work must include a sufficient contingency to reasonably anticipate development of the project's design documents. This is particularly necessary for projects where construction begins before design is fully complete.

Former section 3.2.6 was relocated to Section 3.2.4.

> **§ 3.2.8** The Construction Manager shall review recommendations for systems, materials, or equipment for the impact upon cost, schedule, sequencing, constructability, and coordination among the Contractors. The Construction Manager shall discuss its findings with the Owner and the Architect, and coordinate resolution, as necessary, of any such impacts.

New Section 3.2.8 requires the construction manager to review and compare recommendations from all contractors for systems, materials, and equipment and to evaluate their impacts on cost, schedule, sequencing, constructability, and coordination to prevent conflicts or circumstances that may disrupt the project schedule. Before making any decisions, however, the construction manager is to discuss its findings with the owner and architect and coordinate any resolution with them.

> ~~**§ 3.2.13** The Construction Manager shall expedite~~**§ 3.2.14** The Construction Manager shall make recommendations about, and coordinate the ordering and delivery of, materials in support of the schedule, including those that must be ordered ~~well~~ in advance of construction.

Section 3.2.14 clarifies that the construction manager must make recommendations about the ordering and delivery of materials, but is not required to expedite that delivery.

> **§ 3.2.~~14~~15** The Construction Manager shall assist the Owner in selecting, retaining, and coordinating the professional services of surveyors, geotechnical engineers, special consultants, and construction materials testing ~~laboratories~~ required for the Project.

Minor changes to Section 3.2.15 add assisting the owner with geotechnical engineering and construction materials testing to the construction manager's coordination duties with regard to professional services.

> **§ 3.2.~~17~~18** Following the Owner's approval of the Drawings and Specifications, the Construction Manager shall update and submit the latest estimate of the Cost of the Work and the Project schedule for the Architect's review and the Owner's approval.

Section 3.2.18 was relocated to Section 3.2.20.

> **§ 3.2.19** The Construction Manager, in consultation with the Owner, shall develop bidders' interest in the Project and establish bidding schedules. The Construction Manager shall assist the Owner and the Architect with the development of the Bidding Documents, which consist of bidding requirements and proposed Contract Documents. The Construction Manager, with the assistance of the Architect, shall issue ~~bidding documents~~Bidding Documents to bidders and conduct pre-bid conferences with prospective bidders. The Construction Manager shall issue the current Project schedule with each set of ~~bidding documents.~~Bidding Documents. The Construction Manager shall assist the Architect with regard to questions from bidders and with the issuance of addenda.

The only substantive change to Section 3.2.18 requires the construction manager to assist the owner and architect in the development of the bid documents (defined as including the bidding requirements and the proposed Contract Documents).

> **§ 3.2.21** The Construction Manager, with the assistance of the Architect, shall review bids, and prepare bid analyses, and make recommendations to the Owner for the Owner's award of Contracts for Construction or rejection of bids.

Changes to Section 3.2.21 require the construction manager to work with the architect to review bids, prepare bid analyses, and make recommendations to the owner on awarding or rejecting bids.

> ~~**§ 3.3 Construction Phase Administration of the Construction Contract**~~
> **§ 3.2.24** If the Owner identified a Sustainable Objective in Article 1, the Construction Manager shall fulfill its Preconstruction Phase responsibilities as required in AIA Document E235™–2019, Sustainable Projects Exhibit, Construction Manager as Adviser Edition, attached to this Agreement.

New Section 3.2.24 requires the construction manager to fulfill its preconstruction phase responsibilities in accordance with any sustainable objectives the owner has elected.

> **§ 3.3 Construction Phase**
>
> **§ 3.3.1** The Construction Manager shall provide on-site administration of the Contracts for Construction in cooperation with the Architect as set forth below and in AIA Document A232™–2019, General Conditions of the Contract for Construction, Construction Manager as Adviser Edition. If the Owner and Contractor modify AIA Document A232–2019, those modifications shall not affect the Construction Manager's services under this Agreement unless the Owner and the Construction Manager amend this Agreement.

Section 3.3.1 was relocated from Section 3.3.3 and states that any revisions affecting the construction manager's services that the owner and contractor make to the A232–2019 are binding on the construction manager only if those changes are reflected in the C132. The drafting of the C132 and the A232, therefore, needs to be coordinated.

> ~~**§ 3.3.3** The Construction Manager shall provide on-site administration of the Contracts for Construction in cooperation with the Architect as set forth below and in AIA Document A232™–2009, General Conditions of the Contract for Construction, Construction Manager as Adviser Edition. If the Owner and Contractor modify AIA Document A232–2009, those modifications shall not affect the Construction Manager's services under this Agreement unless the Owner and the Construction Manager amend this Agreement.~~

Section 3.3.3 was relocated to Section 3.3.1.

> **§ 3.3.8** The Construction Manager shall ~~schedule~~coordinate all tests and inspections required by the Contract Documents or governmental authorities, observe the on-site testing and inspections, and arrange for the delivery of test and inspection reports to the Owner and Architect.

The only substantive change to Section 3.3.8 requires the construction manager to observe the on-site testing and inspections required by the contract documents and governmental authorities.

> **§ 3.3.11** The Construction Manager shall develop cash flow reports and forecasts for the Project and include them in the Construction Manager's progress reports.

The only substantive change to Section 3.3.11 requires the construction manager to include the cash flow reports and forecasts it develops in its progress reports.

> **§ 3.3.12.3** The Construction Manager's certification for payment shall constitute a representation to the Owner, based on the Construction Manager's evaluations of the Work and on the data comprising the Contractors' Applications for Payment, that, to the best of the Construction Manager's knowledge, information and belief, the Work has progressed to the point indicated ~~and~~, the quality of the Work is in accordance with the Contract Documents~~.~~, and the Contractors are entitled to payment in the amount certified. The foregoing representations are subject to (1) an evaluation of the Work for conformance with the Contract Documents upon Substantial Completion~~, to~~; (2) results of subsequent tests and inspections~~, to~~; (3) correction of minor deviations from the Contract Documents prior to completion; and ~~to~~(4) specific qualifications expressed by the Construction Manager. The issuance of a Certificate for Payment shall further constitute a recommendation to the Architect and Owner that the Contractor be paid the amount certified.

Section 3.3.12.3 now provides for the construction manager's certification that the contractors are entitled to payment for the amount certified. This addition entitles the owner to rely on the construction manager's certifications regarding the status, quality, and value of the contractor's work.

§ 3.3.20 The Construction Manager shall promptly review all Shop Drawings, Product Data, Samples, and other submittals from the ~~Multiple Prime~~ Contractors for compliance with the submittal requirements of the Contract, coordinate submittals with information contained in related documents, and transmit to the Architect those that the Construction Manager recommends for approval. The Construction Manager's actions shall be taken in accordance with the Project submittal schedule approved by the Architect, or in the absence of an approved Project submittal schedule, with such reasonable promptness as to cause no delay in the Work or in the activities of the ~~Contractor, other Multiple Prime~~ Contractors, the Owner, or the Architect.

~~§ 3.3.20~~**§ 3.3.20.1** If professional design services or certifications by a design professional related to systems, materials, or equipment are specifically required of the Contractors by the Contract Documents, the Construction Manager shall review those submittals for sequencing, constructability, and coordination impacts on the other Contractors. The Construction Manager shall discuss its findings with the Owner and the Architect, and coordinate resolution, as necessary, of any such impacts.

New Section 3.3.20.1 addresses situations in which contractors are required to provide design services related to systems, materials, or equipment. In those cases, the construction manager is required to review the contractor's design submittals for sequencing, constructability, and coordination impacts on the other contractors. The construction manager is to coordinate the resolution of any impacts.

§ 3.3.21 The Construction Manager shall keep a daily log containing a record of weather, each Contractor's Work on the site, number of workers, identification of equipment, Work accomplished, problems encountered, and other similar relevant data as the Owner may require.

~~§ 3.3.20.1~~**§ 3.3.21.1** The Construction Manager shall collect, review for accuracy, and compile the Contractors' daily logs; and include them in the Construction Manager's reports prepared and submitted in accordance with section 3.3.21.2.

New Section 3.3.21.1 requires the construction manager to collect and review all contractors' daily logs for accuracy and include this information in its reports.

§ 3.3.21.2 The Construction Manager shall record the progress of the Project. On a monthly basis, or otherwise as agreed to by the Owner, the Construction Manager shall submit written progress reports to the Owner and Architect, showing percentages of completion and other information identified below:

.1 Work completed for the period;
.2 Project schedule status;
.3 Submittal schedule and status report, including a summary of remaining and outstanding submittals;

.4 Request for information, Change Order, and Construction Change Directive status reports;
.5 Tests and inspection reports;
.6 Status report of nonconforming and rejected Work;
.7 Daily logs;
.8 Summary of all ~~Multiple Prime~~ Contractors' Applications for Payment;
.9 Cumulative total of the Cost of the Work to date including the Construction Manager's compensation and reimbursable expenses at the job site, if any;
.10 Cash-flow and forecast reports; ~~and~~
.11 Photographs to document the progress of the Project;
.12 Status reports on permits and approvals of authorities having jurisdiction; and
.13 Any other items the Owner may require:

Section 3.3.21.2 identifies the information that should be included in construction manager's monthly progress reports. Revisions to this Section for 2019 include the requirement of photographs to document the progress of the Project and status reports on permits and approvals of authorities having jurisdiction.

§ 3.3.~~20.2~~21.3 In addition, for Projects constructed on the basis of the Cost of the Work, the Construction Manager shall include the following additional information in its progress reports:

.1 ~~Contractor's~~Contractors' work force ~~report~~reports;
.2 Equipment utilization report
.3 Cost summary, comparing actual costs to updated cost estimates; and
.4 Any other items as the Owner may require:

§ 3.3.~~21~~22 Utilizing the documents provided by the ~~Contractor~~Contractors, the Construction Manager shall ~~maintain~~make available, at the Project site ~~one copy of all Contracts, Drawings, Specifications, addenda,~~, the Contract Documents, including Change Orders, Construction Change Directives, and other Modifications, in good order and marked currently to ~~record all~~indicate field changes and selections made during construction, and ~~in addition,~~the approved Shop Drawings, Product Data, Samples, and similar required submittals. ~~The Construction Manager shall maintain records, in duplicate, of principal building layout lines, elevations of the bottom of footings, floor levels and key site elevations certified by a qualified surveyor~~These shall be in electronic form or ~~professional engineer. The Construction Manager shall make all such records~~paper copy, available to the Owner, Architect, and ~~the Contractor, and upon~~Contractors. Upon completion of the Project, the Construction Manager shall deliver them to the Owner.

Changes to Section 3.3.22 eliminate the requirement that the construction manager maintain duplicate records and instead require all contract documents and other documents identified in this Section to be made available electronically or in paper copy.

§ 3.3.~~27~~28 The Construction Manager shall ~~deliver all~~coordinate receipt, and delivery to the Owner, of other items provided by the Contractors, such as keys, manuals, and record drawings ~~and maintenance stocks to the Owner~~. The Construction Manager shall forward to the Architect a final Project Application for Payment and Project Certificate for Payment, or a final Application for Payment and final Certificate for Payment, upon the ~~Contractor's~~Contractors' compliance with the requirements of the Contract Documents.

Changes to Section 3.3.28 clarify that the construction manager is required to coordinate the delivery of certain items to the owner, not actually create them.

ARTICLE 4 SUPPLEMENTAL AND ADDITIONAL SERVICES

Changes to Article 4 distinguish between Supplemental Services and Additional Services. "Supplemental Services" are services that are beyond the architect's basic services but are agreed upon at the time of the signing of the contract. "Additional Services" also are beyond the architect's basic services but are added after the contract is signed and may increase the architect's compensation. As in the 2009 version, this version of the C132 includes a table of services with a column to designate the party responsible for the service (construction manager, owner, or not provided).

§ 4.1.2 ~~Insert a~~Description of Supplemental Services

§ 4.1.2.1 A description of each ~~Additional~~Supplemental Service ~~designated~~identified in Section 4.1.1 as the Construction Manager's responsibility is provided below.

(Describe in detail the Construction Manager's Supplemental Services identified in Section 4.1.1 or, if ~~not further described~~set forth in an exhibit, identify the exhibit.)

§ 4.1.2.2 A description of each Supplemental Service identified in Section 4.1.1 as the Owner's responsibility is provided below.

(Describe in detail the Owner's Supplemental Services identified in Section 4.1.1 or, if set forth in an exhibit, identify the exhibit.)

§ 4.1.3 If the Owner identified a Sustainable Objective in Article 1, the Construction Manager shall provide, as a Supplemental Service, the Sustainability Services required in AIA Document E235™–2019, Sustainable Projects Exhibit, Construction Manager as Adviser Edition, attached to this ~~document~~Agreement. The Owner shall compensate the Construction Manager as provided in Section 11.2.

Section 4.1.3 requires the owner to compensate the construction manager as provided in Section 11.2 if the owner has identified a sustainable objective.

~~§ 4.3~~ § 4.2 Construction Manager's Additional Services

§ 4.2.1 The Construction Manager may provide Additional Services ~~may be provided~~ after execution of this Agreement, without invalidating this Agreement. Except for services required due to the fault of the Construction Manager, any Additional Services provided in accordance with this Section 4.~~3~~2 shall entitle the Construction Manager to compensation pursuant to Section 11.3.

§ 4.~~3.1~~2.2 Upon recognizing the need to perform the following Additional Services, the Construction Manager shall notify the Owner with reasonable promptness and explain the facts and circumstances giving rise to the need. The Construction Manager shall not proceed to provide the following ~~services~~Additional Services until the Construction Manager receives the Owner's written authorization:

.1 Services necessitated by a change in the Initial Information, previous instructions or approvals given by the Owner, or a material change in the Project including~~, but not limited to,~~ size, quality, complexity, the Owner's schedule or budget for Cost of the Work, or procurement or delivery method, or bid packages in addition to those listed in Section 1.1.6~~;~~ . Services necessitated by sections 6.4 and 6.6 shall not be considered additional services;

.2 Services necessitated by the enactment or revision of codes, laws ~~or~~, regulations or official interpretations after the date of this Agreement;

.3 Services necessitated by decisions of the Owner not rendered in a timely manner or any other failure of performance on the part of the Owner or the Owner's other consultants or contractors;

.4 Preparation of documentation for alternate bid or proposal requests proposed by the Owner;

.~~4~~5 Preparation for, and attendance at, a public presentation, meeting or hearing;

.~~5~~6 Preparation for, and attendance at, a dispute resolution proceeding or legal proceeding, except where the Construction Manager is party thereto;

~~.6 Providing consultation~~**.7** Consultation concerning replacement of Work resulting from fire or other cause during construction and furnishing services required in connection with the replacement of such Work; or

.~~7~~8 Assistance to the Initial Decision Maker~~, if other than the Architect; or~~ .

~~.8 Service as the Initial Decision Maker.~~

The only substantive changes to Section 4.2.2 are in subpart 1 and 3, stating that services necessitated by sections 6.4 and 6.6 are not Additional Services, while services necessitated by the owner failing to provide information in a timely manner are Additional Services.

§ 4.2.3~~.2~~ To avoid delay in the Construction Phase, the Construction Manager shall provide the following Additional Services, notify the Owner with reasonable promptness, and explain the facts and circumstances giving rise to the need. If, upon receipt of the Construction Manager's notice, the Owner ~~subsequently~~ determines that all or parts of ~~those~~the services are not required, the Owner shall give prompt written notice to the Construction Manager~~, and the~~ of the Owner's determination. The Owner shall ~~have no further obligation to~~ compensate the Construction Manager for ~~those~~the services~~;~~ provided prior to the Construction Manager's receipt of the Owner's notice:

~~.1~~ ~~Services~~**.1** Providing assistance to the Initial Decision Maker in evaluating an extensive number of Claims submitted by a Contractor or others in connection with the Work ~~when the Architect is serving as the Initial Decision Maker~~.

~~.2~~ ~~To the extent the Construction Manager's Basic Services are affected, providing Construction Phase Services 60 days after (1) the date of Substantial Completion of the Work or (2) the anticipated date of Substantial Completion, identified in Initial Information, whichever is earlier.~~

~~.3~~**.2** Services required in an emergency to coordinate the activities of a Contractor or ~~Multiple Prime~~ Contractors in the event of risk of personal injury or serious property damage, consistent with Section 3.3.~~13~~15.

Changes to Section 4.2.3 require the construction manager to proceed with certain Additional Services to avoid delay. If the owner determines that the Additional Services are not necessary and so notifies the construction manager, the owner is not obligated to compensate the construction manager for services performed by the construction manager after receiving the owner's notice.

~~§ 4.3.3~~**§ 4.2.4** Except for services required under Section 3.3.30, Construction Phase Services provided more than 60 days after (1) the date of Substantial Completion of the Work, or (2) the anticipated date of Substantial Completion identified in the Initial Information, whichever is earlier, shall be compensated as Additional Services to the extent the Construction Manager incurs additional cost in providing those Construction Phase Services.

New Section 4.2.4 concerns services provided more than 60 days after substantial completion of the project and requires that they be compensated as Additional Services. This was provided for in § 4.2.2.2 of the C132–2009.

ARTICLE 5 OWNER'S RESPONSIBILITIES

§ 5.1 Unless otherwise provided for under this Agreement, the Owner shall provide information in a timely manner regarding requirements for and limitations on the Project, including a written program, which shall set forth the Owner's ~~program, other~~ objectives~~,~~; schedule~~,~~; constraints and criteria~~,~~; special equipment~~,~~; systems~~,~~; and site requirements~~. Within 15 days after receipt of a written request from the Construction Manager, the Owner shall furnish the requested information as necessary and relevant for the Construction Manager to evaluate, give notice of, or enforce any lien rights, if any~~.

Revisions to Section 5.1 add a requirement that the owner provide a written program setting forth the required information. The requirement for the owner to provide information to preserve lien rights was relocated to Section 5.18.

~~§ 5.8~~**§ 5.8** The Owner shall provide the Supplemental Services designated as the Owner's responsibility in Section 4.1.1.

New Section 5.8 requires the owner to provide the Supplemental Services designated as its responsibility in the table of services in Section 4.1.1.

> **§ 5.9** If the Owner identified a Sustainable Objective in Article 1, the Owner shall fulfill its responsibilities as required in AIA Document E235™–2019, Sustainable Projects Exhibit, Construction Manager as Adviser Edition, attached to this Agreement.

New Section 5.9 requires the owner to fulfill its responsibilities related to that sustainable objectives, including the Sustainable Projects Exhibit E235–2019.

> ~~**§ 5.13** Except as otherwise provided in this Agreement, or when direct communications have been specially authorized, the Owner shall endeavor to~~ **§ 5.15** The Owner shall communicate with the ~~Contractor~~Contractors and the Construction Manager's consultants through the Construction Manager about matters arising out of or relating to the Contract Documents. The Owner and Construction Manager shall include the Architect in all communications that relate to or affect the Architect's services or professional responsibilities. The Owner shall promptly notify the ~~Construction Manager~~ Architect of the substance of any direct communications ~~that may affect the Construction Manager's services.~~ between the Owner and the Construction Manager otherwise relating to the Project. Communications by and with the Architect's consultants shall be through the Architect.

Changes to Section 5.13, now renumbered Section 5.15, provide that the owner shall communicate with the contractors and the construction manager's consultants through the construction manager in accordance with other similar provisions of the agreement. Other substantive changes require the owner and construction manager to involve the architect in communications involving the architect's services.

ARTICLE 6 COST OF THE WORK

> **§ 6.1** For purposes of this Agreement, the Cost of the Work shall be the total cost to the Owner to construct all elements of the Project designed or specified by the Architect and shall include the ~~contractors'~~Contractors' general conditions costs, overhead and profit. The Cost of the Work also includes the reasonable value of labor, materials, and equipment, donated to, or otherwise furnished by, the Owner. The Cost of the Work includes the compensation of the Construction Manager and Construction Manager's Consultants during the Construction Phase only, including compensation for reimbursable expenses at the job site, if any. The Cost of the Work does not include the compensation of the Architect~~,~~; the costs of the land, rights-of-way, financing, or contingencies for changes in the Work; or other costs that are the responsibility of the Owner.

The only substantive change to Section 6.1 is inclusion of labor, materials, and equipment furnished by the owner in the calculation of the Cost of the Work.

§ 6.5 If the Construction Manager's estimate of the Cost of the Work ~~at the conclusion of the Design Development Phase~~ exceeds the Owner's budget for the Cost of the Work, the Owner shall

.1 give written approval of an increase in the budget for the Cost of the Work;
~~.2~~**.2** terminate in accordance with Section 9.5;
.3 in consultation with the Construction Manager and Architect, revise the Project program, scope, or quality as required to reduce the Cost of the Work; or
.~~3~~4 implement any other mutually acceptable alternative.

Section 6.5 now includes termination as one of the available options if the construction manager's estimated Cost of the Work exceeds the budget. The owner can exercise any of these options any time this occurs.

§ 6.6 If the Owner chooses to revise the Project program, scope, or quality to reduce the Cost of the Work pursuant to Section 6.5.3, or if the bids or proposals received from the prospective Contractors, in the aggregate, exceed the Owner's budget for the Cost of the Work, and the Owner chooses to revise the Project program, scope, or quality to reduce the Cost of the Work, the Construction Manager shall cooperate with the Owner and Architect to develop the necessary revisions, update the cost estimate, and obtain additional bids. The Construction Manager will perform the services described in Sections 6.4 and 6.6 without additional compensation.

New Section 6.6 governs the construction manager's responsibilities (for no additional compensation) if the owner revises the project program, scope, or quality to reduce the Cost of the Work because the construction manager's cost estimate exceeds the owner's budget.

ARTICLE 7 COPYRIGHTS AND LICENSES

The Construction Manager and the Construction Manager's consultants, if any, shall not own or claim a copyright in the Instruments of Service. The Construction Manager, the Construction Manager's consultants, if any, and the Owner warrant that in transmitting Instruments of Service, or any other information, the transmitting party is the copyright owner of such information or has permission from the copyright owner to transmit such information for its use on the Project. ~~If the Owner and Construction Manager intend to transmit Instruments of Service or any other information or documentation in digital form, they shall endeavor to establish necessary protocols governing such transmissions.~~

The only change to Article 7 eliminates the language requiring the parties to establish necessary protocols for transmitting information electronically because this information and these requirements are now included in a separate exhibit (the E203).

ARTICLE 8 CLAIMS AND DISPUTES

> **§ 8.1.3** The Construction Manager shall indemnify and hold the Owner and the Owner's officers and employees harmless from and against damages, losses and judgments arising from claims by third parties, including reasonable attorneys' fees and expenses recoverable under applicable law, but only to the extent they are caused by the negligent acts or omissions of the Construction Manager, its employees and its consultants in the performance of professional services under this Agreement. The Construction Manager's obligation to indemnify and hold the Owner and the Owner's officers and employees harmless does not include a duty to defend. The Construction Manager's duty to indemnify the Owner under this ~~provision~~Section 8.1.3 shall be limited to the available proceeds of the insurance coverage required by this Agreement.

Like the B132–2019, changes to Section 8.1.3 eliminate the duty to defend from the construction manager's indemnity obligations to the owner and the duty to indemnify is limited to the available proceeds of the insurance required by this Agreement.

> **§ 8.4** The provisions of this Article 8 shall survive the termination of this Agreement.

New Section 8.4 states that the provisions of Article 8, which includes the indemnity obligation, remain in effect after termination of the agreement.

ARTICLE 9 TERMINATION OR SUSPENSION

> **§ 9.1** If the Owner fails to make payments to the Construction Manager in accordance with this Agreement, such failure shall be considered substantial nonperformance and cause for termination or, at the Construction Manager's option, cause for suspension of performance of services under this Agreement. If the Construction Manager elects to suspend services, the Construction Manager shall give seven days' written notice to the Owner before suspending services. In the event of a suspension of services, the Construction Manager shall have no liability to the Owner for delay or damage caused the Owner because of such suspension of services. Before resuming services, the Owner shall pay the Construction Manager ~~shall be paid~~ all sums due prior to suspension and any expenses incurred in the interruption and resumption of the Construction Manager's services. The Construction Manager's fees for the remaining services and the time schedules shall be equitably adjusted.
>
> . . . .
>
> **§ 9.6** ~~In~~If the ~~event of termination not the fault of~~ Owner terminates this Agreement for its convenience pursuant to Section 9.5, or the Construction Manager, terminates this Agreement pursuant to Section 9.3, the Owner shall compensate the Construction Manager ~~shall be compensated~~ for services performed prior to termination, ~~together with~~ Reimbursable Expenses ~~then due and all Termination Expenses as defined in Section 9.7.~~

> **§ 9.7** ~~Termination Expenses are in addition to compensation for the Construction Manager's services and include expenses directly~~ incurred, and costs attributable to termination ~~for which~~, including the costs attributable to the Construction Manager's termination of consultant agreements.

The only substantive change to Article 9 is the inclusion of a termination fee (at the parties' election) for an owner termination for convenience in lieu of anticipated profit on unperformed services.

> **§ 9.8** Except as otherwise expressly provided herein, this Agreement shall terminate one year from the date of Substantial Completion.

Similar to the B132–2019, Section 9.8 states that the agreement terminates one year from the date of Substantial Completion unless otherwise noted.

ARTICLE 10 MISCELLANEOUS PROVISIONS

> **§ 10.1** This Agreement shall be governed by the law of the place where the Project is located, ~~except that if~~excluding that jurisdiction's choice of law rules. If the parties have selected arbitration as the method of binding dispute resolution, the Federal Arbitration Act shall govern Section 8.3.

The only substantive change to Section 10.1 emphasizes that the agreement is governed by the law of the state where the project is located, regardless of that jurisdiction's choice of law rules.

> **§ 10.3** The Owner and Construction Manager, respectively, bind themselves, their agents, successors, assigns, and legal representatives to this Agreement. Neither the Owner nor the Construction Manager shall assign this Agreement without the written consent of the other, except that the Owner may assign this Agreement to a lender providing financing for the Project if the lender agrees to assume the Owner's rights and obligations under this Agreement~~.~~ , including any payments due to the Construction Manager by the Owner prior to the assignment.

Revised Section 10.3 clarifies that the owner may assign the agreement to a lender if the lender assumes the owner's responsibilities under the agreement, including the owner's outstanding payment obligations to the construction manager.

> **§ 10.7** The Construction Manager shall have the right to include photographic or artistic representations of the design of the Project among the Construction Manager's promotional and professional materials. The Construction Manager shall provide professional credit for the Architect and the Contractors in the Construction Manager's promotional materials for the Project. The Construction Manager shall be given reasonable access to the completed

Project to make such representations. However, the Construction Manager's materials shall not include the Owner's confidential or proprietary information if the Owner has previously advised the Construction Manager in writing of the specific information considered by the Owner to be confidential or proprietary. The Owner shall provide professional credit for the Construction Manager in the Owner's promotional materials for the Project. This Section 10.7 shall survive the termination of this Agreement unless the Owner terminates this Agreement for cause pursuant to Section 9.4.

Changes to Section 10.7 require the construction manager to provide professional credit for the architect and contractors in any promotional materials.

§ 10.8 If the Construction Manager or Owner receives information specifically designated ~~by the other party~~ as "confidential" or "business proprietary," the receiving party shall keep such information strictly confidential and shall not disclose it to any other person except ~~to (1) its employees, (2) those who need to know the content of such information in order to perform services or construction solely and exclusively for the Project, or (3) its consultants and contractors whose contracts include similar restrictions on the use of confidential information.~~ as set forth in Section 10.8.1. This Section 10.8 shall survive the termination of this Agreement.

§ 10.8.1 The receiving party may disclose "confidential" or "business proprietary" information after 7 days' notice to the other party, when required by law, arbitrator's order, or court order, including a subpoena or other form of compulsory legal process issued by a court or governmental entity, or to the extent such information is reasonably necessary for the receiving party to defend itself in any dispute. The receiving party may also disclose such information to its employees, consultants, or contractors in order to perform services or work solely and exclusively for the Project, provided those employees, consultants and contractors are subject to the restrictions on the disclosure and use of such information as set forth in this Section 10.8.

Changes to Sections 10.8 and new Section 10.8.1 mirror similar provisions in the B132–2019. These Sections define when and how information designated as confidential can be disclosed. While previous Section 10.8 permitted disclosure of such information for purposes of construction, new Section 10.8.1 also provides for disclosure when required by law. Section 10.8 further states that the restriction on sharing confidential information survives termination of the agreement.

§ 10.9 The invalidity of any provision of the Agreement shall not invalidate the Agreement or its remaining provisions. If it is determined that any provision of the Agreement violates any law, or is otherwise invalid or unenforceable, then that provision shall be revised to the extent necessary to make that provision legal and enforceable. In such case the Agreement shall be construed, to the fullest extent permitted by law, to give effect to the parties' intentions and purposes in executing the Agreement.

New Section 10.9, which mirrors a similar section in the B132–2019, contains a savings clause, which states that any provisions of the agreement held to be invalid or unenforceable will be revised to the extent necessary to allow them to be enforced.

ARTICLE 11 COMPENSATION

§ 11.1 For the Construction Manager's Basic Services described under Article 3, the Owner shall compensate the Construction Manager as follows:

§ 11.1.1 For Preconstruction Phase Services in Section 3.2:

(Insert amount of, or basis for, compensation, including stipulated sums, multiples or percentages.)

§ 11.1.2 For Construction Phase Services in Section 3.3:

(Insert amount of, or basis for, compensation, including stipulated sums, multiples or percentages.)

§ 11.2 For ~~Additional~~the Construction Manager's Supplemental Services designated in Section 4.1.1, and for any Sustainability Services required pursuant to Section 4.1.3, the Owner shall compensate the Construction Manager as follows:

(Insert amount of, or basis for, compensation. If necessary, list specific services to which particular methods of compensation apply.)

§ 11.3 For Additional Services that may arise during the course of the Project, including those under Section 4.~~3~~2, the Owner shall compensate the Construction Manager as follows:

(Insert amount of, or basis for, compensation.)

§ 11.4 Compensation for Supplemental and Additional Services of the Construction Manager's consultants when not included in Sections 11.2 or 11.3, shall be the amount invoiced to the Construction Manager plus percent (%), or as ~~otherwise stated below~~follows:

(Insert amount of, or basis for computing, Construction Manager's consultants' compensation for Supplemental or Additional Services.)

§ 11.5 The hourly billing rates for services of the Construction Manager and the Construction Manager's consultants, ~~if any,~~ are set forth below. The rates shall be adjusted in accordance with the Construction Manager's and Construction Manager's consultants' normal review practices.

(If applicable, attach an exhibit of hourly billing rates or insert them below.)

Employee or Category	Rate ($0.00)

§ 11.6 Compensation for Reimbursable Expenses

§ 11.6.1 Reimbursable Expenses are in addition to compensation for Basic, Supplemental, and Additional Services and include expenses incurred by the Construction Manager and the Construction Manager's consultants directly related to the Project, as follows:

- **.1** Transportation and authorized out-of-town travel and subsistence;
- **.2** Long distance services, dedicated data and communication services, teleconferences, Project ~~Web~~web sites, and extranets;
- **.3** ~~Fees paid for securing approval of~~Permitting and other fees required by authorities having jurisdiction over the Project;
- **.4** Printing, reproductions, plots, and standard form documents;

.5 Postage, handling, and delivery;
.6 Expense of overtime work requiring higher than regular rates, if authorized in advance by the Owner;
.7 Professional photography, and presentation materials requested by the Owner;
.8 If required by the Owner, and with the Owner's prior written approval, the Construction Manager's ~~consultant's expense~~<u>consultants' expenses</u> of professional liability insurance dedicated exclusively to this Project, or the expense of additional insurance coverage or limits ~~if the Owner requests such insurance~~ in excess of that normally ~~carried~~<u>maintained</u> by the Construction Manager's consultants
.9 All taxes levied on professional services and on reimbursable expenses;
.10 Site office expenses; and
.11 Other similar Project-related expenditures.

Section 11.6.1 identifies additional expenses that may be reimbursed to the construction manager. Substantive changes to this Section include the requirement of the owner's prior written approval to reimburse expenses incurred by the construction manager's consultants for project-specific professional liability insurance or professional liability insurance required in excess of what they normally maintain.

§ 11.6.2 For Reimbursable Expenses the compensation shall be the expenses incurred by the Construction Manager and the Construction Manager's consultants plus percent (%) of the expenses incurred.

~~**§ 11.7 Payments to the Construction Manager**~~

~~§ 11.7~~<u>**§ 11.7 Construction Manager's Insurance**. If the types and limits of coverage required in Section 2.8 are in addition to the types and limits the Construction Manager normally maintains, the Owner shall pay the Construction Manager for the additional costs incurred by the Construction Manager for the additional coverages as set forth below.</u>

<u>*(Insert the additional coverages the Construction Manager is required to obtain in order to satisfy the requirements set forth in Section 2.8, and for which the Owner shall reimburse the Construction Manager.)*</u>

Changes to Section 11.7 govern compensation in circumstances in which the owner requires insurance types or limits in excess of that which the construction manager normally carries for itself. In such cases, the owner must pay for any increase in the insurance the construction manager would normally carry.

ARTICLE 12 SPECIAL TERMS AND CONDITIONS

No substantive changes.

ARTICLE 13 SCOPE OF THE AGREEMENT

No substantive changes.

A132–2019: Standard Form of Agreement between Owner and Contractor, Construction Manager as Adviser Edition

The A132–2019 is the standard form of agreement between the owner and the contractor when the owner has also hired a CMa.

ARTICLE 1 THE CONTRACT DOCUMENTS

Article 1 (The Contract Documents) lists the documents and information that should be considered part of the Contract Documents—the governing documents for the project. There were no changes to Articles 1 in the 2019 update.

ARTICLE 2 THE WORK OF THIS CONTRACT

Article 2 (The Work of this Contract) describes the contractor's scope of the work for the project; it is a single sentence. There were no changes to Article 2 in the 2019 update.

ARTICLE 3 DATE OF COMMENCEMENT AND DATES OF SUBSTANTIAL COMPLETION

Article 3 (Date of Commencement and Dates of Substantial Completion) sets forth how the time and duration of the project will be defined and calculated. There were several revisions to Article 3 that provide more flexibility in defining completion dates, partial completion dates, and milestones:

§ 3.1 The date of commencement of the Work shall be:

(Check one of the following boxes.)

[ ] The date of this Agreement ~~unless a different~~.
[ ] A date ~~is stated below or provision is made for the date to be fixed~~set forth in a notice to proceed issued by the Owner.
[ ] Established as follows:
(Insert a date or a means to determine the date of commencement~~, if it differs from~~ of the Work.)

If a date of commencement of the Work is not selected, then the date of commencement shall be the date of this Agreement~~or, if applicable, state that the date will be fixed in a notice to proceed.)~~.

~~If, prior to the commencement of the Work, the Owner requires time to file mortgages, mechanics' liens and other security interests, the Owner's time requirement shall be as follows:~~

Section 3.1 was revised to permit parties to simply check the box next to rules setting forth how the dates of commencement and substantial completion will be determined on the project. This is consistent with changes made to the A201 in 2017. The default commencement date if nothing is selected is the date of the agreement.

§ 3.2 The Contract Time shall be measured from the date of commencement of the Work.

This slight revision to 3.2 was made for clarity but under this agreement, the "commencement date" is the same as the "date of commencement of the Work." This could be confusing if the "commencement date" is the date of the agreement but the actual work does not "commence" until several days or weeks later.

§ 3.3 ~~The Contractor shall achieve~~ Substantial Completion of the ~~entire Work not later than ( ) days from~~ Project or Portions Thereof

§ 3.3.1 Subject to adjustments of the Contract Time as provided in the Contract Documents, the date of ~~commencement, or as follows:~~

~~(Insert number of calendar days. Alternatively, a calendar date may be used when coordinated with the date of~~

~~commencement. If appropriate, insert requirements for earlier~~ Substantial Completion of ~~certain~~ the Work of all of the Contractors for the Project will be:

(Insert the date of Substantial Completion of the Work of all Contractors for the Project.)

§ 3.3.2 Subject to adjustments of the Contract Time as provided in the Contract Documents, if portions of the Work~~.)~~ of all of the Contractors for the Project are to be completed prior to Substantial Completion of the entire Work of all of the Contractors for the Project, the Contractors shall achieve Substantial Completion of such portions by the following dates:

Portion of ~~the~~ Work **Substantial Completion Date**

Section 3.3 defines completion of the entire project (all contractors) and, with the new revisions, permits identification of completion dates for particular milestones. This section was changed to permit a date certain to be inserted, or a number of days, for portions of the work and the entire project itself.

§ 3.4 When the Work of this Contract, or any Portion Thereof, is Substantially Complete

§ 3.4.1 Subject to adjustments of ~~this~~the Contract Time as provided in the Contract Documents., the Contractor shall substantially complete the entire Work of this Contract:

~~*(Insert provisions, if any, for liquidated damages relating to failure to achieve Substantial Completion on time or for bonus payments for early completion of the Work.)*~~

(Check one of the following boxes and complete the necessary information.)

[ ] Not later than ( ) calendar days from the date of commencement of the Work.

[ ] By the following date:

Section 3.4 provides for the date of substantial completion by the contractor entering into that particular A132.

§ 3.4.2 Subject to adjustments of the Contract Time as provided in the Contract Documents, if portions of the Work of this Contract are to be substantially complete prior to when the entire Work of this Contract shall be substantially complete, the Contractor shall substantially complete such portions by the following dates:

Portion of Work	Date to be substantially complete

§ 3.4.3 If the Contractor fails to substantially complete the Work of this Contract, or portions thereof, as provided in this Section 3.4, liquidated damages, if any, shall be assessed as set forth in Section 4.5.

Section 3.4.3 refers the parties to the liquidated damages provision in Section 4.5. This puts the parties to the contract on notice of this later section without including it in its entirety here.

ARTICLE 4 CONTRACT SUM

§ 4.1 The Owner shall pay the Contractor the Contract Sum in current funds for the Contractor's performance of the Contract. The Contract Sum shall be one of the following:

(Check the appropriate box.)

[ ] Stipulated Sum, in accordance with Section 4.2 below
[ ] Cost of the Work plus the Contractor's Fee ~~without a Guaranteed Maximum Price~~, in accordance with Section 4.3 below
[ ] Cost of the Work plus the Contractor's Fee with a Guaranteed Maximum Price, in accordance with Section 4.4 below

(Based on the selection above, complete Section 4.2, 4.3 or 4.4 ~~below. Based on the selection above, also complete either Section 5.1.4, 5.1.5 or 5.1.6~~ below.)

The only revision made to this section was to delete "without a Guaranteed Maximum Price" from the second option. This does not materially change the meaning of this option or the section. The third option still includes the GMP in its definition, distinguishing it from the second option.

§ 4.2 Stipulated Sum

§ 4.2.1 The ~~Stipulated~~ Contract Sum shall be ($), subject to additions and ~~deletions~~deductions as provided in the Contract Documents.

Changing "Stipulated Sum" to "Contract Sum" in Section 4.2 is consistent with the rest of the document's use of the defined term "Contract Sum" and explains how a Contract Sum based on a stipulated sum is calculated. Many of the remaining revisions to Section 4.2 simplify the definitions and methods for calculating the Contract Sum and remove unnecessary words, particularly as it relates to alternates, unit prices, and allowances in 4.2.2 through 4.2.4.

§ 4.2.2 ~~**The Stipulated Sum is based on the following alternates**~~ **Alternates**

§ 4.2.2.1 Alternates, if any, ~~which are described~~ included in the Contract ~~Documents and are hereby accepted by the Owner~~Sum:

~~(State the numbers or other identification of accepted alternates. If the bidding or proposal documents permit the Owner to accept other alternates subsequent to the execution of this Agreement, attach a schedule of such other alternates showing the amount for each and the date when that amount expires.)~~

~~**§ 4.2.3** Unit prices, if any:~~

~~(Identify and state the unit price, and state the quantity limitations, if any, to which the unit price will be applicable.)~~

Item	~~**Units and Limitations**~~	~~**Price per Unit ($0.00)**~~

~~**§ 4.2.4** Allowances included in the Stipulated Sum, if any:~~

~~(Identify allowance and state exclusions, if any, from the allowance price.)~~

§ 4.2.2.2 Subject to the conditions noted below, the following alternates may be accepted by the Owner following execution of this Agreement. Upon acceptance, the Owner shall issue a Modification to this Agreement.

(Insert below each alternate and the conditions that must be met for the Owner to accept the alternate.)

Item	~~**Allowance**~~**Price**	**Conditions for Acceptance**

§ 4.2.3 Allowances, if any, included in the Contract Sum:

(Identify each allowance.)

Item	**Price**

§ 4.2.4 Unit prices, if any:

(Identify the item and state the unit price, and quantity limitations, if any, to which the unit price will be applicable.)

Item	**Units and Limitations**	**Price per Unit ($0.00)**

In Section 4.3, “Contract Sum” has been replaced with “the Cost of the Work” for consistency and clarity. Cost of the Work more accurately describes the sum being calculated in this Section. The calculation of the Cost of the Work has been moved from Exhibit A to Exhibit B because the Insurance and Bond requirements in total have been moved from Section 10 to Exhibit A; Cost of the Work is now the second exhibit attached to the agreement.

§ 4.3 Cost of the Work Plus Contractor’s Fee without a Guaranteed Maximum Price

§ 4.3.1 The ~~Contract Sum is the~~ Cost of the Work is as defined in Exhibit ~~A~~B, Determination of the Cost of the Work, ~~plus the Contractor’s Fee~~.

§ 4.3.2 The Contractor’s Fee:

(State a lump sum, percentage of Cost of the Work or other provision for determining the Contractor’s Fee.)

§ 4.3.3 The method of adjustment of the Contractor's Fee for changes in the Work:

§ 4.3.4 Limitations, if any, on a Subcontractor's overhead and profit for increases in the cost of its portion of the Work:

§ 4.3.5 Rental rates for Contractor-owned equipment shall not exceed percent (%) of the standard rental rate paid at the place of the Project.

§ 4.3.6 Unit prices, if any:

(Identify the item and state the unit price~~; state quantity limitations, if any, to which the unit price will be applicable.)~~ and quantity limitations, if any, to which the unit price will be applicable.)

Item	Units and Limitations	Price per Unit ($0.00)

§ 4.3.7 The Contractor shall prepare and submit to the Construction Manager ~~for the Owner, in writing, a Control Estimate~~ , within 14 days of executing this Agreement., a written Control Estimate for the Owner's review and approval. The Control Estimate shall include the items in Section ~~A~~ B.1 of Exhibit ~~A~~B, Determination of the Cost of the Work.

§ 4.4 Cost of the Work Plus Contractor's Fee with a Guaranteed Maximum Price

§ 4.4.1 The ~~Contract Sum is the~~ Cost of the Work is as defined in Exhibit ~~A~~B, Determination of the Cost of the Work, ~~plus the Contractor's Fee~~.

§ 4.4.2 The Contractor's Fee:

(State a lump sum, percentage of Cost of the Work or other provision for determining the Contractor's Fee.)

§ 4.4.3 The method of adjustment of the Contractor's Fee for changes in the Work:

§ 4.4.4 Limitations, if any, on a Subcontractor's overhead and profit for increases in the cost of its portion of the Work:

§ 4.4.5 Rental rates for Contractor-owned equipment shall not exceed percent (%) of the standard rental rate paid at the place of the Project.

§ 4.4.6 Unit Prices, if any:

(Identify the item and state the unit price, and ~~state the~~ quantity limitations, if any, to which the unit price will be applicable.)

Similar non-substantive changes to simplify, clarify, and use defined terms are prevalent in Section 4.4.7, including changes to alternates and allowances to be consistent with those terms and calculations above.

§ 4.4.7 Guaranteed Maximum Price

§ 4.4.7.1 The ~~sum of the Cost of the Work and the Contractor's Fee~~Contract Sum is guaranteed by the Contractor not to exceed ($), subject to additions and deductions by ~~changes in the Work~~Change Order as provided in the Contract Documents. ~~Such~~This maximum sum is referred to in the Contract Documents as the Guaranteed Maximum Price. Costs which would cause the Guaranteed Maximum Price to be exceeded shall be paid by the Contractor without reimbursement by the Owner.

~~(Insert specific provisions if the Contractor is to participate in any savings.)~~

§ 4.4.7.2 The Guaranteed Maximum Price is based on the following alternates, if any, which are described in the Contract Documents and are hereby accepted by the Owner:

§ 4.4.7.2 Alternates

§ 4.4.7. 2.1 3 AllowancesAlternates, if any, included in the Guaranteed Maximum Price, if any:

(Identify and state the amounts of any allowances, and state whether they include labor, materials, or both.)

Item AllowancePrice

§ 4.4.7.2.2 Subject to the conditions noted below, the following alternates may be accepted by the Owner following execution of this Agreement. Upon acceptance, the Owner shall issue a Modification to this Agreement.

(Insert below each alternate and the conditions that must be met for the Owner to accept the alternate.)

Item	Price	Conditions for Acceptance

§ 4.4.7.3 Allowances, if any, included in the Guaranteed Maximum Price:

(Identify each allowance.)

Item	Price

§ 4.4.7.4 Assumptions, if any, onupon which the Guaranteed Maximum Price is based:

(Identify each assumption.)

§ 4.4.8 To the extent that the Contract Documents are anticipated to require further development, the Guaranteed Maximum Price includes the costs attributable to such further development consistent with the Contract Documents and reasonably inferable therefrom. Such further development does not include changes in scope, systems, kinds and quality of materials, finishes, or equipment, all of which, if required, shall be incorporated by Change Order.

§ 4.4.9 The Owner shall authorize preparation of revisions to the Contract Documents that incorporate the agreed-upon assumptions contained in Section 4.4.7.4. The Owner shall promptly furnish such revised Contract Documents to the Contractor. The Contractor shall notify the Owner and Architect of any inconsistencies between the agreed-upon assumptions contained in Section 4.4.7.4 and the revised Contract Documents.

Additional sections added to the GMP in Sections 4.4.8 and 4.4.9 address common occurrences on many GMP Projects that are fast-tracked or where the Contract Documents are incomplete at the bidding phase and continue to evolve during the Project. These Sections clarify how the parties will determine when later developments and changes are included in the GMP and when an adjustment is necessary.

§ 4.5 Liquidated damages, if any:

(Insert terms and conditions for liquidated damages, if any, to be assessed in accordance with Section 3.4.)

§ 4.6 Other:

(Insert provisions for bonus, cost savings or other incentives, if any, that might result in a change to the Contract Sum.)

Section 4.5 (addressing liquidated damages) and Section 4.6 (addressing other cost calculations) have been added to keep all of the cost information in one place, to provide clarity and flexibility for the parties in their effort to define costs and contract sums, and to bring this agreement into alignment with the A201–2017.

Many of the changes to Article 5 were made to simplify and clarify the meaning of defined terms.

ARTICLE 5 PAYMENTS

§ 5.1 Progress Payments

§ 5.1.1 Based upon Applications for Payment submitted to the Construction Manager by the Contractor, and ~~upon certification of the Project Application and Project Certificate~~Certificates for Payment ~~or Application for Payment and Certificate for Payment~~issued by the Construction Manager and Architect ~~and issuance by the Architect~~, the Owner shall make progress payments on account of the Contract Sum, to the Contractor, as provided below and elsewhere in the Contract Documents.

§ 5.1.2 The period covered by each Application for Payment shall be one calendar month ending on the last day of the month, or as follows:

§ 5.1.3 Provided that an Application for Payment is received by the Construction Manager not later than the day of a month, the Owner shall make payment of the amount certified ~~amount in the Application for Payment~~ to the Contractor not later than the day of the ___ month. If an Application for Payment is received by the Construction Manager after the application date fixed above, payment of the amount certified shall be made by the Owner not later than ( ) days after the Construction Manager receives the Application for Payment.

(Federal, state or local laws may require payment within a certain period of time.)

§ 5.1.4 Progress Payments Where the Contract Sum is Based on a Stipulated Sum

§ 5.1.4.1 Each Application for Payment shall be based on the most recent schedule of values submitted by the Contractor in accordance with the Contract Documents. The schedule of values shall allocate the entire Contract Sum among the various portions of the Work ~~and~~. The schedule of values shall be prepared in such form, and supported by such data to substantiate its accuracy, as the Construction Manager and Architect may require. This schedule~~, unless objected to by the Construction Manager or Architect,~~ of values shall be used as a basis for reviewing the Contractor's Applications for Payment.

Section 5.1.4.3 simplifies the language defining how to calculate the amount of each progress payment. First, the total cost of work to be included in the pay application is calculated, and then all reductions are separately calculated as set forth below, including deducting retainage.

§ 5.1.4.3 In accordance with AIA Document A232™–2019, General Conditions of the Contract for Construction, Construction Manager as Adviser Edition, and subject to other provisions of the Contract Documents, the amount of each progress payment shall be computed as follows:

§ 5.1.4..1 Take that portion of the Contract Sum properly allocable to completed Work as determined by multiplying the percentage completion of each portion of the Work by the share of the total Contract Sum allocated to that portion of the Work in the schedule of values, less retainage of percent (%). Pending final determination of cost to the Owner of changes in the Work, amounts not in dispute may be included as provided in Section 7.3.9 of the General Conditions;

§ 5.1.4.3.1 The amount of each progress payment shall first include:

- **.1** That portion of the Contract Sum properly allocable to completed Work;
- **.2** Add thatThat portion of the Contract Sum properly allocable to materials and equipment delivered and suitably stored at the site for subsequent incorporation in the completed construction (, or, if approved in advance by the Owner, suitably stored off the site at a location agreed upon in writing), less retainage of percent (%);; and
- **.3** Subtract the aggregate of previous payments made by the Owner; and
- **.4** Subtract
- **.3** That portion of Construction Change Directives that the Architect determines, in the Architect's professional judgment, to be reasonably justified.

§ 5.1.4.3.2 The amount of each progress payment shall then be reduced by:

- **.1** The aggregate of any amounts previously paid by the Owner;
- **.2** The amount, if any, for Work that remains uncorrected and for which the Construction Manager or Architect has previously withheld or nullified a Certificate for Payment as provided in SectionArticle 9.5 of the General Conditions.AIA Document A232–2019;

§ 5.1.4.4 The progress payment amount determined in accordance with Section 5.1.4.3 shall be further modified under the following circumstances:

- **.1** Add, upon Substantial Completion of the Work, a sum sufficient to increase the total payments to percent (%) of the Contract Sum, less such amounts as the Construction Manager recommends and the Architect determines for incomplete Work and unsettled claims; and
- **.2** Add, if final completion of the Work is thereafter materially delayed through no fault of
- **.3** Any amount which the Contractor, any additional amounts payable in accordance with Section 9.10.3 of the General Conditions. does not intend to pay a Subcontractor or material supplier, unless the Work has been performed by others the Contractor intends to pay;

§ 5.1.4.5 Reduction or limitation of retainage, if any, shall be as follows:

(If it is intended, prior to Substantial Completion of the entire Work, to reduce or limit the retainage resulting from the percentages inserted in Sections 5.1.4.3.1 and 5.1.4.3.2 above, and this is not explained elsewhere in the Contract Documents, insert here provisions for such reduction or limitation.)

~~.4~~ For Work performed or defects discovered since the last payment application, any amount for which the Architect may withhold payment, or nullify a Certificate of Payment in whole or in part, as provided in Article 9 of AIA Document A232–2019; and

~~.5~~ Retainage withheld pursuant to Section 5.1.7.

Section 5.1.4.5 was relocated to Section 5.1.7.2.

Non-substantive simplifying revisions were made to Section 5.1.5, which concerns the calculation of the Cost of the Work and deductions for purposes of pay applications.

§ 5.1.5 Progress Payments Where the Contract Sum is Based on the Cost of the Work without a Guaranteed Maximum Price

§ 5.1.5.1 With each Application for Payment, the Contractor shall submit the cost control information required in Exhibit ~~A~~B, Determination of the Cost of the Work, along with payrolls, petty cash accounts, receipted invoices, or invoices with check vouchers attached, and any other evidence required by the Owner, Construction Manager or Architect to demonstrate that ~~cash disbursements~~payments already made by the Contractor on account of the Cost of the Work equal or exceed ~~(1)~~ progress payments already received by the Contractor~~; less (2) that portion of those payments attributable to the Contractor's Fee; plus (3)~~, plus payrolls for the period covered by the present Application for Payment, less that portion of the payments attributable to the Contractor's Fee.

§ 5.1.5.2 Applications for Payment shall show the Cost of the Work actually incurred by the Contractor through the end of the period covered by the Application for Payment and for which the Contractor has made or intends to make actual payment prior to the next Application for Payment.

§ 5.1.5.3 ~~Subject~~In accordance with AIA Document A232-2019 and subject to other provisions of the Contract Documents, the amount of each progress payment shall be computed as follows:

§ 5.1 ~~Take the~~**.5.3.1** The amount of each progress payment shall first include:

- **.1** The Cost of the Work as described in Exhibit ~~A~~B, Determination of the Cost of the Work;
- **.2** ~~Add~~ That portion of Construction Change Directives that the Architect determines, in the Architect's professional judgment, to be reasonably justified; and
- **.3** The Contractor's Fee~~, less retainage of percent (%). The Contractor's Fee shall be~~ computed upon the Cost of the Work described in ~~that~~ the preceding Section 5.1.5.3.1.1 at the rate stated in ~~that~~ Section 4.3.2; or if the Contractor's Fee is stated as a fixed sum, in Section 4.3.2 an amount which bears the same ratio to that fixed-sum Fee as the Cost of the Work included in Section 5.1.5.3.1.1 bears to a reasonable estimate of the probable Cost of the Work upon its completion;.
- ~~**.3** Subtract retainage of percent (%) from that portion of the Work that the Contractor self-performs;~~
- **.4** ~~Subtract the~~

§ 5.1.5.3.2 The amount of each progress payment shall then be reduced by:

.1 The aggregate of ~~previous payments made~~any amounts previously paid by the Owner;

~~**.5** Subtract the~~

.2 The amount, if any, for Work that remains uncorrected and for which the Architect has previously withheld a Certificate for Payment as provided in Article 9 of AIA Document A232–2019;

.3 Any amount for which the Contractor does not intend to pay a Subcontractor or material supplier, unless the Work has been performed by others the Contractor intends to pay;

.4 For Work performed or defects discovered since the last payment application, any amount for which the Architect may withhold payment, or nullify a Certificate of Payment in whole or in part, as provided in Article 9 of AIA Document A232–2019;

.5 The shortfall, if any, indicated by the Contractor in the documentation required by ~~Article 5~~Section 5.1.5.1 to substantiate prior Applications for Payment, or resulting from errors subsequently discovered by the Owner's auditors in such documentation; and

~~**.6** Subtract amounts, if any, for which the Construction Manager or Architect has withheld or withdrawn a Certificate for Payment as provided in Section 9.5 of AIA Document A232™–2009, General Conditions~~

.6 Retainage withheld pursuant to Section 5.1.7.

§ 5.1.5.7 If final completion of the Work is materially delayed through no fault of the Contractor, then the Owner shall pay the Contractor any additional amounts in accordance with Article 9 of AIA Document A232–2019.

New Section 5.1.5.7 incorporates sections of the AIA Document 232, General Conditions, and may require the owner to pay the contractor additional amounts if completion is delayed. This change likely arises out of scenarios that might arise on projects when substantial design changes occur during the project. This section seeks to address and prevent disputes when additional amounts are owed to the contractor in the event of delay.

§ 5.1.6 Progress Payments Where the Contract Sum is Based on the Cost of the Work with a Guaranteed Maximum Price

§ 5.1.6.1 With each Application for Payment, the Contractor shall submit payrolls, petty cash accounts, receipted invoices or invoices with check vouchers attached, and any other evidence required by the Owner, Construction Manager or Architect to demonstrate that ~~cash disbursements~~payments already made by the Contractor on account of the Cost of the Work equal or exceed ~~(1)~~ progress payments already received by the Contractor~~; less (2) that portion of those payments attributable to the Contractor's Fee; plus (3)~~ plus payrolls for the period covered by the present Application for Payment, less that portion of the progress payments attributable to the Contractor's Fee.

§ 5.1.6.2 Each Application for Payment shall be based on the most recent schedule of values submitted by the Contractor in accordance with the Contract Documents. The schedule of values shall allocate the entire ~~Contract Sum~~Guaranteed Maximum Price among: (1) the various portions of the Work; (2) any contingency for costs that are included in the Guaranteed Maximum Price but not otherwise allocated to another line item or included in a Change Order; and be prepared in such form and supported by such data to substantiate its accuracy as the Construction Manager and Architect may require. This schedule, unless objected to by the Construction Manager or Architect, shall be used as a basis for reviewing(3) the Contractor's Applications for PaymentFee.

§ 5.1.6.2.1 The schedule of values shall be prepared in such form, and supported by such data to substantiate its accuracy, as the Construction Manager and Architect may require. This schedule of values shall be used as a basis for reviewing the Contractor's Applications for Payment.

§ 5.1.6.2.2 The allocation of the Guaranteed Maximum Price under this Section 5.1.6.2 shall not constitute a separate guaranteed maximum price for the Cost of the Work of each individual line item in the schedule of values.

§ 5.1.6.2.3 When the Contractor allocates costs from a contingency to another line item in the schedule of values, the Contractor shall submit supporting documentation to the Architect and Construction Manager.

§ 5.1.6.3 Applications for Payment shall show the percentage of completion of each portion of the Work as of the end of the period covered by the Application for Payment. The percentage of completion shall be the lesser of (1) the percentage of that portion of the Work which has actually been completed; or (2) the percentage obtained by dividing (a) the expense that has actually been incurred by the Contractor on account of that portion of the Work and for which the Contractor has made payment or intends to make actual payment prior to the next Application for Payment by (b) the share of the Guaranteed Maximum Price allocated to that portion of the Work in the schedule of values.

§ 5.1.6.4 SubjectIn accordance with AIA Document A232–2019, and subject to other provisions of the Contract Documents, the amount of each progress payment shall be computed as follows:

Take that

§ 5.1.6.4.1 The amount of each progress payment shall first include:

.1 That portion of the Guaranteed Maximum Price properly allocable to completed Work as determined by multiplying the percentage of completion of each portion of the Work by the share of the Guaranteed Maximum Price allocated to that portion of the Work in the schedule of values. Pending final determination of cost to the Owner of changes in the Work, amounts not in dispute shall be included as provided in Section 7.3.10 of AIA Document A232–2009most recent schedule of values;

.2 Add thatThat portion of the Guaranteed Maximum Price properly allocable to materials and equipment delivered and suitably stored at the site for subsequent incorporation in the Work,completed construction or, if approved in writing in advance by the Owner, suitably stored off the site at a location agreed upon in writing;

.3 AddThat portion of Construction Change Directives that the Contractor's Fee, less retainage of percent (
%).Architect determines, in the Architect's professional judgment, to be reasonably justified; and

.4 The Contractor's Fee shall be, computed upon the Cost of the Work described in the preceding Sections 5.1.6.4.1.1 and 5.1.6.4.1.2 at the rate stated in Section 4.4.2 or, if the Contractor's Fee is stated as a fixed sum in that Section, shall be an amount that bears the same ratio to that fixed-sum fee as the Cost of the Work included in Sections 5.1.6.4.1.1 and 5.1.6.4.1.2 bears to a reasonable estimate of the probable Cost of the Work upon its completion;.

~~.4 Subtract retainage of percent (%) from that portion of the Work that the Contractor self-performs;~~

.5 ~~Subtract the~~

§ 5.1.6.4.2 The amount of each progress payment shall then be reduced by:

.1 The aggregate of ~~previous payments made~~any amounts previously paid by the Owner;

~~.6 Subtract the~~

.2 The amount, if any, for Work that remains uncorrected and for which the Architect has previously withheld a Certificate for Payment as provided in Article 9 of AIA Document A232–2019;

.3 Any amount for which the Contractor does not intend to pay a Subcontractor or material supplier, unless the Work has been performed by others the Contractor intends to pay;

.4 For Work performed or defects discovered since the last payment application, any amount for which the Architect may withhold payment, or nullify a Certificate of Payment in whole or in part, as provided in Article 9 of AIA Document A232–2019;

.5 The shortfall, if any, indicated by the Contractor in the documentation required by Section 5.1.6.1 to substantiate prior Applications for Payment, or resulting from errors subsequently discovered by the Owner's auditors in such documentation; and

~~.7 Subtract amounts, if any, for which the Construction Manager or Architect have withheld or nullified a Certificate for Payment as provided in Section 9.5 of AIA Document A232–2009.~~

.6 Retainage withheld pursuant to Section 5.1.7.

Like Section 5.1.5, the changes to Section 5.1.6 are not substantive, but merely meant to clarify and simplify the method for calculating the amount of pay applications and progress payments. Additional changes regarding the schedule of values, allocation of the GMP, and contingency address commonly confusing additions and reductions to the amount of the pay application. Additional references to the A232 are incorporated in Section 5.1.6 for clarification and continuity across the forms.

§ 5.1.6.5 The Owner and the Contractor shall agree upon a ~~(1)~~ mutually acceptable procedure for review and approval of payments to Subcontractors and ~~(2)~~ the percentage of retainage held on Subcontracts, and the Contractor shall execute subcontracts in accordance with those agreements.

§ 5.1.6.6 In taking action on the Contractor's Applications for Payment, the Construction Manager and Architect shall be entitled to rely on the accuracy and completeness of the information furnished by the Contractor and such action shall not be deemed to ~~represent~~be a representation that (1) the Construction Manager or Architect have made a detailed examination, audit, or arithmetic verification of the documentation submitted in accordance with Section 5.1.6.1 or other supporting data; (2) that the Construction

Manager or Architect have made exhaustive or continuous on-site inspections; or (3) that the Construction Manager or Architect have made examinations to ascertain how or for what purposes the Contractor has used amounts previously paid on account of the Contract. Such examinations, audits, and verifications, if required by the Owner, will be performed by the Owner's auditors acting in the sole interest of the Owner.

§ 5.1.6.7 Except with the Owner's prior approval, the Contractor shall not make advance payments to suppliers for materials or equipment which have not been delivered and stored at the site.

§ 5.1.6.8 If final completion of the Work is materially delayed through no fault of the Contractor, then the Owner shall pay the Contractor any additional amounts in accordance with Article 9 of AIA Document A232–2019.

Revisions to Sections 5.1.6.5 and 5.1.6.6 are identical to the revisions to Sections 5.1.5.4. and 5.1.5.5 above and are merely stylistic and for clarification. A similar addition was made in Section 5.1.6.8 addressing delays that are not the fault of the Contractor, like in Section 5.1.5.7.

§ 5.1.7 Retainage

§ 5.1.7.1 For each progress payment made prior to when the Work of this Contract is substantially complete, the Owner may withhold the following amount, as retainage, from the payment otherwise due:

(Insert a percentage or amount to be withheld as retainage from each Application for Payment. The amount of retainage may be limited by governing law.)

§ 5.1.7.1.1 The following items are not subject to retainage:

(Insert any items not subject to the withholding of retainage, such as general conditions, insurance, etc.)

§ 5.1.7.2 Reduction or limitation of retainage, if any, shall be as follows:

(If the retainage established in Section 5.1.7.1 is to be modified prior to when the entire Work of this Contract is substantially complete, including modifications for completion of portions of the Work as provided in Section 3.4.2, insert provisions for such modifications.)

§ 5.1.7.3 Except as set forth in this Section 5.1.7.3, when the Work of this Contract is substantially complete, the Contractor may submit an Application for Payment that includes the retainage withheld from prior Applications for Payment pursuant to this Section 5.1.7. The Application for Payment submitted when the Work of this Contract is substantially complete shall not include retainage as follows:

(Insert any other conditions for release of retainage when the Work of this Contract is substantially complete, or upon Substantial Completion of the Work of all Contractors on the Project or portions thereof.)

Section 5.1.7 sets forth provisions used to calculate retainage, including when retainage can be withheld altogether. None of the subparts of Section 5.1.7 change how or when retainage is calculated or paid, but instead clarify the calculation by making retainage its own section, similar to changes made in the A201–2017.

§ 5.2 Final Payment

~~§ 5.2~~**§ 5.2.1 Final Payment Where the Contract Sum is Based on a Stipulated Sum**

§ 5.2.1.1 Final payment, constituting the entire unpaid balance of the Contract Sum, shall be made by the Owner to the Contractor when

.1 the Contractor has fully performed the Contract except for the Contractor's responsibility to correct Work as provided in ~~Section~~Article 12~~.2~~ of AIA Document A232–~~2009~~2019, and to satisfy other requirements, if any, which extend beyond final payment; and

.2 a final Certificate for Payment or Project Certificate for Payment has been issued by the Architect.

§ 5.2.1.2 The Owner's final payment to the Contractor shall be made no later than 30 days after the issuance of the final Certificate for Payment or Project Certificate for Payment, or as follows:

§ 5.2.2 Final Payment Where the Contract Sum is Based on the Cost of the Work with or without a Guaranteed Maximum Price

§ 5.2.2.1 Final payment, constituting the entire unpaid balance of the Contract Sum, shall be made by the Owner to the Contractor when

.1 the Contractor has fully performed the Contract except for the Contractor's responsibility to correct Work as provided in Article 12 of AIA Document A232–2019, and to satisfy other requirements, if any, which extend beyond final payment;

.2 the Contractor has submitted a final accounting for the Cost of the Work, pursuant to Exhibit ~~A~~B, Determination of the Cost of the Work ~~when payment is on the basis of the Cost of the Work, with or without a Guaranteed Maximum payment~~and a final Application for Payment; and

.3 a final Certificate for Payment or Project Certificate for Payment has been issued by the Architect~~; such~~ in accordance with Exhibit B, Determination of the Cost of the Work.

§ 5.2.2.2 The Owner's final payment to the Contractor shall be made ~~by the Owner not more~~no later than 30 days after the issuance of the final Certificate for Payment or Project Certificate for Payment, or as follows:

Section 5.2 separates the calculation of final payment based on a stipulated sum from final payment based on a GMP. Like many of the changes in the A132, these changes are intended to clarify calculation of payment to avoid delays in payment and disputes as to amounts.

§ 5.3 Payments due and unpaid under the Contract shall bear interest from the date payment is due at the rate stated below, or in the absence thereof, at the legal rate prevailing from time to time at the place where the Project is located. *(Insert rate of interest agreed upon, if any.)*

%

ARTICLE 6 DISPUTE RESOLUTION

§ 6.1 Initial Decision Maker

The Architect will serve as Initial Decision Maker pursuant to ~~Section~~Article 15~~.2~~ of AIA Document A232–~~2009~~2019, unless the parties appoint below another individual, not a party to this Agreement, to serve as Initial Decision Maker.

(If the parties mutually agree, insert the name, address and other contact information of the Initial Decision Maker, if other than the Architect.)

§ 6.2 Binding Dispute Resolution

For any Claim subject to, but not resolved by, mediation pursuant to ~~Section~~Article 15~~.3~~ of AIA Document A232– ~~2009~~2019, the method of binding dispute resolution shall be as follows:

(Check the appropriate box. ~~If the Owner and Contractor do not select a method of binding dispute resolution below, or do not subsequently agree in writing to a binding dispute resolution method other than litigation, Claims will be resolved by litigation in a court of competent jurisdiction.~~)

[ ] Arbitration pursuant to ~~Section~~Article 15~~.4~~ of AIA Document A232–201~~0~~9.
[ ] Litigation in a court of competent jurisdiction.
[ ] Other: *(Specify)*

If the Owner and Contractor do not select a method of binding dispute resolution or do not subsequently agree in writing to a binding dispute resolution method other than litigation, Claims will be resolved by litigation in a court of competent jurisdiction.

Small non-substantive changes to Article 6 simply revise references to the A232 to refer to the correct Article or Section in that document.

ARTICLE 7 TERMINATION OR SUSPENSION

Previous Section 7.1 stated that the Contract could be terminated in accordance with the A232. Current Section 7.1 added Section 7.1.1.1, which provides for a termination fee to be paid to the contractor.

§ 7.1.1.1 If the Contract is terminated for the Owner's convenience in accordance with Article 14 of AIA Document A232–2019, then the Owner shall pay the Contractor a termination fee as follows:

(Insert the amount of, or method for determining, the fee, if any, payable to the Contractor following a termination for the Owner's convenience.)

§ 7.2 Where the Contract Sum is Based on the Cost of the Work with or without a Guaranteed Maximum Price

§ 7.2.1 ~~Subject to the provisions of Section~~ **Termination**

§ 7.2.~~2 below, the~~1.1 The Contract may be terminated by the Owner or the Contractor as provided in Article 14 of AIA Document A232–~~2009~~2019.

§ 7.2.1.2 Termination by the Owner for Cause

§ 7.2 .1.2.1~~The Contract may be terminated by~~ If the Owner terminates the Contract for cause as provided in Article 14 of AIA Document A232–~~2009; however~~2019, the Owner shall then only pay the Contractor an amount ~~calculated~~ as follows:

.1 Take the Cost of the Work incurred by the Contractor to the date of termination;

.2 Add the Contractor's Fee, computed upon the Cost of the Work to the date of termination at the rate stated in ~~Sections~~Section 4.3.2 or 4.4.2, as applicable, or, if the Contractor's Fee is stated as a fixed sum in that Section, an amount that bears the same ratio to that fixed-sum Fee as the Cost of the Work at the time of termination bears to a reasonable estimate of the probable Cost of the Work upon its completion;~~and~~

.3 Subtract the aggregate of previous payments made by the Owner; and

.~~3~~4 Subtract the ~~aggregate of previous payments made~~costs and damages incurred, or to be incurred, by the Owner under Article 14 of AIA Document A232–2019.

§ 7.2.1.2.2.~~3~~ ~~If the Owner terminates the Contract for cause when~~ When the Contract Sum is based on the Cost of the Work with a Guaranteed Maximum Price, ~~and~~ if the Owner terminates the Contract for cause as provided in Article 14 of AIA Document A232~~–2009~~–2019, the amount, if any, to be paid to the Contractor under ~~Section~~Article 14~~.2.4~~ of AIA Document A232~~–2009~~–2019 shall not cause the Guaranteed Maximum Price to be exceeded, nor shall it exceed the amount calculated in Section 7.2.1.2.1.

§ 7.2.~~4~~1.2.3 The Owner shall also pay the Contractor fair compensation, either by purchase or rental at the election of the Owner, for any equipment owned by the Contractor that the Owner elects to retain and that is not otherwise included in the Cost of the Work under Section 7.2.1.2.1.1. To the extent that the Owner elects to take legal assignment of subcontracts and purchase orders (including rental agreements), the Contractor shall, as a condition of receiving the payments referred to in this Article 7, execute and deliver all such papers and take all such steps, including the legal assignment of such subcontracts and other contractual rights of the Contractor, as the Owner may require for the purpose of fully vesting in the Owner the rights and benefits of the Contractor under such subcontracts or purchase orders. All Subcontracts, purchase orders and rental agreements entered into by the Contractor will contain provisions allowing for assignment to the Owner as described above.

Most of the changes to Section 7.2, Termination, are not substantive with the exception of a provision in Section 7.2.1.2.3 that requires all subcontracts, purchase orders, and rental agreements between the contractor and others to contain provisions allowing assignment of those agreements to the owner upon termination.

§ 7.2.~~5~~ 1.3 Termination by the Owner for Convenience

If the Owner terminates the Contract for convenience in accordance with Article 14 of AIA Document A232–2019, then the Owner shall pay the Contractor a termination fee as follows:

(Insert the amount of or method for determining the fee, if any, payable to the Contractor following a termination for the Owner's convenience.)

Section 7.2.1.3 mirrors Section 7.1.1.1 and requires the owner to pay the contractor a termination fee upon termination for convenience.

§ 7.3 Suspension

The Work may be suspended by the Owner as provided in Article 14 of AIA Document A232–~~2009~~2019; in such case, the Contract Sum and Contract Time shall be increased as provided in ~~Section~~Article 14~~.3.2~~ of AIA Document A232– ~~2009~~2019, except that the term ~~'profit'~~"profit" shall be understood to mean the Contractor's Fee as described in ~~Sections~~Section 4.3.2 ~~and~~or 4.4.2, as applicable, of this Agreement.

Changes to Section 7.3, Suspension, are not substantive.

ARTICLE 8 MISCELLANEOUS PROVISIONS

§ 8.1 Where reference is made in this Agreement to a provision of AIA Document A232–~~2009~~2019 or another Contract Document, the reference refers to that provision as amended or supplemented by other provisions of the Contract Documents.

The provision permitting recovery of interest on unpaid contract balances has been moved from Article 8 to Section 5.3.

§ 8.~~3~~2 The Owner's representative:

(Name, address, email address, and other information)

§ 8.~~4~~3 The Contractor's representative:

(Name, address, email address, and other information)

§ 8.~~5~~4 Neither the Owner's nor the Contractor's representative shall be changed without ten ~~days written~~days' prior notice to the other party.

Email addresses were added to identification of the representatives.

~~**§ 8.6 Other provisions:**~~

§ 8.5 Insurance and Bonds

§ 8.5.1 The Owner and the Contractor shall purchase and maintain insurance as set forth in AIA Document A132™– 2019, Standard Form of Agreement Between Owner and Contractor, Construction Manager as Adviser Edition, Exhibit A, Insurance and Bonds, and elsewhere in the Contract Documents.

§ 8.5.2 The Contractor shall provide bonds as set forth in AIA Document A132™–2019, Exhibit A, and elsewhere in the Contract Documents.

§ 8.6 Notice in electronic format, pursuant to Article 1 of AIA Document A232–2019, may be given in accordance with AIA Document E203™–2013, Building Information Modeling and Digital Data Exhibit, if completed, or as otherwise set forth below:

(If other than in accordance with AIA Document E203–2013, insert requirements for delivering notice in electronic format such as name, title, and email address of the recipient and whether and how the system will be required to generate a read receipt for the transmission.)

§ 8.7 Relationship of the Parties

Where the Contract is based on the Cost of the Work plus the Contractor's Fee, with or without a Guaranteed Maximum Price, the Contractor accepts the relationship of trust and confidence established by this Agreement and covenants with the Owner to cooperate with the Architect and exercise the Contractor's skill and judgment in furthering the interests of the Owner; to furnish efficient business administration and supervision; to furnish at all times an adequate supply of workers and materials; and to perform the Work in an expeditious and economical manner consistent with the Owner's interests. The Owner agrees to furnish and approve, in a timely manner, information required by the Contractor and to make payments to the Contractor in accordance with the requirements of the Contract Documents.

§ 8.8 Other provisions:

Other changes to the Miscellaneous Provisions identify the Insurance and Bonds Exhibit (Exhibit A) (in Section 8.5.2) and provide for notice in electronic format (in Section 8.6). Where the agreement is based on the cost of the work plus the contractor's fee, with or without a GMP, it sets forth a relationship of trust and confidence between the contractor and owner (in Section 8.7).

ARTICLE 9 ENUMERATION OF CONTRACT DOCUMENTS

§ 9.1 ~~The Contract Documents, except for Modifications issued after execution of this Agreement, are enumerated in the sections below.~~

~~§ 9.1.1 The~~This Agreement is ~~this executed~~ comprised of the following documents:

.1 AIA Document A132~~–2009~~™–2019, Standard Form of Agreement Between Owner and Contractor, Construction Manager as Adviser Edition.

~~§ 9.1~~**.2** ~~The General Conditions are~~ AIA Document A132™–2019, Exhibit A, Insurance and Bonds Exhibit

.3 AIA Document A232~~–2009~~™–2019, General Conditions of the Contract for Construction, Construction Manager as Adviser Edition.

.4 AIA Document E203™–2013, Building Information Modeling and Digital Data Exhibit, dated as indicated below:

(Insert the date of the E203–2013 incorporated into this Agreement.)

.5 Drawings

.6 Specifications

.7 Addenda, if any:

~~§ 9.1.3 The~~ Portions of Addenda relating to bidding or proposal requirements are not part of the Contract Documents unless the bidding or proposal requirements are also enumerated in this Article 9.

.8 Other Exhibits:

(Check all boxes that apply and include appropriate information identifying the exhibit where required.)

[ ] AIA Document A132™–2019, Exhibit B, Determination of the Cost of the Work

[ ] AIA Document E235™–2019, Sustainable Projects Exhibit, Construction Manager as Adviser Edition, dated as indicated below:

(Insert the date of the E235–2019 incorporated into this Agreement.)

[ ] The Sustainability Plan:

[ ] Supplementary and other Conditions of the Contract:

~~§~~ **.9**~~.1.4~~ ~~The Specifications:~~

~~*(Either list the Specifications here or refer to an exhibit attached to this Agreement.)*~~

~~**§ 9.1.5** The Drawings:~~

~~*(Either list the Drawings here or refer to an exhibit attached to this Agreement.)*~~

~~**§ 9.1.6** The Addenda, if any:~~

~~Portions of Addenda relating to bidding requirements are not part of the Contract Documents unless the bidding requirements are also enumerated in this Article 9.~~

~~**§ 9.1.7** Additional documents, if any, forming part of the Contract Documents are:~~

~~.1 AIA Document A132™–2009, Exhibit A, Determination of the Cost of the Work, if applicable.~~

~~.2 AIA Document E201™–2007, Digital Data Protocol Exhibit, if completed, or the following:~~

~~.3 AIA Document E202™–2008, Building Information Modeling Protocol Exhibit, if completed, or the following:~~

~~.4~~ Other documents, if any, listed below:

(List here any additional documents ~~which~~that are intended to form part of the Contract Documents. AIA Document A232–~~2009~~2019 provides that ~~bidding requirements such as~~the advertisement or invitation to bid, Instructions to Bidders, sample forms ~~and~~, the Contractor's bid or proposal, portions of Addenda relating to bidding or proposal requirements, and other information furnished by the Owner in anticipation of receiving bids or proposals, are not part of the Contract Documents unless enumerated in this Agreement. ~~They~~ Any such documents should be listed here only if intended to be part of the Contract Documents.)

Article 9 (Enumeration of Contract Documents) contains non-substantive changes to refer to other current AIA documents and their exhibits. There is now an option to include the new E235–2019, Sustainable Projects Exhibit, Construction Manager as Advisor Edition.

ARTICLE 10 INSURANCE AND BONDS

Article 10 (Insurance and Bonds) was completely removed from the agreement itself and moved to Exhibit A. This change conforms to changes made throughout the 2019 AIA Construction Manager Agreements, as well as previous revisions to the A201–2017 and its related agreements.

A232–2019: General Conditions of the Contract for Construction, Construction Manager as Adviser Edition

The A232 is the form of General Conditions to be used when the owner hires a construction manager as advisor. It coordinates with the A132 agreement between owner and contractor, the B132 agreement between the owner and architect, and the C132 agreement between the owner and construction manager as advisor. It is important for the parties to use the A232 General Conditions when using a construction manager as advisor because the more commonly used A201 does not integrate the role of a construction manager as advisor.

ARTICLE 1 GENERAL PROVISIONS

§ 1.1 Basic Definitions

§ 1.1.1 The Contract Documents. The Contract Documents are enumerated in the Agreement between the Owner and Contractor (hereinafter the Agreement~~)~~,) and consist of the Agreement, Conditions of the Contract (General, Supplementary and other Conditions), Drawings, Specifications, Addenda issued prior to execution of the Contract, other documents listed in the Agreement, and Modifications issued after execution of the Contract. A Modification is (1) a written amendment to the Contract signed by both parties, (2) a Change Order, (3) a Construction Change Directive, or (4) a written order for a minor change in the Work issued by the Architect. Unless specifically enumerated in the Agreement, the Contract Documents do not include the advertisement or invitation to bid, Instructions to Bidders, sample forms, other information furnished by the Owner in anticipation of receiving bids or proposals, the Contractor's bid or proposal, or portions of addenda relating to bidding or proposal requirements~~)~~.

. . .

§ 1.1.4 The Project. The Project is the total construction. of which the Work performed under the Contract Documents may be the whole or a part and which may include construction by other ~~Multiple Prime~~ Contractors, and by the Owner's own forces~~, including persons or entities under separate contracts not administered by the Construction Manager~~ and Separate Contractors.

~~**§ 1.1.5 The Drawings.**~~ **§ 1.1.5 Contractors.** Contractors are persons or entities, other than the Contractor or Separate Contractors, who perform Work under contracts with the Owner that are administered by the Architect and Construction Manager.

§ 1.1.6 Separate Contractors. Separate Contractors are persons or entities who perform construction under separate contracts with the Owner not administered by the Architect and Construction Manager.

§ 1.1.7 The Drawings. The Drawings are the graphic and pictorial portions of the Contract Documents showing the design, location and dimensions of the Work, generally including plans, elevations, sections, details, schedules, and diagrams.

. . .

§ 1.1.~~8~~10 Initial Decision Maker. The Initial Decision Maker is the person identified in the Agreement to render initial decisions on Claims in accordance with Section 15.2 ~~and certify termination of the Agreement under Section 14.2.2~~. The Initial Decision Maker shall not show partiality to the Owner or Contractor and shall not be liable for results of interpretations or decisions rendered in good faith.

The change to the definition of the Initial Decision Maker clarifies that the Initial Decision Maker should be impartial and not an agent of the owner (preferable for contractors), and insulates the Initial Decision Maker from liability for its decisions.

§ 1.2.1.1 The invalidity of any provision of the Contract Documents shall not invalidate the Contract or its remaining provisions. If it is determined that any provision of the Contract Documents violates any law, or is otherwise invalid or unenforceable, then that provision shall be revised to the extent necessary to make that provision legal and enforceable. In such case the Contract Documents shall be construed, to the fullest extent permitted by law, to give effect to the parties' intentions and purposes in executing the Contract.

New Section 1.2.1.1 upholds and protects the enforceability of the contract as a whole if any provision is illegal or unenforceable in a particular state or territory, or as laws change; and provides that any unenforceable provision should be revised to make that provision valid.

§ 1.5 Ownership and Use of Drawings, Specifications, and Other Instruments of Service

§ 1.5.1 The Architect and the Architect's consultants shall be deemed the authors and owners of their respective Instruments of Service, including the Drawings and Specifications, and ~~will~~ retain all common law, statutory, and other reserved rights in their Instruments of Service, including copyrights. The Contractor, Subcontractors, sub-subcontractors, and ~~material or equipment~~ suppliers shall not own or claim a copyright in the Instruments of Service. Submittal or distribution to meet official regulatory requirements or for other purposes in connection with ~~this~~the Project is not to be construed as publication in derogation of the ~~Architect,~~Architect's or Architect's consultants' reserved rights.

§ 1.5.2 The Contractor, Subcontractors, Sub-subcontractors, and ~~material or equipment~~ suppliers are authorized to use and reproduce the Instruments of Service provided to them, subject to any protocols established pursuant to Sections 1.7 and 1.8, solely and exclusively for execution of the Work. All copies made under this authorization shall bear the copyright notice, if any, shown on the Instruments of Service. The Contractor, Subcontractors, Sub-subcontractors, and ~~material or equipment~~ suppliers may not use the Instruments of Service on other projects or for additions to ~~this~~the Project outside the scope of the Work without the specific written consent of the Owner, Architect, and the Architect's consultants.

§ 1.6 Notice

§ 1.6.1 Except as otherwise provided in Section 1.6.2, where the Contract Documents require one party to notify or give notice to the other party, such notice shall be provided in writing to the designated representative of the party to whom the notice is addressed and shall be deemed to have been duly served if delivered in person, by mail, by courier, or by electronic transmission if a method for electronic transmission is set forth in the Agreement.

§ 1.6.2 Notice of Claims as provided in Section 15.1.3 shall be provided in writing and shall be deemed to have been duly served only if delivered to the designated representative of the party to whom the notice is addressed by certified or registered mail, or by courier providing proof of delivery.

New Section 1.6 outlines how notices should be given under the agreement. Proper service of notice is often a critical factor in preserving the validity of a claim. Section 1.6 allows notification of some events to be given electronically—i.e. via email—which reflects changes in technology and in the way parties of construction projects work, including the need to give real-time notice and exchange of information instantaneously through technology rather than traditional mail. Changed conditions, accidents, shutdowns, and other issues can be resolved more quickly under this provision. This new section also requires that all "notices" referenced throughout the agreement be in writing.

However, official notice of "Claims" under Article 15 must still be sent via traditional, physical mail with proof of delivery. Electronic transmission in addition to traditional mail may be advisable, although it is not necessary.

§ 1.7 Digital Data Use and Transmission ~~of Data in Digital Form~~

~~If the~~The parties ~~intend to transmit~~shall agree upon protocols governing the transmission and use of Instruments of Service or any other information or documentation in digital form~~, they shall endeavor~~. The parties will use AIA Document E203™–2013, Building Information Modeling and Digital Data Exhibit, to establish ~~necessary protocols governing such transmissions, unless otherwise already provided in the Agreement or the Contract Documents~~the protocols for the development, use, transmission, and exchange of digital data.

§ 1.8 Building Information Models Use and Reliance

Any use of, or reliance on, all or a portion of a building information model without agreement to protocols governing the use of, and reliance on, the information contained in the model and without having those protocols set forth in AIA Document E203™–2013, Building Information Modeling and Digital Data Exhibit, and the requisite AIA Document G202™–2013, Project Building Information Modeling Protocol Form, shall be at the using or relying party's sole risk and without liability to the other party and its contractors or consultants, the authors of, or contributors to, the building information model, and each of their agents and employees.

New Section 1.7 directs the parties to agree to protocols for the use and transmission of Instruments of Service and any other electronic data. AIA Document E203–2013 is required to be used for the development, use, transmission, and exchange of digital data, including Building Information Modeling. New Section 1.8, however, limits liability for those providing BIM or other models if the parties have not agreed to protocols governing the use and reliance on the information contained in the model and those protocols are not set forth and agreed to in AIA Documents E203–2013 and G202–2013.

ARTICLE 2 OWNER

§ 2.1 General

§ 2.1.1 The Owner is the person or entity identified as such in the Agreement and is referred to throughout the Contract Documents as if singular in number. The Owner shall designate in writing a representative who shall have express authority to bind the Owner with respect to all matters requiring the Owner's approval or authorization.

Except as otherwise provided in ~~Article~~Section 4.2.1, the Construction Manager and the Architect do not have such authority. The term "Owner" means the Owner or the Owner's authorized representative.

§ 2.1.2 The Owner shall furnish to the Contractor, within fifteen days after receipt of a written request, information necessary and relevant for the Contractor to evaluate, give notice of, or enforce mechanic's lien rights. Such information shall include a correct statement of the record legal title to the property on which the Project is located, usually referred to as the site, and the Owner's interest therein.

§ 2.2 ~~Information and Services Required~~Evidence of the ~~Owner~~Owner's Financial Arrangements

§ 2.2.1 Prior to commencement of the Work, and upon written request by the Contractor ~~may request in writing that~~, the Owner ~~provide~~shall furnish to the Contractor reasonable evidence that the Owner has made financial arrangements to fulfill the Owner's obligations under the Contract. ~~Thereafter, the~~The Contractor ~~may only request~~ shall have no obligation to commence the Work until the Owner provides such evidence. If commencement of the Work is delayed under this Section 2.2.1, the Contract Time shall be extended appropriately.

Changes to Section 2.2 clarify the language regarding the contractor's request and the owner's obligation to provide financial information before commencement of work, and, importantly, permits an extension of the project schedule if the owner delays in providing reasonable evidence that financial arrangements have been made to fulfill the Owner's obligations under the Contract.

§ 2.2.2 Following commencement of the Work and upon written request by the Contractor, the Owner shall furnish to the Contractor reasonable evidence that the Owner has made financial arrangements to fulfill the Owner's obligations under the Contract only if (1) the Owner fails to make payments to the Contractor as the Contract Documents require; (2~~) a change in the Work materially changes the Contract Sum; or (3~~) the Contractor identifies in writing a reasonable concern regarding the Owner's ability to make payment when due~~. The Owner shall furnish such evidence as a condition precedent to commencement or continuation of the Work or the portion of the Work affected by a material change. After the Owner furnishes the evidence~~; or (3) a change in the Work materially changes the Contract Sum. If the Owner fails to provide such evidence, as required, within fourteen days of the Contractor's request, the Contractor may immediately stop the Work and, in that event, shall notify the Owner that the Work has stopped. However, if the request is made because a change in the Work materially changes the Contract Sum under (3) above, the Contractor may immediately stop only that portion of the Work affected by the change until reasonable evidence is provided. If the Work is stopped under this Section 2.2.2, the Contract Time shall be extended appropriately and the Contract Sum shall be increased by the amount of the Contractor's reasonable costs of shutdown, delay and start-up, plus interest as provided in the Contract Documents.

Similarly, changes to Section 2.2.2 clarify the language regarding the Contractor's request and the circumstances under which the owner is obligated to give financial information during construction of the project. This Section also permits an extension of the project schedule and the contract sum if the owner delays in providing assurance of adequate financial arrangements to fulfill its obligations within 14 days.

§ 2.2.3 After the Owner furnishes evidence of financial arrangements under this Section 2.2, the Owner shall not materially vary such financial arrangements without prior notice to the Contractor.

Additional language in Section 2.2.3 clarifies that the owner must not make changes to financial arrangements (without notice) after providing such information to the contractor. Presumably it is free to change such arrangements without notice if the contractor has never requested this information or if the owner has never provided such information to the contractor.

~~§ 2.2.2~~**§ 2.2.4** Where the Owner has designated information furnished under this Section 2.2 as "confidential," the Contractor shall keep the information confidential and shall not disclose it to any other person. However, the Contractor may disclose "confidential" information, after seven (7) days' notice to the Owner, where disclosure is required by law, including a subpoena or other form of compulsory legal process issued by a court or governmental entity, or by court or arbitrator(s) order. The Contractor may also disclose "confidential" information to its employees, consultants, sureties, Subcontractors and their employees, Sub-subcontractors, and others who need to know the content of such information solely and exclusively for the Project and who agree to maintain the confidentiality of such information.

New Section 2.2.4 outlines how confidential information should be handled during the project and the notice required if the contractor is compelled by law to disclose confidential information.

§ 2.3 Information and Services Required of the Owner

§ 2.3.1 Except for permits and fees that are the responsibility of the Contractor under the Contract Documents, including those required under Section 3.7.1, the Owner shall secure and pay for necessary approvals, easements, assessments and charges required for construction, use or occupancy of permanent structures or for permanent changes in existing facilities. Unless otherwise provided under the Contract Documents, the Owner, ~~through~~assisted by the Construction Manager, shall secure and pay for the building permit.

§ 2.3.2 The Owner shall retain an architect lawfully licensed to practice architecture, or an entity lawfully practicing architecture, in the jurisdiction where the Project is located. That person or entity is identified as the Architect in the Agreement and is referred to throughout the Contract Documents as if singular in number.

§ 2.3.3 The Owner shall retain a construction manager adviser lawfully practicing construction management in the jurisdiction where the Project is located. That person or entity is identified as the Construction Manager in the Agreement and is referred to throughout the Contract Documents as if singular in number.

~~§ 2.2.3~~**§ 2.3.4** If the employment of the Construction Manager or Architect terminates, the Owner shall employ a successor construction manager or architect to whom the Contractor has no reasonable objection and whose status under the Contract Documents shall be that of the Construction Manager or Architect, respectively.

New Sections 2.3.2 and 2.3.3 require that the owner retain an architect or architectural firm that is licensed and that both the architect and the construction manager hired by the owner be lawfully practicing in the jurisdiction where the project is located. New Section 2.3.4 outlines succession and selection of a new architect or construction manager if either terminates its engagement before completion of the project.

> **§ 2.~~2.6~~3.8** The Owner shall ~~endeavor to~~ forward all communications to the Contractor through the Construction Manager ~~and~~. Other communication shall ~~contemporaneously provide the same communications to the Architect about matters arising out of or relating to the Contract Documents~~be made as set forth in Section 4.2.6.

Section 2.3.8, along with Section 4.2.6, set the flow of communications and require that all communications from the owner to the contractor go through the construction manager. Similarly, the owner and construction manager must involve the architect in communications to the extent the architect or the architect's obligations are implicated.

> **§ 2.~~4~~5 Owner's Right to Carry Out the Work**
>
> If the Contractor defaults or neglects to carry out the Work in accordance with the Contract Documents and fails within a ten-day period after receipt of ~~written~~ notice from the Owner to commence and continue correction of such default or neglect with diligence and promptness, the Owner may, without prejudice to other remedies the Owner may have, correct such ~~deficiencies. In such case an appropriate Change Order shall be issued deducting from payments then or thereafter due the Contractor~~default or neglect. Such action by the Owner and amounts charged to the Contractor are both subject to review by the Construction Manager and prior approval of the Architect, and the Construction Manager or Architect may, pursuant to Section 9.5.1, withhold or nullify a Certificate for Payment in whole or in part, to the extent reasonably necessary to reimburse the Owner for the reasonable cost of correcting such deficiencies, including Owner's expenses and compensation for the Construction Manager's and Architect's and their respective consultants' additional services made necessary by such default, neglect, or failure. ~~Such action by the Owner~~If current and ~~amounts charged to the Contractor are both subject to prior approval of the Architect, after consultation with the Construction Manager. If~~ future payments ~~then or thereafter due the Contractor~~ are not sufficient to cover such amounts, the Contractor shall pay the difference to the Owner. If the Contractor disagrees with the actions of the Owner or the Architect, or the amounts claimed as costs to the Owner, the Contractor may file a Claim pursuant to Article 15.

If the contractor defaults or fails to carry out the work and fails to commence and continue to correct the default after ten days' written notice, the owner can carry out the work. The owner's actions and the amounts claimed are subject to the construction manager's review and prior approval by the Architect. If the contractor disagrees with these actions, the contractor can file a claim. In accordance with Section 1.6, notice of default may be transmitted electronically, but the notice of claim must be served by certified or registered mail, or by courier providing proof of delivery.

ARTICLE 3 CONTRACTOR

§ 3.1.2 The ~~plural term "Multiple Prime Contractors" refers to persons or entities who perform construction under contracts with the Owner that are administered by the Construction Manager. The term does not include the Owner's own forces, including persons or entities under separate contracts not administered by the Construction Manager.~~

Section 3.1.2 and other sections throughout the A232 remove the use of "Multiple Prime Contractors" in favor of the more general "other Contractors." The drafters of the A232 and other CMa documents assumed that the owner would engage multiple contractors and that each would enter into separate A132 agreements with the owner.

§ 3.2.4 If the Contractor believes that additional cost or time is involved because of clarifications or instructions the Architect issues in response to the Contractor's notices or requests for information pursuant to Sections 3.2.2 or 3.2.3, the Contractor shall ~~make~~submit Claims as provided in Article 15. If the Contractor fails to perform the obligations of Sections 3.2.2 or 3.2.3, the Contractor shall pay such costs and damages to the Owner, subject to section 15.1.7, as would have been avoided if the Contractor had performed such obligations. If the Contractor performs those obligations, the Contractor shall not be liable to the Owner or Architect for damages resulting from errors, inconsistencies or omissions in the Contract Documents, for differences between field measurements or conditions and the Contract Documents, or for nonconformities of the Contract Documents to applicable laws, statutes, ordinances, codes, rules and regulations, and lawful orders of public authorities.

§ 3.3 Supervision and Construction Procedures

§ 3.3.1 The Contractor shall supervise and direct the Work, using the Contractor's best skill and attention. The Contractor shall be solely responsible for, and have control over, construction means, methods, techniques, sequences, and procedures, and for coordinating all portions of the Work under the Contract~~, unless the Contract Documents give other specific instruction concerning these matters~~. If the Contract Documents give specific instructions concerning construction means, methods, techniques, sequences, or procedures, the Contractor shall evaluate the jobsite safety thereof and~~, except as stated below,~~ shall be ~~fully and~~ solely responsible for the jobsite safety of such means, methods, techniques, sequences, or procedures. If the Contractor determines that such means, methods, techniques, sequences or procedures may not be safe, the Contractor shall give timely ~~written~~ notice to the Owner, the Construction Manager, and the Architect, and shall ~~not proceed with that portion of the Work without further written instructions from the Architect, through the Construction Manager. If the Contractor is then instructed to proceed with the required~~propose alternative means, methods, techniques, sequences, or procedures ~~without acceptance of changes~~ . The Architect shall evaluate the proposed ~~by the Contractor, the Owner shall be~~alternative solely ~~responsible~~ for ~~any loss~~conformance with the design intent for the completed construction. The Construction Manager shall review the proposed alternative for sequencing, constructability, and coordination impacts on the other Contractors. Unless the Architect or ~~damage arising solely from those Owner-required~~the Construction Manager objects to the Contractor's proposed alternative, the Contractor shall perform the Work using its alternative means, methods, techniques, sequences, or procedures.

In addition to the contractor being required to not proceed with work that the contractor determines to be unsafe, revisions to Section 3.3.1 require the contractor to propose alternative means, methods, techniques, sequences, or procedures that are to be evaluated by both the architect and construction manager. This is consistent with changes made to the A201–2017. Again, in accordance with Section 1.6, notice may be given electronically.

> **§ 3.5.2** All material, equipment, or other special warranties required by the Contract Documents shall be issued in the name of the Owner, or shall be transferable to the Owner, and shall commence in accordance with Section 9.8.4.

New Section 3.5.2 requires that all required warranties be issued in the name of the owner and that these warranties be transferable. A similar section was added in the A201–2017. The referenced Section 9.8.4 provides for when these warranties commence.

> **§ 3.7.4 Concealed or Unknown Conditions.** If the Contractor encounters conditions at the site that are (1) subsurface or otherwise concealed physical conditions that differ materially from those indicated in the Contract Documents or unknown physical conditions of an unusual nature that differ materially from those ordinarily found to exist and generally recognized as inherent in construction activities of the character provided for in the Contract Documents, the Contractor shall promptly provide notice to the Owner, Construction Manager, and the Architect before conditions are disturbed and in no event later than ~~21~~14 days after first observance of the conditions. The Architect and Construction Manager will promptly investigate such conditions and, if the Architect, in consultation with the Construction Manager, determines that they differ materially and cause an increase or decrease in the Contractor's cost of, or time required for, performance of any part of the Work, will recommend that an equitable adjustment be made in the Contract Sum or Contract Time, or both. If the Architect, in consultation with the Construction Manager, determines that the conditions at the site are not materially different from those indicated in the Contract Documents and that no change in the terms of the Contract is justified, the Architect shall promptly notify the Owner, Construction Manager, and Contractor ~~in writing~~, stating the reasons. If the Owner or Contractor disputes the Architect's determination or recommendation, either party may ~~proceed~~submit a Claim as provided in Article 15.

A few changes to 3.7.4 shorten the time for a contractor to give notice of concealed or unknown conditions from 21 days to 14 days and permit the architect to given electronic rather than written notice to the owner, construction manager, and contractor if it determines that the conditions are not materially different from those indicated in the Contract Documents.

> **§ 3.10 Contractor's Construction and Submittal Schedules**
>
> **§ 3.10.1** The Contractor, promptly after being awarded the Contract, shall ~~prepare and~~ submit for the Owner's and Architect's information, and the Construction Manager's ~~approval~~use in developing the Project schedule, a Contractor's construction schedule for the Work. The schedule shall contain detail appropriate for the Project, including (1) the date of commencement of the Work, interim schedule milestone dates, and the date of

Substantial Completion; (2) an apportionment of the Work by construction activity; and (3) the time required for completion of each portion of the Work. The schedule shall provide for the orderly progression of the Work to completion and shall not exceed time limits current under the Contract Documents~~,~~. The schedule shall be revised at appropriate intervals as required by the conditions of the Work and Project~~, shall be related to the entire Project schedule to the extent required by the Contract Documents, and shall provide for expeditious and practicable execution of the Work~~. The Contractor shall cooperate with the Construction Manager in scheduling and performing the Contractor's Work to avoid conflict with, and as to cause no delay in, the work or activities of other ~~Multiple Prime~~ Contractors, or the construction or operations of the Owner's own forces~~.~~ or Separate Contractors.

Section 3.10 was revised to include submittal schedules in addition to construction schedules. Section 3.10.1 outlines several baseline details that should be included in all schedules. The role of the construction manager in this section was changed from approving the construction schedules to using them in the construction manager's preparation and development of its own project schedules.

§ 3.10.2 The Contractor ~~shall prepare a submittal schedule~~, promptly after being awarded the Contract and thereafter ~~update it~~ as necessary to maintain a current submittal schedule, ~~and~~ shall submit ~~the~~a submittal schedule~~(s)~~ for the Construction Manager's and Architect's approval. The Architect and Construction Manager's approval shall not be unreasonably ~~be~~ delayed or withheld. The submittal schedule shall (1) be coordinated with the Contractor's construction schedule, and (2) allow the Construction Manager and Architect reasonable time to review submittals. If the Contractor fails to submit a submittal schedule, or fails to provide submittals in accordance with the approved submittal schedule, the Contractor shall not be entitled to any increase in Contract Sum or extension of Contract Time based on the time required for review of submittals.

Although the construction manager's responsibility to approve the submittal schedule was removed from Section 3.10.1, it is still included in Section 3.10.2. Most of the revisions to Section 3.10.2 clarify this section without making any substantive changes. One change, however, is significant: this section now provides that a contractor's failure to provide submittals in accordance with its submittal schedule will deny the contractor an opportunity for an increase in the Contract Time or Contract Sum on account of a delay in reviewing the submittals.

§ 3.12.10.1 If professional design services or certifications by a design professional related to systems, materials, or equipment are specifically required of the Contractor by the Contract Documents, the Owner and the Architect will specify all performance and design criteria that such services must satisfy. The Contractor shall be entitled to rely upon the adequacy and accuracy of the performance and design criteria provided in the Contract Documents. The Contractor shall cause such services or certifications to be provided by ~~a properly~~an appropriately licensed design professional, whose signature and seal shall appear on all drawings, calculations, specifications, certifications, Shop Drawings, and other submittals prepared by such professional. Shop Drawings, and other submittals related to the Work, designed or certified by such professional, if prepared by others, shall bear such professional's written approval when submitted to the Architect.

The Owner, the Architect, and the ~~Architect~~Construction Manager shall be entitled to rely upon the adequacy, and accuracy ~~and completeness~~ of the services, certifications, and approvals performed or provided by such design professionals, provided the Owner and Architect have specified to the Contractor ~~all~~the performance and design criteria that such services must satisfy. Pursuant to this Section 3.12.10, the Architect will review, and approve or take other appropriate action on submittals only for the limited purpose of checking for conformance with information given and the design concept expressed in the Contract Documents. The ~~Contractor~~Construction Manager shall ~~not be responsible~~review submittals for ~~the adequacy of the performance~~sequencing, constructability, and ~~design criteria specified in the Contract Documents~~coordination impacts on other Contractors.

Changes to Section 3.12.10 provides that the contractor is entitled to rely on the adequacy and accuracy of the performance and design criteria provided in the Contract Documents.

This section continues to provide that the owner, architect, and construction manager are entitled to rely on the adequacy and accuracy of the design professional's services, certifications, and approvals but eliminates the concept of "completeness" in that reliance. The drafters reasoned that the concept of "completeness" is included within "adequacy"; i.e., if the design professional's services are not complete, these services would not be adequate.

Finally, the construction manager, not the contractor, is required to review submittals for sequencing, constructability, and coordination impacts.

§ 3.12.10.2 If the Contract Documents require the Contractor's design professional to certify that the Work has been performed in accordance with the design criteria, the Contractor shall furnish such certifications to the Construction Manager and Architect at the time and in the form specified by the Architect.

New Section 3.12.10.2 requires a contractor that engages in design-assistance to certify that the work has been performed in accordance with the design criteria. The form and timing of the certifications shall be in accordance with what the architect specifies. This change is an example of how parties are collaborating and overlapping on new delivery methods, particularly where design is not fully complete before construction begins.

ARTICLE 4 ARCHITECT AND CONSTRUCTION MANAGER

§ 4.2.2 The Architect will visit the site at intervals appropriate to the stage of construction, or as otherwise agreed with the Owner, to become generally familiar with the progress and quality of the portion of the Work completed, and to determine in general if the Work observed is being performed in a manner indicating that the Work, when fully completed, will be in accordance with the Contract Documents. However, the Architect will not be required to make exhaustive or continuous on-site inspections to check the quality or quantity of the Work. On the basis of the site visits, the Architect will keep the Owner and the Construction Manager reasonably informed about the progress and quality of the portion of the Work completed, and promptly report to the Owner and Construction

Manager ~~(1)~~ known deviations from the Contract Documents and ~~from the most recent Project schedule prepared by the Construction Manager, and (2)~~ defects and deficiencies observed in the Work.

Changes to Section 4.2.2 require the architect to keep the owner and construction manager informed of the progress and quality of the work, but removed the architect's duty to inform the owner of the progress in relation to the most recent project schedule. This Section and Section 4.2.3 acknowledge the necessary collaboration among the owner, architect, and construction manager.

§ 4.2.6 Communications ~~**Facilitating Contract Administration.** Except as otherwise provided in the Contract Documents or when direct communications have been specially authorized, the~~. The Owner ~~and Contractor~~ shall ~~endeavor to~~ communicate with ~~each other through~~ the Contractor and the Construction ~~Manager, and shall contemporaneously provide the same communications to the Architect~~ Manager's consultants through the Construction Manager about matters arising out of or relating to the Contract Documents. The Owner and Construction Manager shall include the Architect in all communications that relate to or affect the Architect's services or professional responsibilities. The Owner shall promptly notify the Architect of the substance of any direct communications between the Owner and the Construction Manager otherwise relating to the Project. Communications by and with the Architect's consultants shall be through the Architect. Communications by and with Subcontractors and ~~material~~ suppliers shall be through the Contractor. Communications by and with other ~~Multiple Prime~~ Contractors shall be through the Construction Manager ~~and shall be contemporaneously provided to the Architect if those communications are about matters arising out of or related to the Contract Documents.~~.

Communications by and with the Owner's own forces and Separate Contractors shall be through the Owner. The Contract Documents may specify other communication protocols.

The changes to Section 4.2.6 are similar to those in Section 2.3.8 and direct the owner to communicate with the contractor and construction manager's consultants only through the construction manager and to include the architect in those communications to the extent the communications relate to the architect's services or responsibilities. Similarly, communications with the architect's consultants must be through the architect and communications with subcontractors must be through the contractor. This section specifies the communication protocols for the project.

~~**§ 4.2.9**~~**§ 4.2.9** Utilizing the submittal schedule provided by the Contractor, the Construction Manager shall prepare, and revise as necessary, a Project submittal schedule incorporating information from other Contractors, the Owner, Owner's consultants, Owner's Separate Contractors and vendors, governmental agencies, and participants in the Project under the management of the Construction Manager. The Project submittal schedule and any revisions shall be submitted to the Architect for approval.

New Section 4.2.9 requires the construction manager to take the initial submittal schedule from the contractor and incorporate submittals from all other entities, parties, consultants, and subcontractors who may not be in privity with the contractor, including those engaged by the owner or architect, and create a project submittal schedule that is submitted to the Architect for approval.

> **§ 4.2.1617** If the Owner and Architect agree, the Architect will provide one or more projectProject representatives to assist in carrying out the Architect's responsibilities at the site. TheThe Owner shall notify the Construction Manager of any change in the duties, responsibilities and limitations of authority of such projectthe Project representatives shall be as set forth in an exhibit to be incorporated in the Contract Documents.

Revised Section 4.2.17 permits the architect to provide project representatives and requires the owner and architect to inform the construction manager of any changes in the representatives' responsibilities, but no longer requires those responsibilities to be set forth in an Exhibit to the Contract Documents.

ARTICLE 5 SUBCONTRACTORS

No substantive changes were made to Article 5.

ARTICLE 6 CONSTRUCTION BY OWNER OR BY SEPARATE CONTRACTORS

> **§ 6.2.2** If part of the Contractor's Work depends for proper execution or results upon construction or operations by the Owner's own forces or other Multiple Prime, Separate Contractors or other Contractors, the Contractor shall, prior to proceeding with that portion of the Work, promptly report tonotify the Construction Manager and Architect of apparent discrepancies or defects in such otherthe construction or operations by the Owner or Separate Contractor or other Contractors that would render it unsuitable for such proper execution and results. of the Contractor's Work. Failure of the Contractor soto notify the Construction Manager and the Architect of apparent discrepancies or defects prior to reportproceeding with the Work shall constitute an acknowledgment that the Owner's own forcesor Separate Contractor's or other Multiple Prime Contractors' completed or partially completed construction is fit and proper to receive the Contractor's Work, except as to defects not then reasonably discoverable. The Contractor shall not be responsible for discrepancies or defects in the construction or operations by the Owner or Separate Contractors or other Contractors that are not apparent.

Changes to Section 6.2.2 replace ambiguous "report to" language with "notify." This section requires the contractor to inspect the work of others before performing its own and to identify defects, or be responsible for assumption of those defects, unless the defects are hidden or otherwise not apparent. This Section does not define what would be "apparent"—whether that is visible or knowable without destruction or taking previous work apart.

ARTICLE 7 CHANGES IN THE WORK

§ 7.3.4 If the Contractor does not respond promptly or disagrees with the method for adjustment in the Contract Sum, the Construction Manager shall determine the adjustment on the basis of reasonable expenditures and savings of those performing the Work attributable to the change, including, in case of an increase in the Contract Sum, an amount for overhead and profit as set forth in the Agreement, or if no such amount is set forth in the Agreement, a reasonable amount. In such case, and also under Section 7.3.3.3, the Contractor shall keep and present, in such form as the Construction Manager may prescribe, an itemized accounting together with appropriate supporting data.

Unless otherwise provided in the Contract Documents, costs for the purposes of this Section 7.3.4 shall be limited to the following:

.1 Costs of labor, including applicable payroll taxes, fringe benefits required by agreement or custom, workers' compensation insurance, and other employee costs approved by the Construction Manager and Architect;

.2 Costs of materials, supplies, and equipment, including cost of transportation, whether incorporated or consumed;

.3 Rental costs of machinery and equipment, exclusive of hand tools, whether rented from the Contractor or others;

.4 Costs of premiums for all bonds and insurance, permit fees, and sales, use, or similar taxes, directly related to the change; and

.5 Costs of supervision and field office personnel directly attributable to the change.

Section 7.3.4 was moved from Section 7.3.7 and governs adjustment to the Contract Sum for Changes in the Work in the absence of the parties' agreement on the terms of the change. It sets forth the method for calculating adjustment of the Contract Sum and permits the construction manager to determine adjustments to the Contract Sum if the contractor disagrees with the owner's calculation. The unit price and quantity language has been eliminated from this Section.

§ 7.4 Minor Changes in the Work

The Architect ~~has authority to~~ may order minor changes in the Work that are consistent with the intent of the Contract Documents and do not ~~involving~~involve an adjustment in the Contract Sum or an extension of the Contract Time ~~and not inconsistent with the intent of the Contract Documents. Such~~. The Architect's order for minor changes shall be in writing. If the Contractor believes that the proposed minor change in the Work will ~~be effected by written order issued through~~affect the Contract Sum or Contract Time, the Contractor shall notify the Construction Manager and shall ~~be binding on the Owner and Contractor.~~ not proceed to implement the change in the Work. If the Contractor performs the Work set forth in the Architect's order for a minor change without prior notice to the Construction Manager that such change will affect the Contract Sum or Contract Time, the Contractor waives any adjustment to the Contract Sum or extension of the Contract Time.

Changes to Section 7.4, Minor Changes in the Work, largely mirror those made in the A201–2017. It provides that the architect may order the contractor to perform minor changes in the work as long as they are consistent with the intent of the Contract Documents (rather than "not inconsistent" as in the previous version) and that direction must be in writing. If the contractor disagrees with the architect's determination of a minor change, it must notify the construction manager—not the architect—prior to proceeding with the work. If it proceeds with the work without providing notice of its disagreement, it waives the right to any adjustment in the contract sum or contract time. Previously, the contractor was required to perform the changed work and preserve its claim.

ARTICLE 8 TIME

§ 8.3 Delays and Extensions of Time

§ 8.3.1 If the Contractor is delayed at any time in the commencement or progress of the Work by (1) an act or neglect of the Owner, ~~Owner's own forces,~~ Architect, Construction Manager, ~~Architect, any of the other Multiple Prime Contractors~~ or an employee of any of them, or of the Owner's own forces, Separate Contractors, or other Contractors; (2) by changes ordered in the Work~~, or~~; (3) by labor disputes, fire, unusual delay in deliveries, unavoidable casualties, adverse weather conditions documented in accordance with Section 15.1.6.2, or other causes beyond the Contractor's control; ~~or~~(4) by delay authorized by the Owner pending mediation and ~~arbitration, or~~binding dispute resolution; or (5) by other causes that the Contractor asserts and the Architect, based on the recommendation of the Construction Manager, determines ~~may~~ justify delay, then the Contract Time shall be extended ~~by Change Order~~ for such reasonable time as the Architect may determine.

Changes to Section 8.3.1 incorporate the definition of Separate Contractors, eliminate unnecessary terms, and rearrange terms to provide clarity and consistency. Item (3) specifically adds adverse weather conditions as a potential basis for a delay claim.

ARTICLE 9 PAYMENTS AND COMPLETION

§ 9.1 Contract Sum

§ 9.1.1 The Contract Sum is stated in the Agreement and, including authorized adjustments, is the total amount payable by the Owner to the Contractor for performance of the Work under the Contract Documents.

§ 9.1.2 If unit prices are stated in the Contract Documents or subsequently agreed upon, and if quantities originally contemplated are materially changed so that application of such unit prices to the actual quantities causes substantial inequity to the Owner or Contractor, the applicable unit prices shall be equitably adjusted.

New Section 9.1.2 specifically allows for equitable adjustment of unit prices if quantities are materially changed so that the original quantities cause an inequity. This provision acknowledges the reality that construction may begin before design documents are complete, often causing changes in unit prices and quantities that were not known during bidding. Rather than unfairly enforcing bid and unit prices based on preliminary information, this provision specifically permits equitable adjustment to either the contractor or owner; i.e., it is not a one-way provision.

> **§ 9.4.~~3~~2.1** Within seven days after the Architect receives the Project Application and Project Certificate for Payment and the Summary of Contractors' Applications for Payment from the Construction Manager, the Architect will either (1) issue to the Owner a Project Certificate for Payment, with a copy to the Construction Manager,; or (2) issue to the Owner a Project Certificate for Payment for such amount as the Architect determines is properly due, ~~or~~and notify the Construction Manager and Owner ~~in writing~~ of the Architect's reasons for withholding certification in ~~whole or in~~ part as provided in Section 9.5.1; or (3) withhold certification of the entire Project Application for Payment, and notify the Construction Manager and Owner of the Architect's reason for withholding certification in whole as provided in Section 9.5.1. The Construction Manager will promptly forward the Architect's notice of withholding certification to the Contractors.

Changes to Section 9.4.2.1 now permit an owner to withhold certification of a payment application in its entirety if appropriate.

> **§ 9.5.2** When ~~the above~~either party disputes the Architect's decision regarding a Certificate for Payment under Section 9.5.1, in whole or in part, that party may submit a Claim in accordance with Article 15.

Section 9.5.2 clarifies that either the contractor or the owner may submit a Claim under Article 15 if either of them disagree with the architect's decision on a Certificate for Payment.

> **§ 9.6.4** The Owner has the right to request written evidence from the Contractor that the Contractor has properly paid Subcontractors and ~~material and equipment~~ suppliers amounts paid by the Owner to the Contractor for subcontracted Work. If the Contractor fails to furnish such evidence within seven days, the Owner shall have the right to contact Subcontractors and suppliers to ascertain whether they have been properly paid. Neither the Owner, Construction Manager nor Architect shall have an obligation to pay, or to see to the payment of money to, a Subcontractor or supplier, except as may otherwise be required by law.

Changes to Section 9.6.4 clarify that the owner may contact and require assurances not only from subcontractors, but also from suppliers.

> **§ 9.6.8** Provided the Owner has fulfilled its payment obligations under the Contract Documents, the Contractor shall defend and indemnify the Owner from all loss, liability, damage or expense, including reasonable attorney's fees and litigation expenses, arising out of any lien claim or other claim for payment by any Subcontractor or supplier of any tier. Upon receipt of notice of a lien claim or other claim for payment, the Owner shall notify the Contractor. If approved by the applicable court, when required, the Contractor may substitute a surety bond for the property against which the lien or other claim for payment has been asserted.

New Section 9.6.8 requires the contractor to defend and indemnify the owner for lien claims not caused by the owner's breach of the agreement.

> **§ 9.10.3** If, after Substantial Completion of the Work, final completion thereof is materially delayed through no fault of the Contractor or by issuance of Change Orders affecting final completion, and the Construction Manager and Architect so confirm, the Owner shall, upon application by the Contractor and certification by the Construction Manager and Architect, and without terminating the Contract, make payment of the balance due for that portion of the Work fully completed, corrected, and accepted. If the remaining balance for Work not fully completed or corrected is less than retainage stipulated in the Contract Documents, and if bonds have been furnished, the written consent of the surety to payment of the balance due for that portion of the Work fully completed and accepted shall be submitted by the Contractor to the Architect through the Construction Manager prior to certification of such payment. Such payment shall be made under terms and conditions governing final payment, except that it shall not constitute a waiver of Claims.
>
> **§ 9.10.4** The making of final payment shall constitute a waiver of Claims by the Owner except those arising from
>
> **.1** liens, Claims, security interests, or encumbrances arising out of the Contract and unsettled;
> **.2** failure of the Work to comply with the requirements of the Contract Documents; ~~or~~
> **.3** terms of special warranties required by the Contract Documents.; or
> **.4** audits performed by the Owner, if permitted by the Contract Documents, after final payment.

The only substantive change to Section 9.10.3 potentially permits post-completion audits by the owner, if otherwise permitted by the Contract Documents.

ARTICLE 10 PROTECTION OF PERSONS AND PROPERTY

> **§ 10.2.5** The Contractor shall promptly remedy damage and loss (other than damage or loss insured under property insurance required by the Contract Documents) to property referred to in Sections 10.2.1.2, 10.2.1.3 and 10.2.1.4 caused in whole or in part by the Contractor, a Subcontractor, a Sub-subcontractor, or anyone directly or indirectly employed by any of them, or by anyone for whose acts they may be liable and for which

the Contractor is responsible under Sections 10.2.1.2, 10.2.1.3 and 10.2.1.4~~, except damage or loss~~. The Contractor may make a Claim for the cost to remedy the damage or loss to the extent such damage or loss is attributable to acts or omissions of the Owner, Construction Manager or Architect or anyone directly or indirectly employed by any of them, or by anyone for whose acts any of them may be liable, and not attributable to the fault or negligence of the Contractor. The foregoing obligations of the Contractor are in addition to the Contractor's obligations under Section 3.18.

The only substantive change to Section 10.2.5 expressly permits the contractor to make a claim for the cost to remedy damage or loss attributable to the owner, construction manager, or architect.

§ 10.3.5 The Contractor shall ~~indemnify~~reimburse the Owner for the cost and expense the Owner incurs (1) for remediation of ~~a material~~hazardous materials or ~~substance~~substances the Contractor brings to the site and negligently handles, or (2) where the Contractor fails to perform its obligations under Section 10.3.1, except to the extent that the cost and expense are due to the Owner's fault or negligence.

Rather than require the contractor to indemnify the owner, changes to Section 10.3.5 require the contractor to merely reimburse costs and expenses incurred by the owner for remediation of hazardous materials and substances.

§ 10.3.6 If, without negligence on the part of the Contractor, the Contractor is held liable by a government agency for the cost of remediation of a hazardous material or substance solely by reason of performing Work as required by the Contract Documents, the Owner shall ~~indemnify~~reimburse the Contractor for all cost and expense thereby incurred.

Changes to Section 10.3.6 also require reimbursement rather than indemnification from the owner to the contractor if the contractor is required to bear the costs of remediating hazardous materials or substances.

ARTICLE 11 INSURANCE AND BONDS

§ 11.1 Contractor's ~~Liability~~ Insurance and Bonds

§ 11.1.1 The Contractor shall purchase and maintain insurance of the types and limits of liability, containing the endorsements, and subject to the terms and conditions, as described in the Agreement or elsewhere in the Contract Documents. The Contractor shall purchase and maintain the required insurance from an insurance company or insurance companies lawfully authorized to issue insurance in the jurisdiction where the Project is located. The Owner, Construction Manager and Construction Manager's consultants, and the Architect and Architect's consultants, shall be named as additional insureds under the Contractor's commercial general liability policy or as otherwise described in the Contract Documents.

~~**§ 11.1.1** The Contractor shall purchase from and maintain in a company or companies lawfully authorized to do business in the jurisdiction in which the Project is located such insurance as will protect the Contractor from claims set forth below which may arise out of or result from the Contractor's operations and completed operations under the Contract and for which the Contractor may be legally liable, whether such operations be by the Contractor or by a Subcontractor or by anyone directly or indirectly employed by any of them, or by anyone for whose acts any of them may be liable:~~

~~**.1** Claims under workers' compensation, disability benefit and other similar employee benefit acts which are applicable to the Work to be performed;~~

~~**.2** Claims for damages because of bodily injury, occupational sickness or disease, or death of the Contractor's employees;~~

~~**.3** Claims for damages because of bodily injury, sickness or disease, or death of any person other than the Contractor's employees;~~

~~**.4** Claims for damages insured by usual personal injury liability coverage;~~

~~**.5** Claims for damages, other than to the Work itself, because of injury to or destruction of tangible property, including loss of use resulting therefrom;~~

~~**.6** Claims for damages because of bodily injury, death of a person or property damage arising out of ownership, maintenance or use of a motor vehicle; and~~

~~**.7** Claims for bodily injury or property damage arising out of completed operations; and~~

~~**.8** Claims involving contractual liability insurance applicable to the Contractor's obligations under Section 3.18.~~

~~**§ 11.1.2** The insurance required by Section 11.1.1 shall be written for not less than limits of liability specified in the Contract Documents or required by law, whichever coverage is greater. Coverages, whether written on an occurrence or claims-made basis, shall be maintained without interruption from the date of commencement of the Work until the date of final payment and termination of any coverage required to be maintained after final payment and, with respect to the Contractor's completed operations coverage, until the expiration of the period for correction of Work or for such other period for maintenance of completed operations coverage as specified in the Contract Documents.~~

~~**§ 11.1.3** Certificates of insurance acceptable to the Owner shall be submitted to the Construction Manager for transmittal to the Owner with a copy to the Architect prior to commencement of the Work and thereafter upon renewal or replacement of each required policy of insurance. These certificates and the insurance policies required by this Section 11.1 shall contain a provision that coverages afforded under the policies will not be canceled or allowed to expire until at least 30 days' prior written notice has been given to the Owner. An additional certificate evidencing continuation of liability coverage, including coverage for completed operations, shall be submitted with the final Application for Payment as required by Section 9.10.2 and thereafter upon renewal or replacement of such coverage until the expiration of the time required by Section 11.1.2. Information concerning reduction of coverage shall be furnished by the Contractor with reasonable promptness.~~

~~**§ 11.1.4** The Contractor shall cause the commercial liability coverage required by the Contract Documents to include (1) the Construction Manager, the Construction Manager's consultants, the Owner, the Architect, and the Architect's consultants as additional insureds for claims caused in whole or in part by the Contractor's negligent acts or omissions during the Contractor's operations; and (2) the Owner as an additional insured for claims caused in whole or in part by the Contractor's negligent acts or omissions during the Contractor's completed operations.~~

~~§ 11.2 Owner's Liability Insurance~~

~~The Owner shall be responsible for purchasing and maintaining the Owner's usual liability insurance.~~

~~§ 11.3 Property Insurance~~

~~**§ 11.3.1** Unless otherwise provided, the Owner shall purchase and maintain, in a company or companies lawfully authorized to do business in the jurisdiction in which the Project is located, property insurance written on a builder's risk "all risk" or equivalent policy form in the amount of the initial Contract Sum, plus value of subsequent Contract modifications and cost of materials supplied or installed by others, comprising total value for the entire Project at the site on a replacement cost basis without optional deductibles. Such property insurance shall be maintained, unless otherwise provided in the Contract Documents or otherwise agreed in writing by all persons and entities who are beneficiaries of such insurance, until final payment has been made as provided in Section 9.10 or until no person or entity other than the Owner has an insurable interest in the property required by this Section 11.3 to be covered, whichever is later. This insurance shall include interests of the Owner, the Contractor, Subcontractors and Sub- subcontractors in the Project.~~

~~**§ 11.3.1.1** Property insurance shall be on an "all-risk" or equivalent policy form and shall include, without limitation, insurance against the perils of fire (with extended coverage) and physical loss or damage including, without duplication of coverage, theft, vandalism, malicious mischief, collapse, earthquake, flood, windstorm, falsework, testing and startup, temporary buildings and debris removal including demolition occasioned by enforcement of any applicable legal requirements, and shall cover reasonable compensation for the Architect's, Contractor's, and Construction Manager's services and expenses required as a result of such insured loss.~~

~~**§ 11.3.1.2** If the Owner does not intend to purchase such property~~

§ 11.1.2 The Contractor shall provide surety bonds of the types, for such penal sums, and subject to such terms and conditions as required by the Contract Documents. The Contractor shall purchase and maintain the required bonds from a company or companies lawfully authorized to issue surety bonds in the jurisdiction where the Project is located.

§ 11.1.3 Upon the request of any person or entity appearing to be a potential beneficiary of bonds covering payment of obligations arising under the Contract, the Contractor shall promptly furnish a copy of the bonds or shall authorize a copy to be furnished.

§ 11.1.4 Notice of Cancellation or Expiration of Contractor's Required Insurance. Within three (3) business days of the date the Contractor becomes aware of an impending or actual cancellation or expiration of any insurance required by the Contract Documents, the Contractor shall provide notice directly to the Owner, and separately to the Construction Manager, of such impending or actual cancellation or expiration. Upon receipt of notice from the Contractor, the Owner shall, unless the lapse in coverage arises from an act or omission of the Owner, have the right to stop the Work until the lapse in coverage has been cured by the procurement of replacement coverage by the Contractor. The furnishing of notice by the Contractor shall not relieve the Contractor of any contractual obligation to provide any required coverage.

§ 11.2 Owner's Insurance

§ 11.2.1 The Owner shall purchase and maintain insurance of the types and limits of liability, containing the endorsements, and subject to the terms and conditions, as described in the Agreement or elsewhere in the Contract Documents. The Owner shall purchase and maintain the required insurance ~~required by the Contract and~~ from an insurance company or insurance companies lawfully authorized to issue insurance in the jurisdiction where the Project is located.

Article 11 of the A232 underwent major changes in 2019. Similar to what the AIA did with the A201 in 2017, it removed most of the insurance and bond requirements from the A232 and transferred them to a new Insurance and Bonds Exhibit, which is Exhibit A to the A132–2019. Relocating the insurance and bond requirements to an exhibit to the project agreement helps the parties and their respective insurance advisors set project-specific terms. The insurance exhibit is only a few pages long and easier for a third-party to review than the full General Conditions.

In the 2019 version, Article 11 of the A232 has only five Sections: Contractor's Insurance and Bonds (Section 11.1); Owner's Insurance (Section 11.2); Waivers of Subrogation (Section 11.3); Loss of Use, Business Interruption, Delay in Completion Insurance (Section 11.4); and Adjustment and Settlement of Insured Loss (Section 11.5).

§ 11.2.2 Failure to Purchase Required Property Insurance. If the Owner fails to purchase and maintain the required property insurance, with all of the coverages and in the ~~amount~~amounts described ~~above~~in the Agreement or elsewhere in the Contract Documents, the Owner shall ~~so~~ inform both the Contractor and the Construction Manager, separately and in writing, prior to commencement of the Work. ~~The~~Upon receipt of notice from the Owner, the Contractor may ~~then effect~~delay commencement of the Work and may obtain insurance that will protect the interests of the Contractor, Subcontractors, and Sub-Subcontractors in the Work. When the failure to provide coverage has been cured or resolved, the Contract Sum and Contract Time shall be equitably adjusted. In the event the Owner fails to procure coverage, the Owner waives all rights against the Contractor, Subcontractors, and Sub-subcontractors ~~in the Work, and by appropriate Change Order the~~to the extent the loss to the Owner would have been covered by the insurance to have been procured by the Owner. The cost ~~thereof~~ of the insurance shall be charged to the Owner~~. If~~ by a Change Order. If the Owner does not provide written notice, and the Contractor is damaged by the failure or neglect of the Owner to purchase or maintain the required insurance ~~as described above, without so notifying the Contractor in writing, then~~, the Owner shall ~~bear~~reimburse the Contractor for all reasonable costs ~~properly~~and damages attributable thereto.

Section 11.2.2 permits the contractor to purchase property insurance if the owner fails provide the required level of insurance and charge the cost to the owner. The contractor may delay commencement of the work until the proper insurance has been obtained.

§ 11.2.3.~~1.3~~ ~~If the~~ Notice of Cancellation or Expiration of Owner's Required Property Insurance. Within three (3) business days of the date the Owner becomes aware of an impending or actual cancellation or expiration of any property insurance required by the Contract Documents, the Owner shall provide notice directly to the Contractor, and separately to the Construction Manager, of such impending or actual cancellation or expiration. Unless the lapse in coverage arises from an act or omission of the Contractor: (1) the Contractor, upon receipt of notice from the Owner, shall have the right to stop the Work until the lapse in coverage has been cured by the procurement of replacement coverage by either the Owner or the Contractor; (2) the Contract Time and Contract Sum shall be equitably adjusted; and (3) the Owner waives all rights against the Contractor, Subcontractors, and Sub-subcontractors to the extent any loss to the Owner would have been covered by the insurance had it not expired or been cancelled. If the Contractor purchases replacement coverage, the cost of the insurance shall be charged to the Owner by an appropriate Change Order. The furnishing of notice by the Owner shall not relieve the Owner of any contractual obligation to provide required insurance.

~~Within three (3) business days of the date the Owner becomes aware of an impending or actual cancellation or expiration of any property insurance requires deductibles, the Owner shall pay costs not covered because of such deductibles.~~

~~**§ 11.3.1.4** This property insurance shall cover portions of the Work stored off the site, and also portions of the Work in transit.~~

~~**§ 11.3.1.5** Partial occupancy or use in accordance with Section 9.9 shall not commence until the insurance company or companies providing property insurance have consented to such partial occupancy or use by endorsement or otherwise. The Owner and the Contractor shall take reasonable steps to obtain consent of the insurance company or companies and shall, without mutual written consent, take no action with respect to partial occupancy or use that would cause cancellation, lapse or reduction of insurance.~~

~~**§ 11.3.2 Boiler and Machinery Insurance.** The Owner shall purchase and maintain boiler and machinery insurance required by the Contract Documents or by law, which shall specifically cover such insured objects during installation and until final acceptance by the Owner; this insurance shall include interests of the Owner, Construction Manager, Contractor, Subcontractors and Sub-subcontractors in the Work, and the Owner and Contractor shall be named insureds.~~

~~**§ 11.3.3 Loss of Use Insurance.** The Owner, at the Owner's option, may purchase and maintain such insurance as will insure the Owner against loss of use of the Owner's property due to fire or other hazards, however caused. The Owner waives all rights of action against the Contractor for loss of use of the Owner's property, including consequential losses due to fire or other hazards however caused.~~

~~**§ 11.3.4** If the Contractor requests in writing that insurance for risks other than those described herein or other special causes of loss be included in the property insurance policy, the Owner shall, if possible, include such insurance, and the cost thereof shall be charged to the Contractor by appropriate Change Order.~~

Section 11.2.3 requires the owner to give notice directly to the contractor and construction manager that insurance has been or will be cancelled, in which case the contractor may stop the work, purchase the required insurance at the owner's expense, and seek an adjustment to the Contract Time and Contract Sum. In all cases, the owner is not relieved of its obligations to provide insurance simply because it follows these notice provisions.

§ 11.4 Loss of Use, Business Interruption, and Delay in Completion Insurance

The Owner, at the Owner's option, may purchase and maintain insurance that will protect the Owner against loss of use of the Owner's property, or the inability to conduct normal operations, due to fire or other causes of loss. The Owner waives all rights of action against the Contractor, Architect, and Construction Manager for loss of use of the Owner's property, due to fire or other hazards however caused.

Section 11.4 allows the owner to purchase additional insurance to protect it from damages arising from loss of use of the property due to fire or other common losses and waives its rights to make such claims or seek such damages from the other parties. This provision does not condition the waiver on the owner purchasing this insurance.

ARTICLE 12 UNCOVERING AND CORRECTION OF WORK

§ 12.1 Uncovering of Work

§ 12.1.1 If a portion of the Work is covered contrary to the Construction Manager's or Architect's request or to requirements specifically expressed in the Contract Documents, it must, if requested in writing by either, be uncovered for their ~~observation~~examination and be replaced at the Contractor's expense without change in the Contract Time.

Article 12 covers situations when the architect or construction manager require the contractor to uncover work-in-place to determine if it was performed in accordance with the Contract Documents. The previous version of Section 12.1.1 required the contractor to uncover the work enough for the construction manager's or architect's observation. The revised section requires the work to be uncovered enough for examination. Since examination is a more thorough activity than observation, this change may result in a greater obligation on the contractor and presumably a higher cost, both in the uncovering and recovering of the work.

§ 12.1.2 If a portion of the Work has been covered ~~which~~that the Construction Manager or Architect has not specifically requested to ~~observe~~examine prior to its being covered, the Construction Manager or Architect may request to see such Work and it shall be uncovered by the Contractor. If such Work is in accordance with the Contract Documents, ~~costs of uncovering and replacement~~the Contractor shall~~, by~~ be entitled to an equitable adjustment to the Contract Sum and Contract Time as may be appropriate ~~Change Order, be at the Owner's expense.~~. If such Work is not in accordance with the Contract Documents, ~~such~~the costs of uncovering the Work, and the cost of correction, shall be at the Contractor's expense ~~unless the condition was caused by the Owner or one of the other Contractors in which event the Owner shall be responsible for payment of such costs~~.

The previous version of Section 12.1.2 provided that the cost of uncovering and correcting Work that was found to be not in conformance with the Contract

Documents was at the contractor's expense unless the non-conformance was caused by the owner or other contractors. That exception was removed in the 2019 version, although the contractor still could make a Claim under Article 15 for increased costs caused by the fault of the owner or one of the other contractors.

The only substantive change in Section 12.2.1 is that it now separates out the requirements for correction of the work before and after substantial completion.

ARTICLE 13 MISCELLANEOUS PROVISIONS

There are only two major changes to Article 13: Section 13.7 ("Time Limits on Claims") was relocated to Article 15 ("Claims"), and Section 13.4.1 was revised to require the owner to both directly arrange and pay for tests, inspections, and approvals required by building codes or applicable law. The previous version only required the owner to pay for these tests.

ARTICLE 14 TERMINATION OR SUSPENSION OF THE CONTRACT

For the most part, the 2019 changes to Article 14 were minor. Changes to two sections, however, were significant and both relate to the contractor's ability to recover profit and overhead on unperformed work.

§ 14.1 Termination by the Contractor

. . .

§ 14.1.3 If one of the reasons described in Section 14.1.1 or 14.1.2 exists, the Contractor may, upon seven days' ~~written~~ notice to the Owner, Construction Manager and Architect, terminate the Contract and recover from the Owner payment for Work executed ~~including~~, as well as reasonable overhead and profit~~;~~ on Work not executed, and costs incurred by reason of such termination~~, and damages~~.

Under Section 14.1.3, when the contractor terminates the agreement on account of the owner's default, the contractor always has been entitled to recover payment for all Work performed through the date of termination. Under the 2019 revisions, the contractor is also now entitled to recover profit and overhead on Work not executed. This change, which is consistent with changes made to the A201 in 2017, recognizes that the contractor should be able to realize the benefit of its bargain when the owner's breach results in a termination of the agreement.

§ 14.4 Termination by the Owner for Convenience

. . .

§ 14.4.3 In case of such termination for the Owner's convenience, the Owner shall pay the Contractor ~~shall be entitled to receive payment~~ for Work properly executed~~, and~~; costs incurred by reason of ~~such~~the termination, ~~along with reasonable overhead and profit on the Work not executed~~including costs attributable to termination of Subcontracts; and the termination fee, if any, set forth in the Agreement.

While the contractor gained the right to overhead and profit on unexecuted work upon a termination for the owner's default, it lost that right upon the owner's termination for convenience. Under the previous version of Section 14.4.3, the contractor was automatically entitled to profit and overhead on unexecuted work upon the owner's termination for convenience. With the 2019 revisions, however, the contractor instead may receive whatever "termination fee" the parties negotiated and inserted into the A132, in addition to the contractor's payment for work executed through the date of termination plus costs attributable to the termination. For this reason, contractors should not simply overlook the opportunity to negotiate a termination fee in the agreement.

ARTICLE 15 CLAIMS AND DISPUTES

§ 15.1 Claims

§ 15.1.1 Definition. A Claim is a demand or assertion by one of the parties seeking, as a matter of right, payment of money, a change in the Contract Time, or other relief with respect to the terms of the Contract. The term "Claim" also includes other disputes and matters in question between the Owner and Contractor arising out of or relating to the Contract. The responsibility to substantiate Claims shall rest with the party making the Claim. This Section 15.1.1 does not require the Owner to file a Claim in order to impose liquidated damages in accordance with the Contract Documents.

Section 15.1.1 has been revised to include changes in Contract Time as part of Claims. The previous version of Article 15 described claims as including only claims for money.

Section 15.1.1 also clarifies that an agreement as to liquidated damages is self-executing and the owner need not assert a Claim to impose liquidated damages. This change was also made in the A201–2017 and may have been prompted by cases holding that a claim for liquidated damages was a "Claim" that an owner waived if it did not timely assert it. It also recognizes that disputes over timely completion are often resolved during project closeout, which may occur months after the delay first occurred, thereby putting the liquidated damages remedy at risk.

§ 15.1.2 ~~Notice of~~ Time Limits on Claims.

The Owner and Contractor shall commence all Claims and causes of action against the other and arising out of or related to the Contract, whether in contract, tort, breach of warranty or otherwise, in accordance with the requirements of the binding dispute resolution method selected in the Agreement and within the period specified by applicable law, but in any case not more than 10 years after the date of Substantial Completion of the Work. The Owner and Contractor waive all Claims and causes of action not commenced in accordance with this Section 15.1.2.

This Section was relocated from Section 13.7 to this Section.

§ 15.1.3 Notice of Claims

§ 15.1.3.1 Claims by either the Owner or Contractor ~~must~~, where the condition giving rise to the Claim is first discovered prior to expiration of the period for correction of the Work set forth in Section 12.2.2, shall be initiated by ~~written~~ notice to the other party and to the Initial Decision Maker with a copy sent to the Construction Manager and Architect, if the ~~Construction Manager and or~~ Architect is not serving as the Initial Decision Maker. Claims by either party ~~must~~under this Section 15.1.3.1 shall be initiated within 21 days after occurrence of the event giving rise to such Claim or within 21 days after the claimant first recognizes the condition giving rise to the Claim, whichever is later.

§ 15.1.3.2 Claims by either the Owner or Contractor, where the condition giving rise to the Claim is first discovered after expiration of the period for correction of the Work set forth in Section 12.2.2, shall be initiated by notice to the other party. In such event, no decision by the Initial Decision Maker is required.

Changes to Sections 15.1.3.1 and 15.1.3.2 distinguish Claims discovered before the expiration of the period for correction of the Work, and after the expiration of that period. Claims discovered before the correction period expires must be served upon the Initial Decision Maker, construction manager, and architect within 21 days. Claims discovered after the correction period must be served only on the other party within the time limit for all Claims set forth in Section 15.1.2.

§ 15.1.4 Continuing Contract Performance

§ 15.1.4.1 Pending final resolution of a Claim, except as otherwise agreed in writing or as provided in Section 9.7 and Article 14, the Contractor shall proceed diligently with performance of the Contract and the Owner shall continue to make payments in accordance with the Contract Documents. ~~The Construction Manager will prepare Change Orders and the Architect will issue a Certificate for Payment or Project Certificate for Payment in accordance with the decisions of the Initial Decision Maker.~~

§ 15.1.4.2 The Contract Sum and Contract Time shall be adjusted in accordance with the Initial Decision Maker's decision, subject to the right of either party to proceed in accordance with this Article 15. The Architect will issue Certificates for Payment in accordance with the decision of the Initial Decision Maker.

The previous version of Section 15.1.4.1 required the construction manager to prepare change orders and the architect to issue certificates for payment to implement decisions of the Initial Decision Maker. This requirement was removed in 2019 because change orders, by definition, require the consent of the owner and contractor. It is unlikely that a decision by the Initial Decision Maker will have both parties' consent. Instead, as stated in new Section 15.1.4.2, if the parties disagree with the Initial Decision Maker's decision, they may pursue a Claim.

§ 15.2 Initial Decision

§ 15.2.1 Claims, excluding those where the condition giving rise to the Claim is first discovered after expiration of the period for correction of the Work set forth in Section 12.2.2 or arising under Sections 10.3, 10.4, ~~11.3.9,~~ and 11.~~3.10~~5, shall be referred to the Initial Decision Maker for initial decision. The Architect will serve as the Initial Decision Maker, unless otherwise indicated in the Agreement. Except for those Claims excluded by this Section 15.2.1, an initial decision shall be required as a condition precedent to mediation of any Claim ~~arising prior to the date final payment is due, unless~~. If an initial decision has not been rendered within 30 days ~~have passed~~ after the Claim has been referred to the Initial Decision Maker ~~with no~~, the party asserting the Claim may demand mediation and binding dispute resolution without a decision having been rendered. Unless the Initial Decision Maker and all affected parties agree, the Initial Decision Maker will not decide disputes between the Contractor and persons or entities other than the Owner.

Changes to Section 15.2.1 are made for consistency with 15.1.3.2 regarding claims where the period for correction of the Work has expired. Other changes in the order of terms clarify that section without making any substantive changes.

§ 15.2.6.1 Either party may, within 30 days from the date of receipt of an initial decision, demand in writing that the other party file for mediation ~~within 60 days of the initial decision.~~. If such a demand is made and the party receiving the demand fails to file for mediation within ~~the time required~~30 days of receipt thereof, then both parties waive their rights to mediate or pursue binding dispute resolution proceedings with respect to the initial decision.

The only substantive change to Section 15.2.6.1 is a reduction of the time period to file for mediation from 60 days after the initial decision to 30 days after being demanded to do so.

§ 15.3.3 Either party may, within 30 days from the date that mediation has been concluded without resolution of the dispute or 60 days after mediation has been demanded without resolution of the dispute, demand in writing that the other party file for binding dispute resolution. If such a demand is made and the party receiving the demand fails to file for binding dispute resolution within 60 days after receipt thereof, then both parties waive their rights to binding dispute resolution proceedings with respect to the initial decision.

New Section 13.2.2 provides a mechanism for a party to demand that the other party file for binding dispute resolution if mediation efforts fail. It allows one party that desires finality of a dispute to force the other party to pursue a binding remedy immediately or be deemed to have waived it.

§ 15.4 Arbitration

§ 15.4.1 If the parties have selected arbitration as the method for binding dispute resolution in the Agreement, any Claim subject to, but not resolved by, mediation shall be subject to arbitration which, unless the parties mutually agree otherwise, shall be administered by the American Arbitration Association in accordance with its Construction Industry Arbitration Rules in effect on the date of the Agreement. <u>The Arbitration shall be conducted in the place where the Project is located, unless another location is mutually agreed upon.</u> A demand for arbitration shall be made in writing, delivered to the other party to the Contract, and filed with the person or entity administering the arbitration. The party filing a notice of demand for arbitration must assert in the demand all Claims then known to that party on which arbitration is permitted to be demanded.

Changes to Section 15.4.1 require the arbitration to occur at the location of the project, which is consistent with many state laws requiring construction disputes to be resolved in the state where the project is located.

B132–2019: Standard Form of Agreement between Owner and Architect, Construction Manager as Adviser Edition

The B132 is an owner-architect agreement to be used when the owner also hires a construction manager as advisor. Most of the changes to Article 1 are minor or stylistic.

ARTICLE 1 INITIAL INFORMATION

§ 1.1 This Agreement is based on the Initial Information set forth in this Section 1.1.

(~~Note the disposition for the following items by inserting the requested~~For each item in this section, insert the information or a statement such as "not applicable," or "unknown at time of execution~~" or "to be determined later by mutual agreement.")~~".)

§ 1.1.1 The Owner's program for the Project:

(~~Identify~~Insert the Owner's program, identify documentation that establishes the Owner's program, or state the manner in which the program will be developed.)

§ 1.1.2 The Project's physical characteristics:

(Identify or describe~~, if appropriate, size, location, dimensions, or other~~ pertinent information about the Project's physical characteristics, such as size; location; dimensions; geotechnical reports; site~~, boundary and~~ boundaries; topographic surveys; traffic and utility studies; availability of public and private utilities and services; legal description of the site; etc.)

§ 1.1.3 The Owner's budget for the Cost of the Work, as defined in Section 6.1:

(Provide total and, if known, a line item breakdown.)

§ 1.1.4 The Owner's anticipated design and construction ~~schedule~~milestone dates:

.1 Design phase milestone dates, if any:
.2 ~~Commencement of construction~~Construction commencement date:
.3 Substantial Completion date or dates:
.4 Other milestone dates:
~~**.4** Other:~~

§ 1.1.5 The Owner intends ~~to retain a Construction Manager adviser and:~~

~~(Note that, if Multiple Prime Contractors are used,~~ the ~~term "Contractor" as referred to throughout this Agreement will be as if plural in number.)~~following procurement method for the Project:

~~[ ] One Contractor~~
~~[ ] Multiple Prime Contractors~~
~~[ ] Unknown at time of execution~~

(Identify method such as competitive bid or negotiated contract.)

Section 1.1.5 previously was intended for the owner to indicate whether it intended to use a single contractor or multiple contractors. The AIA now assumes that the owner will retain multiple contractors when using a construction manager as advisor, with each contractor entering into a separate A132. The revised Section 1.1.5 allows the owner to identify the procurement method for those contractors (e.g., competitive bid, negotiated contract).

§ 1.1.6 The Owner's requirements for accelerated or fast-track ~~scheduling~~design and construction, multiple bid packages, or phased construction are set forth below:

~~(List~~(Identify any requirements for fast-track scheduling or phased construction and, if applicable, list number and type of bid/procurement packages.)

Section 1.1.6 was revised to acknowledge that concurrent design and construction phases drive fast-track projects and requires the identification of any requirements for fast-track scheduling or phased construction.

§ 1.1.7 ~~Other Project information:~~

~~(Identify special characteristics or needs of~~The Owner's anticipated Sustainable Objective for the Project ~~not provided elsewhere, such as environmentally responsible design or historic preservation requirements.)~~:

(Identify and describe the Owner's Sustainable Objective for the Project, if any.)

§ 1.1.7.1 If the Owner identifies a Sustainable Objective, the Owner and Architect shall complete and incorporate AIA Document E235–2019, Sustainable Projects Exhibit, Construction Manager as Adviser Edition, into this Agreement to define the terms, conditions and services related to the Owner's Sustainable Objective. If E235–2019 is incorporated into this Agreement, the Owner and Architect shall incorporate the completed E235–2019 into the agreements with the consultants and contractors performing services or Work in any way associated with the Sustainable Objective.

Both the B132 and B133 permit inclusion of the owner's "Sustainable Objective" in Sections 1.1.7 and 1.1.7.1. These provisions reflect industry awareness and consideration of energy and sustainability practices and the desire to incorporate such measures into projects. The 2019 version provides owners with the option of incorporating a new Exhibit, E235–2019, to set these goals.

§ 1.1.8 The Owner identifies the following representative in accordance with Section 5.4:

(List name, address, and other contact information.)

§ 1.1.9 The persons or entities, in addition to the Owner's representative, who are required to review the Architect's submittals to the Owner are as follows:

(List name, address, and other contact information.)

§ 1.1.10 The Owner ~~will~~shall retain the following consultants and Contractors:

(List name, legal status, address, and other contact information.)

.1 Construction Manager:
(The Construction Manager is identified on the cover page. If a Construction Manager has not been retained as of the date of this Agreement, state the anticipated date of retention~~:~~. If the Architect is to assist the Owner in selecting the Construction Manager, complete Section 4.1.1.1.)

Section 1.1.10.1 now refers owners and architects to Section 4.1.1.1 if the construction manager has not been selected and the architect is to assist the owner in that selection.

.2 ~~Cost Consultant (if in addition to the Construction Manager):~~
~~(If a Cost Consultant is retained, appropriate references to the Cost Consultant should be inserted in Sections 3.2.6, 3.2.7, 3.3.2, 3.3.3, 3.4.5, 3.4.6, 5.4, 6.3, 6.3.1, 6.4 and 11.6.)~~
.3 Land Surveyor:
.~~4~~3 Geotechnical Engineer:
.~~5~~4 Civil Engineer:
.~~6~~5 Other consultants and Contractors:

(List any other consultants and Contractors retained by the Owner~~, such as a Project or Program Manager, or scheduling consultant~~.)

The reference to a Cost Consultant in addition to the construction manager has been eliminated from Section 1.1.10.2, though such a Consultant could be included in subsection 5, "Other consultants and Contractors," if one was to be engaged.

§ 1.2 The Owner and Architect may rely on the Initial Information. Both parties, however, recognize that ~~such information~~the Initial Information may materially change and, in that event, the Owner and the Architect shall appropriately adjust the Architect's services, schedule, for the Architect's services, and the Architect's compensation. The Owner shall adjust the Owner's budget for the Cost of the Work and the Owner's anticipated design and construction milestones, as necessary, to accommodate material changes in the Initial Information.

Section 1.2 was expanded to include adjustment to the owner's budget and schedule in addition to the architect's scope, schedule, and compensation if the material information substantively changes.

§ 1.3 The parties shall agree upon protocols governing the transmission and use of Instruments of Service or any other information or documentation in digital form. The parties will use AIA Document E203–2013, Building Information Modeling and Digital Data Exhibit, to establish the protocols for the development, use, transmission, and exchange of digital data.

§ 1.3.1 Any use of, or reliance on, all or a portion of a building information model without agreement to protocols governing the use of, and reliance on, the information contained in the model and without having those protocols set forth in AIA Document E203–2013, Building Information Modeling and Digital Data Exhibit, and the requisite AIA Document G202–2013, Project Building Information Modeling Protocol Form, shall be at the using or relying party's sole risk and without liability to the other party and its contractors or consultants, the authors of, or contributors to, the building information model, and each of their agents and employees.

New Section 1.3 recognizes the advancements in technology and changes in how parties share and transmit information using that technology. Section 1.3 directs the parties to use the E203–2013. If building information modeling is used without establishing protocols governing use of and reliance on this information utilizing AIA Documents G202–2013 and E203–2013, use and reliance on this information will be at the sole risk of the using or relying party.

ARTICLE 2 ARCHITECT'S RESPONSIBILITIES

> **§ 2.1** The Architect shall provide ~~the~~ professional services as set forth in this Agreement. The Architect represents that it is properly licensed in the jurisdiction where the Project is located to provide the services required by this Agreement, or shall cause such services to be performed by appropriately licensed design professionals.

Revised Section 2.1 requires the architect to make certain representations regarding being licensed or that it has engaged others who are appropriately licensed. This was always an obligation of the architect, but now it is expressly stated as such in the agreement.

> **§ 2.6.2** Automobile Liability covering vehicles owned, and ~~rented~~non-owned vehicles ~~operated~~used, by the Architect with policy limits of not less than ($) ~~combined single limit and aggregate~~per accident for bodily injury, death of any person, and property damage arising out of the ownership, maintenance and use of those motor vehicles, along with any other statutorily required automobile coverage.

Changes to Section 2.6.2 broaden the scope of vehicles to be covered by automobile insurance by replacing "rented" with "non-owned," as these vehicles could potentially be owned or rented by others or on the site through some other agreement. Additional language clarifies that injury, death, or damage must arise out of ownership, maintenance, and use of the covered automobiles for coverage to exist.

> **§ 2.6.3** The Architect may ~~use umbrella or excess liability insurance to~~ achieve the required limits and coverage for ~~Comprehensive~~Commercial General Liability and Automobile Liability through a combination of primary and excess or umbrella liability insurance, provided ~~that~~ such primary and excess or umbrella ~~or excess~~liability insurance ~~results~~policies result in the same ~~type of~~or greater coverage as ~~required for the individual policies~~the coverages required under Sections 2.6.1 and 2.6.2, and in no event shall any excess or umbrella liability insurance provide narrower coverage than the primary policy. The excess policy shall not require the exhaustion of the underlying limits only through the actual payment by the underlying insurers.

Changes to Section 2.6.3 state that any excess policy combined with the principal or umbrella policy to achieve the required limits must not contain a provision requiring that the underlying insurers pay the underlying limits before the excess policy kicks in. This revision is included to prevent situations where projects have sufficient coverage through multiple policies, but are nevertheless insufficiently insured because the limits of the underlying policy are not exhausted, resulting in the umbrella and excess policies never being triggered.

> **§ 2.6.~~5~~6** Professional Liability covering ~~the Architect's~~ negligent acts, errors and omissions in ~~its~~the performance of professional services with policy limits of not less than ($) per claim and ($) in the aggregate.

Changes to Section 2.6.6 recognize that other than the architect, there may be others who will be providing professional services and have a need for professional liability insurance, including engineers, contractors, or consultants who may have limited design or design-assist obligations.

ARTICLE 3 SCOPE OF ARCHITECT'S BASIC SERVICES

> **§ 3.1.3** As soon as practicable after the date of this Agreement, the Architect shall submit ~~to~~, for the ~~Owner~~Construction Manager's review and the ~~Construction Manager~~Owner's approval, a schedule for the performance of the Architect's services ~~for inclusion in the Project schedule prepared by the Construction Manager~~. The schedule ~~of the Architect's services~~ shall include design phase milestone dates, as well as the anticipated dates ~~when cost estimates or design reviews may occur, and~~ for the commencement of construction and for Substantial Completion of the Work as set forth in the Initial Information. This schedule shall include allowances for periods of time required ~~(1)~~ for the Owner's review, ~~(2)~~ for the Construction Manager's review, ~~(3)~~ for the performance of the Owner's consultants, and ~~(4)~~ for approval of submissions by authorities having jurisdiction over the Project. Once approved by the Owner, time limits established by the schedule shall not, except for reasonable cause, be exceeded by the Architect or Owner. With the Owner's approval, the Architect shall adjust the schedule, if necessary, as the Project proceeds until the commencement of construction.

Under the B132–2009, the architect was required to submit to the owner and construction manager for their respective review the architect's schedule for the performance of its services (including design reviews) to be included in the overall project construction schedule. The B132–2019 clarifies that the submission to the construction manager is for the construction manager's *review* while the submission to the owner is for the owner's *approval*.

This Section includes new language relocated from Section 3.1.5 stating that once the owner approves the schedule, the schedule will not unreasonably be exceeded or delayed by the architect or owner except with the owner's approval.

> **§ 3.1.4** The Architect shall submit information to the Construction Manager and participate in developing and revising the Project schedule as it relates to the Architect's services. The Architect shall review and approve, or take other appropriate action upon, the portion of the Project schedule relating to the performance of the Architect's services.

Revisions to Section 3.1.4 emphasize the architect's responsibility for its portion of the project schedule relating to its services. This portion of the project schedule is subject to the architect's approval.

> ~~**§ 3.1.5** Once the Owner and the Architect agree to the time limits established by the Project schedule, the Owner and the Architect shall not exceed them, except for reasonable cause.~~

Former Section 3.1.5 was relocated to Section 3.1.3.

> ~~**§ 3.1.6**~~ **§ 3.1.5** The Architect shall not be responsible for an Owner's or Construction Manager's directive or substitution, or for the Owner's acceptance of non-conforming Work, made or given without the Architect's written approval.

The change to re-numbered Section 3.1.5 provides that for non-conforming work, the architect is not liable for an owner's or construction manger's directive or substitution or the owner's acceptance of it unless the architect provides written approval.

> **§ 3.2.3** The Architect shall present its preliminary evaluation to the Owner and Construction Manager and shall discuss with the Owner and Construction Manager alternative approaches to design and construction of the Project, ~~including the feasibility of incorporating environmentally responsible design approaches.~~. The Architect shall reach an understanding with the Owner and Construction Manager regarding the requirements of the Project.

Changes to Section 3.2.3 clarify that the architect must reach an understanding of the requirements of the project not only with the owner but also the construction manager. It also eliminates language about "environmentally responsible design approaches" because sustainability is now handled differently in the document.

> **§ 3.4 Construction Documents Phase Services**
>
> **§ 3.4.1** Based on the Owner's approval of the Design Development Documents, and on the Owner's authorization of any adjustments in the Project requirements and the budget for the Cost of the Work, the Architect shall prepare Construction Documents for the ~~Owner's approval and the~~ Construction Manager's review and the Owner's approval. The Construction Documents shall illustrate and describe the further development of the approved Design Development Documents and shall consist of Drawings and Specifications setting forth in detail the quality levels and performance criteria of materials and systems and other requirements for the construction of the Work. The Owner and Architect acknowledge that, in order to ~~construct~~perform the Work, the Contractor will provide additional information, including Shop Drawings, Product Data, Samples and other similar submittals, which the Architect shall review in accordance with Section 3.6.4.

The only substantive change to Section 3.4.1 is the addition of "performance criteria" of materials and systems as a required element of the Construction Documents.

> **§ 3.5.2.3** ~~The~~If the Bidding Documents permit substitutions, upon the Owner's written authorization, the Architect shall, as an Additional Service, consider requests for substitutions, ~~if the Bidding Documents permit substitutions, and shall consult with the Construction Manager~~ and prepare and distribute addenda identifying approved substitutions to all prospective bidders.

The entire Section 3.5 was changed from "Bidding or Negotiation" to "Procurement" to better reflect current practice. Revisions to Section 3.5.2.3 specify that the architect's consideration of a bidder's request for substitutions is classified as an Additional Service (i.e., for an additional fee). This change is consistent with the agreement's definition of Additional Services and recognizes that the value of this service may not be able to ascertained when the agreement is signed.

> **§ 3.5.3.2** The Architect shall assist the Owner and Construction Manager in obtaining proposals by:
>
> **.1** facilitating the ~~reproduction~~distribution of Proposal Documents for distribution to prospective ~~contractors~~Contractors, and requesting their return upon completion of the negotiation process;
>
> **.2** organizing and participating in selection interviews with prospective ~~contractors; and~~Contractors;
>
> **.3** preparing responses to questions from prospective Contractors and providing clarifications and interpretations of the Proposal Documents to the prospective Contractors in the form of addenda; and
>
> **.4** participating in negotiations with prospective ~~contractors.~~ Contractors, and subsequently preparing a summary report of the negotiation results, as directed by the Owner.

Changes to Section 3.5.3.2 require the architect to prepare responses to questions from bidders, provide clarifications and interpretations of the Proposal Documents to bidders, and prepare for the owner a summary report of the results of negotiations with bidders.

> **§ 3.5.3.3** ~~The~~If the Proposal Documents permit substitutions, upon the Owner's written authorization, the Architect shall, as an Additional Service, consider requests for substitutions, ~~if the Proposal Documents permit substitutions, and shall~~ consult with the Construction Manager, and prepare and distribute addenda identifying approved substitutions to all prospective contractors.

Like the revisions to Section 3.5.2.3, revisions to Section 3.5.3.3 specify that the architect's consideration of a bidder's request for substitutions and the issuance of addenda regarding approved substitutions is classified as an Additional Service (i.e., for an additional fee). This change is consistent with the agreement's definition of Additional Services and recognizes that the value of this service may not be able to be ascertained when the agreement is signed.

§ 3.6 Construction Phase Services

§ 3.6.1 General

§ 3.6.1.1 The Architect shall provide administration of the Contract between the Owner and the Contractor as set forth below and in AIA Document A232™–~~2009~~2019, General Conditions of the Contract for Construction, Construction Manager as Adviser Edition. If the Owner and Contractor modify AIA Document A232–~~2009~~2019, those modifications shall not affect the Architect's services under this Agreement unless the Owner and the Architect amend this Agreement.

§ 3.6.1.2 The Architect shall advise and consult with the Owner and Construction Manager during the Construction Phase Services. The Architect shall have authority to act on behalf of the Owner only to the extent provided in this Agreement. The Architect shall not have control over, charge of, or responsibility for the construction means, methods, techniques, sequences or procedures, or for safety precautions and programs in connection with the Work, nor shall the Architect be responsible for the ~~Contractor's~~Contractors' failure to perform the Work in accordance with the requirements of the Contract Documents. The Architect shall be responsible for the Architect's negligent acts or omissions, but shall not have control over or charge of, and shall not be responsible for, acts or omissions of the Construction Manager, or acts or omissions of the ~~Contractor~~Contractors or of any other persons or entities performing portions of the Work.

§ 3.6.1.3 Subject to Section 4.2, and except as provided in Section 3.6.6.5, the Architect's responsibility to provide Construction Phase Services commences with the award of the initial Contract for Construction and terminates on the date the Architect issues the final Certificate for Payment.

Changes to Section 3.6.1.3 clarify that the architect's responsibility to provide Construction Phase Services terminates upon the architect's issuance of the final Certificate for Payment, except that if requested by the owner, the architect must conduct a meeting with the owner and construction manager within one year after substantial completion.

§ 3.6.3.2 The Architect's certification for payment shall constitute a representation to the Owner, based on (1) the Architect's evaluation of the Work as provided in Section 3.6.2, (2) the data comprising the Contractor's Application for Payment or the data comprising the Project Application for Payment, and (3) the recommendation of the Construction Manager, that, to the best of the Architect's knowledge, information and belief, the Work has progressed to the point indicated~~ and that~~, the quality of the Work is in accordance with the Contract Documents., and that the Contractors are entitled to payment in the amount certified. The foregoing representations are subject to (1)~~ to~~ an evaluation of the Work for conformance with the Contract Documents upon Substantial Completion, (2) ~~to~~ results of subsequent tests and inspections, (3) ~~to~~ correction of minor deviations from the Contract Documents prior to completion, and (4)~~ to~~ specific qualifications expressed by the Architect.

The only substantive change to Section 3.6.3.2 states that the architect's certification for payment constitutes a representation to the owner that the contractor is entitled to payment in the amount certified. This addition reflects the reliance owners place on the architect's certifications regarding the status and quality of the contractor's work.

§ 3.6.4.3 If the Contract Documents specifically require the ~~Contractor~~Contractors to provide professional design services or certifications by a design professional related to systems, materials or equipment, the Architect shall specify the appropriate performance and design criteria that such services must satisfy. The Architect shall review ~~shop drawings~~and take appropriate action on Shop Drawings and other submittals related to the Work designed or certified by the Contractors' design ~~professional retained by~~professionals, provided the ~~Contractor that~~submittals bear such ~~professional's~~professionals' seal and signature when submitted to the Architect. The Architect's review shall be for the limited purpose of checking for conformance with information given and the design concept expressed in the Contract Documents. The Architect shall be entitled to rely upon, and shall not be responsible for, the adequacy, and accuracy ~~and completeness~~ of the services, certifications, and approvals performed or provided by such design professionals.

Changes to Section 3.6.4.3 require the architect to do more than simply review the shop drawings and submittals provided by the contractors' design professional, but also to take whatever action the architect determines is appropriate. But this section also adds the familiar qualifier that the architect's review is for the limited purpose of checking the shop drawings for conformance with design concept expressed in the Contract Documents.

§ 3.6.6 Project Completion

§ 3.6.6.1 The Architect, assisted by the Construction Manager, shall:

.1 conduct inspections to determine the date ~~or dates~~ of Substantial Completion and the date of final completion;

.2 issue ~~Certificates~~a Certificate of Substantial Completion prepared by the Construction Manager;~~ receive from the Construction Manager and~~

.3 review written warranties and related documents required by the Contract Documents and ~~assembled by~~received from the ~~Contractor~~Contractors, through the Construction Manager; and,

.4 after receipt of a final Contractor's Application and Certificate for Payment or a final Project Application and Project Certificate for Payment from the Construction Manager, issue a final Certificate for Payment based upon a final inspection indicating that, to the best of the Architect's knowledge, information, and belief, the Work complies with the requirements of the Contract Documents.

Revised Section 3.6.6.1 adds a qualifier to the architect's representation that the contractor's work complies with the requirements of the Contract Documents: that representation now applies only to "the best of the Architect's knowledge, information and belief." This revision conforms the B132 to the language of the AIA's Application for Payment (the G732), which contains a subjective standard for evaluating the architect's determination that work complies with the Contract Documents. That standard may provide a basis for relieving the architect from liability for later claims by the owner or others that the architect approved for payment certain work that did not comply with the Contract Documents.

§ 3.6.6.4 The Architect shall forward to the Owner the following information received from the Contractors, through the Construction Manager: (1) consent of surety or sureties, if any, to reduction in or partial release of retainage or the making of final payment; (2) affidavits, receipts, releases and waivers of liens, or bonds indemnifying the Owner against liens; and (3) any other documentation required of the Contractors under the Contract Documents.

New Section 3.6.6.4 requires the architect to collect and forward certain documents and information to the owner through the construction manager. Consistent with other revisions to the 2019 documents, the construction manager is charged with control of the flow of information among the parties.

§ 3.6.6.5 Upon request of the Owner, and prior to the expiration of one year from the date of Substantial Completion, the Architect shall, without additional compensation, conduct a meeting with the Owner and Construction Manager to review the facility operations and performance.

The only revision to Section 3.6.6.5 is to add the construction manager to the meeting to review the work within one year of substantial completion.

ARTICLE 4 SUPPLEMENTAL AND ADDITIONAL SERVICES

§ 4.1 ~~Additional~~ Supplemental Services

§ 4.1.1 The services listed below are not included in Basic Services but may be required for the Project. The Architect shall provide the listed ~~Additional~~Supplemental Services only if specifically designated in the table below as the Architect's responsibility, and the Owner shall compensate the Architect as provided in Section 11.2. Unless otherwise specifically addressed in this Agreement, if neither the Owner nor the Architect is designated, the parties agree that the listed Supplemental Service is not being provided for the Project.

(Designate the ~~Additional~~Architect's Supplemental Services and the Owner's Supplemental Services required for the Project by indicating whether the Architect or Owner shall ~~provide in the second column of the table below. In~~be responsible for providing the ~~third column indicate whether the service~~identified Supplemental Service. Insert a description ~~is located~~of the Supplemental Services in Section 4.~~2 or in~~1.2 below or attach the description of services as an ~~attached~~ exhibit~~. If in an exhibit, identify the exhibit~~. to this Agreement.)

The 2019 revisions to Article 4 established a distinction between "supplemental" services and "additional" services. The intent of this distinction is to clarify that "Supplemental Services" are services that are beyond the architect's basic services but are agreed upon at the time of the signing of the contract. "Additional Services" also are beyond the architect's basic services but are added after the contract is signed and may increase the architect's compensation. This change was made to the owner/architect agreements in 2017 and carried forward to the B132–2019 owner/architect agreement.

Section 4.1 enumerates a table of services that functions like a checklist of Supplemental Services, which are expressly assigned to either the owner or the architect. If neither the owner nor the architect is identified as providing the supplemental service, then that service is not being provided.

Supplemental Services	**Responsibility** *(Architect, Owner or Not Provided)*	~~**Location of Service Description**~~ ~~*(Section 4.2 below or in an exhibit attached to this document and identified below)*~~
§ 4.1.1.1	Assistance with selection of Construction Manager	
§ 4.1.1.2	Programming	
§ 4.1.1.3	Multiple preliminary designs	
§ 4.1.1.4	Measured drawings	
§ 4.1.1.5	Existing facilities surveys	
§ 4.1.1.6	Site evaluation and planning	
§ 4.1.1.7	Building Information Model management responsibilities	
§ 4.1.1.8	Development of Building Information Models for post construction use	
§ 4.1.1.9	Civil engineering	
§ 4.1.1.10	Landscape design	
§ 4.1.1.11	Architectural interior design	
§ 4.1.1.12	Value analysis	
§ 4.1.1.13	Cost estimating	
§ 4.1.1.14	On-site project representation	
§ 4.1.1.15	Conformed documents for construction	
§ 4.1.1.16	As-designed record drawings	
§ 4.1.1.17	As-constructed record drawings	
§ 4.1.1.18	Post-occupancy evaluation	
§ 4.1.1.19	Facility support services	
§ 4.1.1.20	Tenant-related services	
§ 4.1.1.21	Architect's coordination of the Owner's consultants	
§ 4.1.1.22	Telecommunications/data design	
§ 4.1.1.23	Security evaluation and planning	
§ 4.1.1.24	Commissioning	

§ 4.1.1.25	Sustainable Project Services pursuant to Section 4.1.3	
§ 4.1.1.26	Historic preservation	
§ 4.1.1.27	Furniture, furnishings, and equipment design	
§ 4.1.1.28	Other services provided by specialty Consultants	
§ 4.1.1.29	Other Supplemental Services	

This updated list of Supplemental Services reflects many of the technological changes the industry has seen over the last ten years, including newer sustainability standards and building information modeling.

§ 4.1.2 ~~Insert a~~Description of Supplemental Services

§ 4.1.2.1 A description of each ~~Additional~~Supplemental Service ~~designated~~identified in Section 4.1.1 as the Architect's responsibility is provided below.

(Describe in detail the Architect's Supplemental Services identified in Section 4.1.1 or, if ~~not further described~~set forth in an exhibit, identify the exhibit. The AIA publishes a number of Standard Form of Architect's Services documents that can be included as an exhibit to describe the Architect's Supplemental Services.)

§ 4.1.2.2 A description of each Supplemental Service identified in Section 4.1.1 as the Owner's responsibility is provided below.

(Describe in detail the Owner's Supplemental Services identified in Section 4.1.1 or, if set forth in an exhibit, identify the exhibit.)

If a sustainable objective is identified in Article 1, the new B132 makes clear that such services associated with the sustainable objective are to be paid for as a supplemental service:

§ 4.1.3 If the Owner identified a Sustainable Objective in Article 1, the Architect shall provide, as a Supplemental Service, the Sustainability Services required in AIA Document E235™–2019, Sustainable Projects Exhibit, Construction Manager as Adviser Edition, attached to this ~~document~~Agreement. The Owner shall compensate the Architect as provided in Section 11.2.

The benefit of delineating sustainable objectives as a supplemental service is to clarify that costs associated with obtaining sustainable certifications are not included in the cost of architect's basic services, as such costs are routinely not included in the architect's standard design fee proposals and may vary depending on the level of certification, or certifying agency, the owner requires.

§ 4.~~3~~2 Architect's Additional Services

The Architect may provide Additional Services ~~may be provided~~ after execution of this Agreement, without invalidating the Agreement. Except for services required due to the fault of the Architect, any Additional Services provided in accordance with this Section 4.~~3~~2 shall entitle the Architect to compensation pursuant to Section 11.3 and an appropriate adjustment in the Architect's schedule.

§ 4.~~3~~2.1 Upon recognizing the need to perform the following Additional Services, the Architect shall notify the Owner with reasonable promptness and explain the facts and circumstances giving rise to the need. The Architect shall not proceed to provide the following ~~services~~Additional Services until the Architect receives the Owner's written authorization:

- **.1** Services necessitated by a change in the Initial Information, previous instructions or recommendations given by the Construction Manager or the Owner, ~~or~~ approvals given by the Owner, or a material change in the Project including~~, but not limited to,~~ size, quality, complexity, building systems, the Owner's schedule or budget for Cost of the Work, constructability considerations, procurement or delivery method, or bid packages in addition to those listed in Section 1.1.6;
- **.2** Making revisions in Drawings, Specifications, or other documents (as required pursuant to Section 6.7), when such revisions are required because the Construction Manager's estimate of the Cost of the Work exceeds the Owner's budget, except where such excess is due to changes initiated by the Architect in scope, capacities of basic systems, or the kinds and quality of materials, finishes or equipment;
- **.3** Services necessitated by ~~the Owner's request for extensive environmentally responsible design alternatives, such as unique system designs, in-depth material research, energy modeling,~~enactment or ~~LEED® certification~~revision of codes, laws, or regulations, including changing or editing previously prepared Instruments of Service;
- **.4** Changing or editing previously prepared Instruments of Service necessitated by ~~the enactment or revision of codes, laws or regulations or~~ official interpretations of applicable codes, laws or regulations that are either (a) contrary to specific interpretations by the applicable authorities having jurisdiction made prior to the issuance of the building permit, or (b) contrary to requirements of the Instruments of Service when those Instruments of Service were prepared in accordance with the applicable standard of care;
- **.5** Services necessitated by decisions of the Owner or Construction Manager not rendered in a timely manner or any other failure of performance on the part of the Owner, Construction Manager or the Owner's other consultants or contractors;
- **.6** Preparing digital ~~data~~models or other design documentation for transmission to the Owner's consultants and contractors, or to other Owner -authorized recipients;
- **.7** Preparation of design and documentation for alternate bid or proposal requests proposed by the Owner or Construction Manager;
- **.8** Preparation for, and attendance at, a public presentation, meeting or hearing;
- **.9** Preparation for, and attendance at, a dispute resolution proceeding or legal proceeding, except where the Architect is party thereto;
- **.10** Evaluation of the qualifications of ~~bidders or persons~~entities providing bids or proposals;

.11 Consultation concerning replacement of Work resulting from fire or other cause during construction; or

.12 Assistance to the Initial Decision Maker, if other than the Architect.

The revised Section 4.2.1 removes Sustainable Objectives (previously referred to as "environmentally responsible design") from the list of Additional Services because those objectives are addressed above in Section 4.1.3, which allows the architect to provide them as Supplemental Services. The revisions also clarify when changes necessitated by codes, regulations, and laws—or the official interpretation of those codes, regulations, and laws—are deemed Additional Services.

§ 4.~~3~~2.2 To avoid delay in the Construction Phase, the Architect shall provide the following Additional Services, notify the Owner with reasonable promptness, and explain the facts and circumstances giving rise to the need. If, upon receipt of the Architect's notice, the Owner ~~subsequently~~ determines that all or parts of ~~those~~the services are not required, the Owner shall give prompt written notice to the Architect~~, and the~~ of the Owner's determination. The Owner shall ~~have no further obligation to~~ compensate the Architect for ~~those~~the services~~;~~ provided prior to the Architect's receipt of the Owner's notice:

.1 Reviewing a Contractor's submittal out of sequence from the ~~initial~~ Project submittal schedule ~~agreed to~~approved by the Architect;

.2 Responding to the ~~Contractor's~~Contractors' requests for information that are not prepared in accordance with the Contract Documents or where such information is available to the ~~Contractor~~Contractors from a careful study and comparison of the Contract Documents, field conditions, other Owner-provided information, Contractor-prepared coordination drawings, or prior Project correspondence or documentation;

.3 Preparing Change Orders, and Construction Change Directives that require evaluation of ~~Contractor's~~Contractors' proposals and supporting data, or the preparation or revision of Instruments of Service;

.4 Evaluating an extensive number of Claims as the Initial Decision Maker; or

.5 Evaluating substitutions proposed by the Owner, Construction Manager or ~~Contractor~~Contractors and making subsequent revisions to Instruments of Service resulting therefrom~~; or~~.

.6 ~~To the extent the Architect's Basic Services are affected, providing Construction Phase Services 60 days after (1) the date of Substantial Completion of the Work or (2) the anticipated date of Substantial Completion, identified in Initial Information, whichever is earlier.~~

The architect is required to promptly begin to provide the identified additional services and provide the owner with notice regarding those services. Prior to the 2019 edits, if the owner subsequently determined that the architect's additional services were not needed, the owner could provide written notice to that effect and have no further obligation to pay for those services. The 2019 changes allows for the architect to be paid for those services up to the time that the owner provides its notice that these services are not needed.

§ 4.32.3 The Architect shall provide Construction Phase Services exceeding the limits set forth below as Additional Services. When the limits below are reached, the Architect shall notify the Owner:

.1 ( ) reviews of each Shop Drawing, Product Data item, sample and similar submittals of the ~~Contractor~~Contractors

.2 ( ) visits to the site by the Architect ~~over the duration of the Project~~ during construction

.3 ( ) inspections for any portion of the Work to determine whether such portion of the Work is substantially complete in accordance with the requirements of the Contract Documents

.4 ( ) inspections for any portion of the Work to determine final completion

~~§ 4.3.4~~**§ 4.2.4** Except for services required under Section 3.6.6.5 and those services that do not exceed the limits set forth in Section 4.2.3, Construction Phase Services provided more than 60 days after (1) the date of Substantial Completion of the Work, or (2) the anticipated date of Substantial Completion identified in the Initial Information, whichever is earlier, shall be compensated as Additional Services to the extent the Architect incurs additional cost in providing those Construction Phase Services.

New Section 4.2.4 expressly provides that the architect must be compensated for Construction Phase Services performed more than 60 days after substantial completion or the anticipated date of substantial completion at the time the parties entered into the agreement, whichever is earlier. That additional payment does not include the architect's services in conducting a meeting with the owner and construction manager one year after substantial completion, nor does it apply to reviews, inspections, and visits required by Section 4.2.3.

The mandate to compensate the architect beyond the 60-day time period applies only to the extent the architect incurs *additional* cost in rendering services beyond that time period. Accordingly, a project suspension of 60 days, for example, would not mean that the architect automatically would be entitled to Additional Services payment just because Construction Phase services extended beyond the 60-day time period.

ARTICLE 5 OWNER'S RESPONSIBILITIES

For the most part, the revisions made to Article 5 are minor. For example, the last sentence in Section 5.1 was moved to a standalone provision in Section 5.16:

§ 5.16 Within 15 days after receipt of a written request from the Architect, the Owner shall furnish the requested information as necessary and relevant for the Architect to evaluate, give notice of, or enforce lien rights.

Interestingly, the 2019 revisions included the deletion of Section 5.3, which required the owner to engage the construction manager to create the overall project schedule. Perhaps this section was deleted because the obligation is contained in the owner-construction manager agreement or may be contracted to a separate scheduling consultant.

Further, in order to remain consistent with other parts of the agreement, Section 5.7 (regarding owner's supplemental services) and Section 5.8 (regarding sustainable objectives) were reiterated in Article 5. Finally, and perhaps most significantly, Section 5.13 as revised requires the owner to include the architect on all communications with the construction manager that relate to the architect's services or responsibilities:

> **§ 5.13** The Owner shall ~~endeavor to~~ communicate with the ~~Contractor~~ Contractors and the Construction Manager's consultants through the Construction Manager~~, and shall contemporaneously provide the same communications to the Architect~~ about matters arising out of or relating to the Contract Documents. The Owner and Construction Manager shall include the Architect in all communications that relate to or affect the Architect's services or professional responsibilities. The Owner shall promptly notify the Architect of the substance of any direct communications between the Owner and the Construction Manager otherwise relating to the Project. Communications by and with the Architect's consultants shall be through the Architect.

Previously, the owner had a lesser obligation to contemporaneously provide the architect with any correspondence to the construction manager relating to the construction documents. Now, the owner has an affirmative obligation to include the architect on a broader range of correspondence with the construction manager.

ARTICLE 6 COST OF THE WORK

The Cost of the Work article in the B132 does not relate to the cost of the work relative to the architect's services. That is handled in Article 11. Rather, Article 6's coverage of Cost of the Work explains the architect's design (and re-design) obligations vis-à-vis the owner's budget and the construction manager's Cost of the Work as set forth in the construction management agreement. This Article was not significantly modified. Particularly noteworthy are the changes in Sections 6.1, 6.3 and 6.5:

> **§ 6.1** For purposes of this Agreement, the Cost of the Work shall be the total cost to the Owner to construct all elements of the Project designed or specified by the Architect and shall include the ~~contractors'~~Contractors' general conditions costs, overhead and profit. The Cost of the Work includes the compensation of the Construction Manager and Construction Manager's consultants during the Construction Phase only, including compensation for reimbursable expenses at the job site, if any. The Cost of the Work also includes the reasonable value of labor, materials, and equipment, donated to, or otherwise furnished by, the Owner. The Cost of the Work does not include the compensation of the Architect,; the costs of the land, rights-of-way, financing, or contingencies for changes in the Work; or other costs that are the responsibility of the Owner.

This change clarifies that if items are donated to the owner, or otherwise furnished by the owner, those items are included in the B132's definition of Cost of the Work for purposes of calculating the architect's fee. These types of costs generally are *not* included in the definition of Cost of the Work in the construction management agreement because the construction manager should not earn a fee on owner-furnished items unless the construction manager has contractual responsibility for installing those items. The architect, however, may be responsible for design services relative to the owner-furnished items (such as specifying fixtures or equipment), which is the probable justification for this added language.

> **§ 6.3** The Owner shall require the Construction Manager to include appropriate contingencies for design, bidding or negotiating, price escalation, and market conditions in estimates of the Cost of the Work. The Architect shall be entitled to rely on the accuracy and completeness of estimates of the Cost of the Work the Construction Manager prepares as the Architect progresses with its Basic Services. The Architect shall prepare, as an Additional Service, revisions to the Drawings, Specifications or other documents required due to the Construction Manager's inaccuracies or incompleteness in preparing cost estimates., or due to market conditions the Architect could not reasonably anticipate. The Architect may review the Construction Manager's estimates solely for the Architect's guidance in completion of its services, however, the Architect shall report to the Owner any material inaccuracies and inconsistencies noted during any such review.
>
> **§ 6.3.1** If the Architect is providing ~~detailed~~ cost estimating services as ~~an Additional~~a Supplemental Service, and a discrepancy exists between the Construction Manager's cost estimates and the Architect's cost estimates, the Architect and the Construction Manager shall work ~~cooperatively~~together to ~~conform~~reconcile the cost estimates ~~to one another.~~ .

Section 6.3 added a provision entitling the architect to compensation as a Supplemental Service for any revisions to its documents required due to market conditions that were not reasonably foreseeable. Previously, the architect would be entitled to additional compensation only if the revisions were necessitated due to inaccuracies or incompleteness in the construction manager's cost estimates. Previous Sections 6.3.1 and 6.3.2 were merged into one provision, with the obligation to reconcile cost estimates placed on the architect and construction manager equally. As Section 6.3.1 was written previously, the onus was, instead, on the architect to cooperate with the construction manager to conform the estimates.

> **§ 6.5** If the Construction Manager's estimate of the Cost of the Work at the conclusion of the Design Development Phase exceeds the Owner's budget for the Cost of the Work, the Owner shall
>
> **.1** give written approval of an increase in the budget for the Cost of the Work;
> **.2** terminate in accordance with Section 9.5;
> **.3** in consultation with the Architect and Construction Manager, revise the Project program, scope, or quality as required to reduce the Cost of the Work; or
> **.~~3~~4** implement any other mutually acceptable alternative.

If the construction manager's estimate of the Cost of the Work at the end of the design development stage exceeds the owner's budget, the owner can now terminate the owner-architect agreement for convenience. Previously, the owner's options included increasing its budget, reducing the project criteria to meet the budget, or any other mutually acceptable alternative. Notably, there was no specific obligation on the architect to produce a design that could meet the owner's budget and the construction manager's Cost of the Work. Now, the architect may be faced with a termination of its services if it produces a design that does not meet these requirements.

> **§ 6.6** If the Owner chooses to proceed under Section 6.5.~~2~~3, the Architect, without additional compensation, shall incorporate the ~~required modifications~~revisions in the Construction Documents Phase as necessary to comply with the Owner's budget for the Cost of the Work at the conclusion of the Design Development Phase Services, or the budget as adjusted under Section 6.5.1. The Architect's ~~modification of~~revisions in the Construction Documents Phase shall be the limit of the Architect's responsibility ~~as a Basic Service~~ under this Article 6.

ARTICLE 7 COPYRIGHTS AND LICENSES

The revisions to Article 7 reflect the incorporation of the digital data protocols in Articles 1 and 13 by removing reference to the need to establish digital protocols and clarifying that the reproduction of the Instruments of Service will be subject to the protocols established in Article 1.

> **§ 7.1** The Architect and the Owner warrant that in transmitting Instruments of Service, or any other information, the transmitting party is the copyright owner of such information or has permission from the copyright owner to transmit such information for its use on the Project. ~~If the Owner and Architect intend to transmit Instruments of Service or any other information or documentation in digital form, they shall endeavor to establish necessary protocols governing such transmissions.~~
>
> . . .
>
> **§ 7.3** ~~Upon execution of this Agreement, the~~The Architect grants to the Owner a nonexclusive license to use the Architect's Instruments of Service solely and exclusively for purposes of constructing, using, maintaining, altering and adding to the Project, provided that the Owner substantially performs its obligations under this Agreement, including prompt payment of all sums ~~when~~ due~~, under this Agreement~~ pursuant to Article 9 and Article 11. The Architect shall obtain similar nonexclusive licenses from the Architect's consultants consistent with this Agreement. The license granted under this section permits the Owner to authorize the ~~Contractor~~Contractors, Construction Manager, Subcontractors, Sub-subcontractors, and ~~material or equipment~~ suppliers, as well as the Owner's consultants and ~~separate contractors~~Separate Contractors, to reproduce applicable portions of the Instruments of Service, subject to any protocols established pursuant to Section 1.3, solely and exclusively for use in performing services or construction for the Project. If the Architect rightfully terminates this Agreement for cause as provided in Section 9.4, the license granted in this Section 7.3 shall terminate.

Further, for the avoidance of any doubt, the drafters included express language that Article 7 survives termination of the agreement.

> **§ 7.5** Except as otherwise stated in Section 7.3, the provisions of this Article 7 shall survive the termination of this Agreement.

ARTICLE 8 CLAIMS AND DISPUTES

Article 8, Claims and Disputes, was lightly modified for 2019—mostly to remove the architect's duty to defend the owner and to clarify that disputes will be resolved by arbitration only if the parties expressly agree.

Non-substantive changes include:

> **§ 8.1.1** The Owner and Architect shall commence all claims and causes of action~~, whether in contract, tort, or otherwise,~~ against the other and arising out of or related to this Agreement , whether in contract, tort, or otherwise, in accordance with the requirements of the ~~method of~~ binding dispute resolution method selected in this Agreement and within the period specified by applicable law, but in any case not more than 10 years after the date of Substantial Completion of the Work. The Owner and Architect waive all claims and causes of action not commenced in accordance with this Section 8.1.1.
>
> . . .
>
> **§ 8.2.4** If the parties do not resolve a dispute through mediation pursuant to this Section 8.2, the method of binding dispute resolution shall be the following:
>
> *(Check the appropriate box*~~*. If the Owner and Architect do not select a method of binding dispute resolution below, or do not subsequently agree in writing to a binding dispute resolution method other than litigation, the dispute will be resolved in a court of competent jurisdiction.*~~*)*
>
> [ ] Arbitration pursuant to Section 8.3 of this Agreement
> [ ] Litigation in a court of competent jurisdiction
> [ ] Other: *(Specify)*
>
> If the Owner and Architect do not select a method of binding dispute resolution ~~below~~, or do not subsequently agree in writing to a binding dispute resolution method other than litigation, the dispute will be resolved in a court of competent jurisdiction.

The indemnification provision, however, contains additional language that is substantive:

> **§ 8.1.3** The Architect shall indemnify and hold the Owner and the Owner's officers and employees harmless from and against damages, losses and judgments arising from claims by third parties, including reasonable attorneys' fees and expenses recoverable under applicable law, but only to the extent they are caused by the negligent acts or omissions of the Architect, its employees and its consultants in the performance of professional services under this Agreement. The Architect's obligation to indemnify and hold the Owner and the Owner's officers and employees harmless does not include a duty to defend. The Architect's duty to indemnify the Owner under this ~~provision~~Section 8.1.3 shall be limited to the available proceeds of the insurance coverage required by this Agreement.

Architects generally will not accept a duty to defend contained within an indemnity provision because the costs of defense are not covered by its insurance program, and architects are generally unwilling to accept any liability in excess of what is insurable. Rather than rely on the simple omission from the indemnity obligation (e.g., "The Architect shall indemnify and hold the Owner... harmless"), the new language clearly excludes the duty to defend from the architect's obligations under this Section. As such, there can be no argument that a duty to defend is implied by this provision. Attorneys representing an owner would be wise to insert additional language requiring the architect to reimburse its costs of defense if it is ultimately determined that the architect is liable for indemnity under Section 8.1.3. Additionally, the language added at the end of Section 8.1.3 clarifies that the architect's liability under the indemnification provision is limited to the insurance *required by this Agreement*. As previously drafted, one might infer that the architect's liability extended to its entire insurance program, which may be much greater than the limits prescribed by the agreement. This modification significantly limits the architect's exposure.

Finally, for the avoidance of any doubt, the drafters included express language that Article 8 survives termination of the agreement.

> **§ 8.4** The provisions of this Article 8 shall survive the termination of this Agreement.

ARTICLE 9 TERMINATION OR SUSPENSION

The only substantive change to Article 9 relates to the architect's entitlement to certain payment upon a termination for convenience.

> **§ 9.1** If the Owner fails to make payments to the Architect in accordance with this Agreement, such failure shall be considered substantial nonperformance and cause for termination or, at the Architect's option, cause for suspension of performance of services under this Agreement. If the Architect elects to suspend services, the Architect shall give seven days' written notice to the Owner before suspending services. In the event of a suspension of services, the Architect shall have no liability to the Owner for delay or damage caused the Owner because of such suspension of services. Before resuming services, the Owner shall pay the Architect ~~shall be paid~~ all sums due prior to suspension and any expenses incurred in the interruption and resumption of the Architect's services. The Architect's fees for the remaining services and the time schedules shall be equitably adjusted.
>
> . . .
>
> **§ 9.6** ~~In~~If the ~~event of termination not the fault of~~ Owner terminates this Agreement for its convenience pursuant to Section 9.5, or if the Architect, terminates this Agreement pursuant to Section 9.3, the Owner shall compensate the Architect ~~shall be compensated~~ for services performed prior to termination, ~~together with~~ Reimbursable Expenses ~~then due~~incurred, and ~~all Termination Expenses as defined in Section 9.7.~~
>
> ~~**§ 9.7** Termination Expenses are in addition to compensation for the Architect's services and include expenses directly~~costs attributable to termination ~~for which~~, including the ~~Architect is not otherwise compensated, plus an amount for~~costs attributable to the Architect's ~~anticipated profit on the value~~termination of ~~the services not performed by the Architect~~consultant agreements.
>
> **§ 9.7** In addition to any amounts paid under Section 9.6, if the Owner terminates this Agreement for its convenience pursuant to Section 9.5, or the Architect terminates this Agreement pursuant to Section 9.3, the Owner shall pay to the Architect the following fees:

(Set forth below the amount of any termination or licensing fee, or the method for determining any termination or licensing fee.)

.1 Termination Fee:
.2 Licensing Fee if the Owner intends to continue using the Architect's Instruments of Service:

Accordingly, if the owner terminates the agreement for convenience, or if the architect terminates the agreement for non-payment, the architect is entitled to recover: (1) payment for services rendered before termination; (2) reimbursable expenses incurred; (3) costs associated with termination of the architect's consultant agreements; (4) a termination fee; and (5) a licensing fee if the owner plans to use the architect's Instruments of Service post-termination. While the licensing fee was previously contemplated in Section 11.9 of the previous B132, the termination fee is new. Both construction managers and architects are wise to include a termination fee in a termination for convenience clause so that the owner will give pause before simply terminating the agreement. Some savvy owners may obtain the desired services from the architect and, once the design has progressed to a certain point, may decide to manage the construction administration on its own. In such case, under the prior version of this agreement, all the owner had to pay for were the services and expenses incurred to date. The architect, however, may have priced the agreement based on projected staff costs, projected profit, and other projected costs. While it will be made "whole" for the costs incurred through the date of the termination, there may be a real cost to the architect for lost anticipated profit and overhead. As such, a termination fee can attempt to place the architect in a more equitable financial position if the owner decides to terminate for convenience. And, if appropriately sized, the termination fee can serve as a disincentive for the owner to terminate for convenience (which can be done at any stage in the project).

Finally, Section 9.8 inserts an automatic termination provision, which clarifies the expected duration of the architect's services under the agreement to one year after Substantial Completion:

§ 9.8 Except as otherwise expressly provided herein, this Agreement shall terminate one year from the date of Substantial Completion.

Architects routinely stay engaged on a project longer than originally anticipated under their agreement with the owner. And, in some cases, architects are not adequately reimbursed for those extended services. By including this new language, the parties are clearly setting forth expectations for the duration of the agreement. Obviously, if the architect's services are required beyond the year post-Substantial Completion, the parties may execute a change order to extend the duration of the agreement, which will provide the architect an opportunity to obtain appropriate compensation for such extension.

ARTICLE 10 MISCELLANEOUS PROVISIONS

Article 10 compiles miscellaneous provisions and the 2019 version amended several of those provisions. Section 10.1, the choice of law provision, was amended to make clear that the jurisdiction's choice of law rules are excluded:

> **§ 10.1** This Agreement shall be governed by the law of the place where the Project is located, ~~except that if~~excluding that jurisdiction's choice of law rules. If the parties have selected arbitration as the method of binding dispute resolution, the Federal Arbitration Act shall govern.

In other words, if choice of law rules of the jurisdiction would apply the laws of another jurisdiction, the parties, by contract, agree to overrule that choice of law and, instead, apply the law where the project is located.

> **§ 10.3** The Owner and Architect, respectively, bind themselves, their agents, successors, assigns, and legal representatives to this Agreement. Neither the Owner nor the Architect shall assign this Agreement without the written consent of the other, except that the Owner may assign this Agreement to a lender providing financing for the Project if the lender agrees to assume the Owner's rights and obligations under this Agreement~~.~~ , and including any payments due to the Architect by the Owner prior to the assignment.

Section 10.3, the assignment provision, added language to make clear that the owner could assign the architect's agreement to its lender without the architect's consent *provided the lender agreed to make any payments that were due prior to the assignment*.

> **§ 10.7** The Architect shall have the right to include photographic or artistic representations of the design of the Project among the Architect's promotional and professional materials. The Architect shall be given reasonable access to the completed Project to make such representations. However, the Architect's materials shall not include the Owner's confidential or proprietary information if the Owner has previously advised the Architect in writing of the specific information considered by the Owner to be confidential or proprietary. The Owner shall provide professional credit for the Architect in the Owner's promotional materials for the Project. This Section 10.7 shall survive the termination of this Agreement unless the Owner terminates this Agreement for cause pursuant to Section 9.4.

Section 10.7, which permits the architect to use photographs or artistic representations of the project, was modified to specify that such right survives termination of the agreement unless the architect is terminated for cause.

> **§ 10.8** If the Architect or Owner receives information specifically designated ~~by the other party~~ as "confidential" or "business proprietary," the receiving party shall keep such information strictly confidential and shall not disclose it to any other person except ~~to (1) its employees, (2) those who need to know the content of such information in order to perform services or construction solely and exclusively for the Project, or (3) its consultants and contractors whose contracts include similar restrictions on the use of confidential information.~~ as set forth in Section 10.8.1. This Section 10.8 shall survive the termination of this Agreement.

§ 10.8.1 The receiving party may disclose "confidential" or "business proprietary" information after 7 days' notice to the other party, when required by law, arbitrator's order, or court order, including a subpoena or other form of compulsory legal process issued by a court or governmental entity, or to the extent such information is reasonably necessary for the receiving party to defend itself in any dispute. The receiving party may also disclose such information to its employees, consultants, or contractors in order to perform services or work solely and exclusively for the Project, provided those employees, consultants and contractors are subject to the restrictions on the disclosure and use of such information as set forth in this Section 10.8.

The confidentiality clause in Section 10.8 was expanded in 10.8.1 to permit disclosure of such information after seven days' notice when required by law, court order or subpoena. Additionally, the receiving party can disclose confidential information after seven days' notice if necessary to defend itself in a dispute. Section 10.8 also states that the confidentiality restriction survives termination of the Agreement.

§ 10.9 The invalidity of any provision of the Agreement shall not invalidate the Agreement or its remaining provisions. If it is determined that any provision of the Agreement violates any law, or is otherwise invalid or unenforceable, then that provision shall be revised to the extent necessary to make that provision legal and enforceable. In such case the Agreement shall be construed, to the fullest extent permitted by law, to give effect to the parties' intentions and purposes in executing the Agreement.

Finally, consistent with revisions made to the 2017 suite of AIA forms, a savings clause was added in Section 10.9 to provide that any provisions of the agreement that are invalid or unenforceable will be revised to the extent necessary to allow them to be enforced.

ARTICLE 11 COMPENSATION

Several changes were made to the Compensation article. Specifically, Section 11.1 provides three options for the architect's basis of payment: (1) stipulated sum; (2) percentage basis of the owner's budget for the Cost of the Work; or (3) another basis to be described. For percentage-based compensation, the 2019 changes are quite different:

§ 11.6 When compensation ~~is based on a percentage of the Cost of the Work~~identified in Section 11.1 is on a percentage basis, progress payments for each phase of Basic Services shall be calculated by multiplying the percentages identified in this Article by the Owner's most recent budget for the Cost of the Work. Compensation paid in previous progress payments shall not be adjusted based on subsequent updates to the Owner's budget for the Cost of the Work.

§ 11.6.1 When compensation is on a percentage basis and any portions of the Project are deleted or otherwise not constructed, compensation for those portions of the Project shall be payable to the extent services are performed on those portions~~, in accordance with the schedule set forth in Section 11.5 based on (1) the lowest bona fide bid or negotiated proposal, or (2) if no such bid or proposal is received, the most recent estimate of the~~

~~Cost of the Work prepared by the Construction Manager for such portions of the Project~~. The Architect shall be entitled to compensation in accordance with this Agreement for all services performed whether or not the Construction Phase is commenced.

Section 11.6 provides for compensation based on a percentage of the owner's *current* budget for the cost of the work, which can be subject to change. If a subsequent budget is downwardly adjusted, the architect is not required to reimburse, or otherwise deduct from its current payment application, the amount it was previously paid based on the higher budget. Although this likely makes sense from an accounting perspective, the practical result is that the architect may receive a windfall. Further, if work is deleted, the owner must still pay the architect on a percentage basis as though the value of the work was not deducted from the budget but only if the architect performed services for the deleted work. The previous version of this agreement tied the percentage-based compensation to bids or proposals received or estimates of the cost of the work.

Changes also were made to align with Article 4, which now includes references to both "Supplemental" and "Additional Services"; such references were carried through to Article 11 to be clear that the architect's compensation for both types of services are captured.[1] Several revisions were also made to the reimbursable expenses provision:

§ 11.8 Compensation for Reimbursable Expenses

§ 11.8.1 Reimbursable Expenses are in addition to compensation for Basic, Supplemental, and Additional Services and include expenses incurred by the Architect and the Architect's consultants directly related to the Project, as follows:

.1 Transportation and authorized out-of-town travel and subsistence;
.2 Long distance services, dedicated data and communication services, teleconferences, Project ~~Web~~web sites, and extranets;
.3 ~~Fees paid for securing approval of~~Permitting and other fees required by authorities having jurisdiction over the Project;
.4 Printing, reproductions, plots, and standard form documents;
.5 Postage, handling, and delivery;
.6 Expense of overtime work requiring higher than regular rates, if authorized in advance by the Owner;
.7 Renderings, physical models, mock-ups, professional photography, and presentation materials requested by the Owner or required for the Project;
.8 ~~Architect's Consultant's expense~~
.8 If required by the Owner, and with the Owner's prior written approval, the Architect's consultants' expenses of professional liability insurance dedicated exclusively to this Project, or the expense of additional insurance coverage or limits ~~if the Owner requests such insurance~~ in excess of that normally ~~carried~~maintained by the Architect's consultants;
.9 All taxes levied on professional services and on reimbursable expenses;
.10 Site office expenses; ~~and~~
.11 Registration fees and any other fees charged by the Certifying Authority or by other entities as necessary to achieve the Sustainable Objective; and
.12 Other similar Project-related expenditures.

1. *See* B132-2019, §§11.2, 11.4 and 11.10.2.3.

Section 11.8.1.3 is an interesting change in that the intent of the original provision was to allow permitting fees to be paid to the architect as a reimbursable expense; however, it also implied that the architect had the responsibility to "secure" the permits, which may have other implications for the architect's liability. And, the prior language could have also been read to exclude reimbursement for fees that were incurred if the architect did not actually receive approvals. The revisions remove these possibilities and make clear that permitting fees are reimbursable expenses.

Section 11.8.1.8 also clears up confusion regarding project-specific professional liability insurance, which is typically not maintained by architects as part of the insurance program and can be expensive to procure. So that there is no confusion as to whether this is required (and therefore, a reimbursable expense), the owner must require project-specific professional liability insurance and agree to reimburse those costs. Similarly, if the owner requires (and approves the reimbursement for) insurance over what the architect ordinarily maintains as part of its insurance program, then such expenses also are reimbursable.[2]

Finally, if a sustainability certification is required by the agreement (e.g., LEED certification), an upfront payment will be made to the architect for registration fees with the certifying authority. (Section 11.10.1.2.) Additional fees charged by the sustainable certifying authority are also reimbursable expenses. (Section 11.8.1.11.)

ARTICLE 12 SPECIAL TERMS AND CONDITIONS

No substantive changes.

ARTICLE 13 SCOPE OF THE AGREEMENT

Section 13.2 specifically includes the Sustainability Exhibit (AIA E234–2019) and BIM and Digital Data Exhibit (AIA E203–2013) as referenced in the Article 1 revisions. The owner and architect should be careful to review these Exhibits and comport them with their understanding or strike the inclusion of this document in the enumeration of Exhibits in Section 13.2 and delete references to these documents in the body of the agreement. Whereas previously, the use of these Exhibits was optional, the 2019 CM agreements make their use mandatory.

2. *See* B132-2019, §11.9.

§ 13.2 This Agreement is comprised of the following documents ~~listed~~identified below:

.1 AIA Document B132™–~~2009~~2019, Standard Form Agreement Between Owner and Architect, Construction Manager as Adviser Edition

.2 AIA Document ~~E201™–2007,~~E203™–2013, Building Information Modeling and Digital Data ~~Protocol~~ Exhibit, dated as indicated below, if completed, or the following:
(Insert the date of the E203–2013 incorporated into this Agreement.)

.3 Exhibits:
(Check the appropriate box for any exhibits incorporated into this Agreement.)

[ ] AIA Document ~~E202™–2008, Building Information Modeling Protocol~~E235™–2019, Sustainable Projects Exhibit, ~~if completed, or the following:~~Construction Manager as Adviser Edition, dated as indicated below:
(Insert the date of the E235–2019 incorporated into this Agreement.)

[ ] Other Exhibits incorporated into this Agreement:
(Clearly identify any other exhibits incorporated into this Agreement, including any exhibits and scopes of services identified as exhibits in Section 4.1.2.)

.4 Other documents:
(List other documents, if any, ~~including additional scopes of service~~ forming part of the Agreement.)

PART II
Construction Manager as Constructor Series

The A133–2019 is the base contract where the construction manager provides preconstruction phase services and serves as the constructor (rather than just as an advisor), with the contract priced as cost of the work plus a fee subject to a guaranteed maximum price ("GMP"). The A134–2019 is essentially the same form of contract but does not include a GMP. Rather, with the A134, the construction manager provides the owner with a control estimate to help the owner monitor and manage costs.

Because the delivery method is similar in these two standard forms, the 2019 revisions are similar as between them. Further, the 2019 revisions dovetail with the recent revisions to the A201–2017 General Conditions, which is incorporated into both agreements. The 2019 revisions to the A133 and A134 also align with the 2019 revisions to the B133–2019 agreement between the architect and owner, which is part of the "construction manager as constructor" series of AIA documents.

A133–2019/A134–2019: Standard Form of Agreement between Owner and Construction Manager as Constructor (Cost-Plus with GMP/without GMP)

ARTICLE 1 INITIAL INFORMATION

Both the A133–2019 and A134–2019 insert a new Article 1, Initial Information, setting forth basic contracting information such as the parties' representatives, anticipated milestones, and consultants). Specifically, the Initial Information includes:

- the owner's program
- physical characteristics of project
- the owner's budget
- anticipated milestones and accelerated or phased construction
- sustainable objectives for the project
- the owner's representatives and consultants
- the architect's representative
- the construction manager's representative
- the construction manager's preconstruction staffing plan
- the subcontractor procurement plan
- catch-all provisions for other project information

Despite the section's name, it is not intended to be just informational. Indeed, the parties are entitled to rely on the Initial Information and must adjust certain information if it materially changes throughout the project.[1]

Article 1 also includes a specific requirement that if the parties use the new E234-2019 exhibit for sustainable projects, both parties must incorporate that exhibit into their respective other agreements for the project. That is, the owner must incorporate the E234 into its agreement with the architect, and the construction manager must incorporate it into its subcontractor agreements.[2]

The new Article 1 also precludes the parties from changing their designated representatives without ten days' notice to the other party.[3] In recent years, owners have become more stringent on accepting changes to construction manager's personnel, as construction managers often pitch particular individuals to work on the project when they are trying to win the work, and owners expect that those individuals will actually be involved in the project from start to finish. As a result, some owners have begun identifying certain construction manager personnel as "key personnel" and then imposing financial penalties if the construction manager unilaterally changes those key personnel. Construction managers, on the other hand, should negotiate language allowing for reasonable departures of key personnel who leave the construction manager's employ or otherwise become unavailable for the project.

ARTICLE 2 GENERAL PROVISIONS

With the new addition of Article 1, all remaining articles have numerically changed. Article 2 on General Provisions, therefore, was in Article 1 in the 2009 version of the A133 and A134.

Most of the changes to Article 2 are the same in the A133 as they are in the A134. Material differences are discussed below.

1. Section 1.2.
2. Section 1.1.6.1.
3. Section 1.3.

§ ~~1~~2.1 The Contract Documents

The Contract Documents consist of this Agreement, Conditions of the Contract (General, Supplementary and other Conditions), Drawings, Specifications, Addenda issued prior to ~~the~~ execution of this Agreement, other documents listed in this Agreement, and Modifications issued after execution of this Agreement, all of which form the Contract and are as fully a part of the Contract as if attached to this Agreement or repeated herein. Upon the Owner's acceptance of the Construction Manager's Guaranteed Maximum Price proposal, the Contract Documents will also include the documents described in Section ~~2~~3.2.3 and identified in the Guaranteed Maximum Price Amendment and revisions prepared by the Architect and furnished by the Owner as described in Section ~~2~~3.2.8. The Contract represents the entire and integrated agreement between the parties hereto and supersedes prior negotiations, representations or agreements, either written or oral. If anything in the other Contract Documents, other than a Modification, is inconsistent with this Agreement, this Agreement shall govern. An enumeration of the Contract Documents, other than a Modification, appears in Article 15.

This text is from the A133-2019. It is identical in the A134-2019, except that the A134 refers to the Control Estimate in place of the A133's reference to the Guaranteed Maximum Price proposal.

The added text at the end makes clear that all Contract Documents are enumerated in Article 15,[4] except for a Modification. Obviously, Modifications (change orders, etc.) would not be known at the time of contract execution, but all other documents that are intended to be incorporated into the Contract Documents should be identified in Article 15 at the time of contracting for the protection of both parties.

§ ~~1~~2.2 Relationship of the Parties

The Construction Manager accepts the relationship of trust and confidence established by this Agreement and covenants with the Owner to cooperate with the Architect and exercise the Construction Manager's skill and judgment in furthering the interests of the Owner; to furnish efficient construction administration, management services, and supervision; to furnish at all times an adequate supply of workers and materials; and to perform the Work in an expeditious and economical manner consistent with the Owner's interests. The Owner agrees to furnish or approve, in a timely manner, information required by the Construction Manager and to make payments to the Construction Manager in accordance with the requirements of the Contract Documents.

§ ~~1~~2.3 General Conditions

§ 2.3.1 For the Preconstruction Phase, AIA Document A201™–~~2007~~2017, General Conditions of the Contract for Construction, shall apply as follows: Section 1.5, Ownership and Use of Documents; Section 1.7, Digital Data Use and Transmission; Section 1.8, Building Information Model Use and Reliance; Section 2.2.4, Confidential Information; Section 3.12.10, Professional Services; Section 10.3, Hazardous Materials; Section 13.1, Governing Law. The term "Contractor" as used in A201–2017 shall mean the Construction Manager.

§ 2.3.2 ~~only as specifically provided in this Agreement.~~ For the Construction Phase, the general conditions of the contract shall be as set forth in A201–~~2007~~2017, which document is incorporated herein by reference. The term "Contractor" as used in A201–~~2007~~2017 shall mean the Construction Manager.

4. New Article 15 was old Article 12 in both agreements.

This section was updated to incorporate the 2017 version of the A201 General Conditions. In addition, more substantively, the 2009 versions of the agreements did not specifically enumerate which portions of the A201 applied to the preconstruction phase. Both the A133 and the A134 now specifically incorporate certain sections of the A201 that apply to the preconstruction phase.

Both construction managers and owners should carefully review the cross-referenced General Conditions sections and comport those sections with their respective understandings of the services, obligations, and liabilities that flow from the preconstruction phase. Sections that do not apply should be deleted from this Section 2.3.1, and additional sections that do apply should be added.

§ ~~1~~2.4 Contract Sum, Contract Time and Changes in the Work

The Contract Sum is the actual Cost of the Work as defined in Section ~~6~~ 7.1.1 plus the Construction Manager's Fee as defined in Section ~~5~~ 6.1. The Contract Time is the period of time, including authorized adjustments, allotted in the Contract Documents for Substantial Completion of the Work as certified by the Architect in accordance with Section 9.8 of AIA Document A201–~~2007~~2017. The Contract Time shall be measured from the date of commencement of the ~~Construction Phase as established pursuant to Section 2.3.1.2 of this Agreement.~~Work. Changes in the Work shall be governed by ~~Section 5.2 of this Agreement and not by~~ Article 7 of A201–~~2007. If, however, the Contract Time has been established in accordance with Section 2.2.4.5, Article 7 of A201–2007 shall control adjustments to the Contract Time~~2017.

This Section 2.4 defines the Contract Sum and Contract Time and identifies where in the Contract Documents Changes in the Work are analyzed. This section exists only in the A134, as the A133 handles these issues elsewhere.[5]

The 2009 version of the A134 made a distinction between changes for increased costs (which were governed by Article 5.2 of the A134 and not Article 7 of the General Conditions) and changes for increased time where the Contract Time had been established (which were governed by Article 7 of the General Conditions). To reduce confusion and potentially inequitable application of the various change provisions, the 2019 changes simplify matters and remove the distinction; that is, all changes under the A134 are governed by Article 7 of the A201–2017.

ARTICLE 3 CONSTRUCTION MANAGER'S RESPONSIBILITIES

The Construction Manager's Preconstruction Phase responsibilities are set forth in Sections ~~2~~3.1 and ~~2.2.~~3.2, and in the applicable provisions of A201-2017 referenced in Section 2.3.1. The Construction Manager's Construction Phase responsibilities are set forth in Section ~~2~~3.3. The Owner and Construction Manager may agree, in consultation with the Architect, for the Construction Phase to commence prior to completion of the Preconstruction Phase, in which case, both phases will proceed concurrently. The Construction Manager shall identify a representative authorized to act on behalf of the Construction Manager with respect to the Project.

5. A133 § 6.1.1 (Contract Sum); A133 § 6.3 (Changes in the Work); A133 § A.2.2 (Contract Time).

At first glance, Article 3 (previously Article 2) appears to have undergone major changes. In reality, the AIA simply reorganized this Article to make clearer distinctions between the different phases of the construction manager's services. Further, as reorganized, Article 3 of both the A133 and A134 align their respective subsection number conventions.

The new Article 3 of both the A133 and A134 is organized as follows:

- Section 3.1 – Preconstruction Phase
- Section 3.2 – Guaranteed Maximum Price Proposal (A133) or Control Estimate (A134)
- Section 3.3 – Construction Phase

As one would expect, Section 3.2 of the A133 is significantly different from the same section in the A134. Otherwise, the changes are largely the same for the two documents.

~~§ 2.1.8~~ § 3.1.1 Extent of Responsibility

The Construction Manager shall exercise reasonable care in ~~preparing schedules and estimates.~~ performing its Preconstruction Services. The Owner and Architect shall be entitled to rely on, and shall not be responsible for, the accuracy, completeness, and timeliness of services and information furnished by the Construction Manager. The Construction Manager, however, does not warrant or guarantee estimates and schedules except as may be included as part of the Guaranteed Maximum Price. The Construction Manager is not required to ascertain that the Drawings and Specifications are in accordance with applicable laws, statutes, ordinances, codes, rules and regulations, or lawful orders of public authorities, but the Construction Manager shall promptly report to the Architect and Owner any nonconformity discovered by or made known to the Construction Manager as a request for information in such form as the Architect may require.

The 2019 revisions expand the construction manager's standard of care from the previous requirement to exercise reasonable care only in preparing schedules and estimates to the broader requirement to exercise reasonable care in the performance of all of its preconstruction services. Counsel for construction managers may seek to narrow this standard or clarify that the construction manager is not a licensed design professional.

Also significant is the addition of the second sentence in Section 3.1.1. Consistent with the expanded scope of the construction manager's standard of care, the owner and architect are now expressly entitled to rely on the accuracy, completeness, and timeliness of the preconstruction services and information furnished by the construction manager.

§ 3.1.3 Consultation

§ 3.1.3.1 The Construction Manager shall schedule and conduct meetings with the Architect and Owner to discuss such matters as procedures, progress, coordination, and scheduling of the Work.

§ 3.1.3.2 The Construction Manager shall advise the Owner and Architect on proposed site use and improvements, selection of materials, building systems, and equipment. The Construction Manager shall also provide recommendations to the Owner and Architect, consistent with the Project requirements, on constructability; availability of materials and labor; time requirements for procurement, installation and construction; prefabrication;

and factors related to construction cost including, but not limited to, costs of alternative designs or materials, preliminary budgets, life-cycle data, and possible cost reductions. The Construction Manager shall consult with the Architect regarding professional services to be provided by the Construction Manager during the Construction Phase.

§ 3.1.3.3 The Construction Manager shall assist the Owner and Architect in establishing building information modeling and digital data protocols for the Project, using AIA Document E203™–2013, Building Information Modeling and Digital Data Exhibit, to establish the protocols for the development, use, transmission, and exchange of digital data.

Section 3.1.3 expanded the construction manager's consultation obligations into three subsections.

Section 3.1.3.1 sets forth the construction manager's obligation to meet with the owner and architect regarding the Work and is not new.

Section 3.1.3.2 sets forth the construction manager's obligation to advise and make recommendations to the owner and architect regarding constructability, budget, procurement, and other issues. Newly added to this provision is the requirement that the construction manager must provide recommendations on prefabrication. This likely was added because long-lead items can impact the progress of the schedule, which may be mitigated if addressed at the preconstruction stage. Also added is the requirement that the construction manager consult with the architect regarding the construction manager's professional services provided during construction.

Newly-added Section 3.1.3.3 requires the construction manager to assist the owner and architect with establishing mutually agreeable digital data protocols. This change is consistent with the revisions made to the B133-2019.

§ 3.1.6.3 If the Architect is providing cost estimating services as a Supplemental Service, and a discrepancy exists between the Construction Manager's cost estimates and the Architect's cost estimates, the Construction Manager and the Architect shall work together to reconcile the cost estimates.

§ 3.1.7 As the Architect progresses with the preparation of the Schematic Design, Design Development and Construction Documents, the Construction Manager shall consult with the Owner and Architect and make recommendations regarding constructability and schedules, for the Architect's review and the Owner's approval.

§ 3.1.8 The Construction Manager shall provide recommendations and information to the Owner and Architect regarding equipment, materials, services, and temporary Project facilities.

§ 3.1.9 The Construction Manager shall provide a staffing plan for Preconstruction Phase services for the Owner's review and approval.

§ 3.1.10 If the Owner identified a Sustainable Objective in Article 1, the Construction Manager shall fulfill its Preconstruction Phase responsibilities as required in AIA Document E234™–2019, Sustainable Projects Exhibit, Construction Manager as Constructor Edition, attached to this Agreement.

§ 3.1.11 Subcontractors and Suppliers

§ 3.1.11.1 If the Owner has provided requirements for subcontractor procurement in section 1.1.14, the Construction Manager shall provide a subcontracting plan, addressing the Owner's requirements, for the Owner's review and approval.

§ 3.1.11.2 The Construction Manager shall develop bidders' interest in the Project.

§ 3.1.11.3 The processes described in Article 9 shall apply if bid packages will be issued during the Preconstruction Phase.

§ 3.1.12 Procurement

The Construction Manager shall prepare, for the Architect's review and the Owner's acceptance, a procurement schedule for items that must be ordered in advance of construction. The Construction Manager shall expedite and coordinate the ordering and delivery of materials that must be ordered in advance of construction. If the Owner agrees to procure any items prior to the establishment of the Guaranteed Maximum Price, the Owner shall procure the items on terms and conditions acceptable to the Construction Manager. Upon the establishment of the Guaranteed Maximum Price, the Owner shall assign all contracts for these items to the Construction Manager and the Construction Manager shall thereafter accept responsibility for them.

§ 3.1.13 Compliance with Laws

The Construction Manager shall comply with applicable laws, statutes, ordinances, codes, rules and regulations, and lawful orders of public authorities applicable to its performance under this Contract, and with equal employment opportunity programs, and other programs as may be required by governmental and quasi-governmental authorities ~~for inclusion in the Contract Documents~~.

~~§ 2~~§ 3.1.14 Other Preconstruction Services

Insert a description of any other Preconstruction Phase services to be provided by the Construction Manager, or reference an exhibit attached to this document

(Describe any other Preconstruction Phase services, such as providing cash flow projections, development of a project information management system, early selection or procurement of subcontractors, etc.)

Sections 3.1.4 through 3.1.6.2 were simply moved from former Sections 2.1.3 through 2.1.4.2. The newly-numbered sections contain minor tweaks, including new language in Section 3.1.5 requiring the construction manager to consider "sequencing" for phased construction.

Section 3.1.6.2 includes a new requirement that cost estimates include allowances for price escalation and market conditions. Since there may be a significant time lapse between design/preconstruction and construction, an accurate budget or estimate should include these often-fluctuating costs.

Section 3.1.6.3 is new and requires the architect and construction manager to work together to reconcile discrepancies in cost estimates if both parties prepare them.

Section 3.1.7 is new and addresses the construction manager's continuing obligation to advise the owner on constructability and schedules as the architect progresses through the design phases.

Other new provisions include the construction manager's obligation to advise the owner and architect regarding equipment and temporary facilities (Section 3.1.8) and to provide a staffing plan for its preconstruction services (Section 3.1.9). Like the newly added section in Section 4.1.6, if Article 1 includes sustainability objectives, then the construction manager is obligated to fulfill its responsibilities as set forth in the Sustainable Projects Exhibit (Section 3.1.10).

Section 3.1.14 adds a catch-all provision where the owner and construction manager can further identify any additional preconstruction services that were not covered in the preceding sections.

A133 SECTION 3.2 – GUARANTEED MAXIMUM PRICE PROPOSAL

§ 3.2 Guaranteed Maximum Price Proposal ~~and Contract Time~~

§ ~~2~~3.2.1 At a time to be mutually agreed upon by the Owner and the Construction Manager ~~and in consultation with the Architect~~, the Construction Manager shall prepare a Guaranteed Maximum Price proposal for the Owner's and Architect's review, and the Owner's acceptance. The Guaranteed Maximum Price in the proposal shall be the sum of the Construction Manager's estimate of the Cost of the Work, ~~including contingencies~~the Construction Manager's contingency described in Section ~~2~~3.2.4, and the Construction Manager's Fee~~.~~ described in Section 6.1.2.

§ ~~2~~3.2.2 To the extent that the ~~Drawings and Specifications~~Contract Documents are anticipated to require further development ~~by the Architect, the Construction Manager shall provide in~~, the Guaranteed Maximum Price ~~for~~includes the costs attributable to such further development consistent with the Contract Documents and reasonably inferable therefrom. Such further development does not include ~~such things as~~ changes in scope, systems, kinds and quality of materials, finishes, or equipment, all of which, if required, shall be incorporated by Change Order.

§ ~~2~~3.2.3 The Construction Manager shall include with the Guaranteed Maximum Price proposal a written statement of its basis, which shall include the following:

- **.1** A list of the Drawings and Specifications, including all Addenda thereto, and the Conditions of the Contract;
- **.2** A list of the clarifications and assumptions made by the Construction Manager in the preparation of the Guaranteed Maximum Price proposal, including assumptions under Section ~~2.2.2, to supplement the information provided by the Owner and contained in the Drawings and Specifications~~3.2.2;
- **.3** A statement of the proposed Guaranteed Maximum Price, including a statement of the estimated Cost of the Work organized by trade categories or systems, including allowances; the Construction Manager's contingency, set forth in Section 3.2.4; and the Construction Manager's Fee;
- **.4** The anticipated date of Substantial Completion upon which the proposed Guaranteed Maximum Price is based; and
- **.5** A date by which the Owner must accept the Guaranteed Maximum Price.

§ ~~2~~3.2.4 In preparing the Construction Manager's Guaranteed Maximum Price proposal, the Construction Manager shall include ~~its~~a contingency for the Construction Manager's exclusive use to cover those costs ~~considered reimbursable as~~ that are included in the ~~Cost of the Work~~Guaranteed Maximum Price but not otherwise allocated to another line item or included in a Change Order.

§ ~~2~~3.2.5 The Construction Manager shall meet with the Owner and Architect to review the Guaranteed Maximum Price proposal. In the event that the Owner ~~and~~or Architect discover any inconsistencies or inaccuracies in the information presented, they shall promptly notify the Construction Manager, who shall make appropriate adjustments to the Guaranteed Maximum Price proposal, its basis, or both.

§ ~~2~~3.2.6 If the Owner notifies the Construction Manager that the Owner has accepted the Guaranteed Maximum Price proposal in writing before the date specified in the Guaranteed Maximum Price proposal, the Guaranteed Maximum Price proposal shall be deemed effective without further acceptance from the Construction Manager. Following acceptance of a Guaranteed Maximum Price, the Owner and Construction Manager shall execute the Guaranteed Maximum Price Amendment amending this Agreement, a copy of which the Owner shall provide to the Architect. The Guaranteed Maximum Price Amendment shall set forth the agreed upon Guaranteed Maximum Price with the information and assumptions upon which it is based.

§ ~~2~~3.2.7 The Construction Manager shall not incur any cost to be reimbursed as part of the Cost of the Work prior to the ~~commencement~~execution of the ~~Construction Phase~~Guaranteed Maximum Price Amendment, unless the Owner provides prior written authorization for such costs.

§ ~~2~~3.2.8 The Owner shall authorize ~~the Architect to provide the~~preparation of revisions to the ~~Drawings and Specifications to~~Contract Documents that incorporate the agreed-upon assumptions and clarifications contained in the Guaranteed Maximum Price Amendment. The Owner shall promptly furnish ~~those~~such revised ~~Drawings and Specifications~~Contract Documents to the Construction Manager ~~as they are revised.~~. The Construction Manager shall notify the Owner and Architect of any inconsistencies between the agreed-upon assumptions and clarifications contained in the Guaranteed Maximum Price Amendment and the revised ~~Drawings and Specifications~~Contract Documents.

§ ~~2~~3.2.9 The Construction Manager shall include in the Guaranteed Maximum Price all sales, consumer, use and similar taxes for the Work provided by the Construction Manager that are legally enacted, whether or not yet effective, at the time the Guaranteed Maximum Price Amendment is executed.

A133 SECTION 3.2 – GUARANTEED MAXIMUM PRICE PROPOSAL

A133 Section 3.2 relates to the Guaranteed Maximum Price Proposal and received minor edits in the 2019 update. Section 3.2.1 was revised to require the architect to review the GMP Proposal. In the 2009 version, the construction manager was expected to consult with the architect in the preparation of the GMP Proposal.

In addition, the references to contingency and fee are now tied to the clauses in the contract where such items are defined. Section 3.2.3 made a similar change to refer specifically to the contingency as defined in section 3.2.4.

Section 3.2.2 deals with the scenario where the Contract Documents (previously, the Drawings and Specifications) contemplate additional development at the time of GMP establishment. Changing the prior reference of "Drawings and Specifications" to "Contract Documents" potentially expands the scope of refinements that the construction manager must account for it in the GMP Proposal. Additionally, the deletion of inclusive language of "such things as" may limit the construction manager's ability to claim a cost was not contemplated in the GMP because this listing may be read as an exclusive enumeration of conditions that will result in a change order, rather than a contingency draw.

Perhaps the most significant change is to Section 3.2.4, which revised the contingency definition. While owners, construction managers, and their counsel likely disagree that the industry has settled on a consistent definition of "contingency," most will agree that for a cost to be chargeable to the contingency, it must be reimbursable as Cost of the Work. Section 3.2.4, however, removes that requirement from the definition and replaces it with a requirement that a contingency expenditure must only be included within the GMP but not otherwise allocated to another line item or included in a change order. This revised language opens the door for construction managers to charge otherwise non-reimbursable costs to the contingency so long as the GMP is not exceeded. For example, many owners modify construction management agreements to disallow reimbursement of costs incurred to correct defective work. If a similar change is not made to this Section 3.2.4, then a construction manager who is not allowed to be reimbursed for corrective costs could nevertheless reimburse itself for those costs out of the contingency if room exists within the GMP.

The drafters, however, note that the AIA Contract Documents Committee did not intend to change the A133 or A134 to create a contingency for the construction manager to cover costs not included within the "Costs to be Reimbursed" as defined in Article 7. Indeed, Section 6.1.1 of the A133/A134 and Section A.1.1 of the A.1.1 in the GMP Amendment are clear that the construction manager is entitled to only two components of payment: the Cost of the Work and its Fee; the contract documents never say that the contingency is to be separately treated. According to the AIA, therefore, the contingency must relate to the costs allowable as Costs to be Reimbursed.

If owner's counsel believes that the modified language creates an ambiguity, a simple edit to cure that ambiguity would be to add "and otherwise reimbursable as Cost of the Work" after "included in the Guaranteed Maximum Price." In addition, adding "All contingency expenditures are subject to the approval of the Owner" at the end of Section 3.2.4 similarly would resolve the issue.

Minor edits to Section 3.2.7 dovetail with the changes made to Section 3.3.1.2; that is, the construction phase cannot commence before the execution of the GMP Amendment (unless otherwise agreed to in writing), and correspondingly, the construction manager cannot incur any costs to be reimbursed before execution of the GMP Amendment (unless the owner agrees otherwise).

Section 3.2.8 carries forward the switch in nomenclature from "Drawings and Specifications" to the broader term of "Contract Documents," which are specifically enumerated in Article 15. Further, the revisions to this section clarify that the construction manager must identify inconsistencies between the agreed-upon clarifications and assumptions in the GMP Amendment and the Contract Documents revised by the architect to purportedly include such agreed-upon items.

A134 SECTION 3.2 – CONTROL ESTIMATE

§ 3.2 Control Estimate

§ ~~2~~3.2.1 At a time to be mutually agreed upon by the Owner and the Construction Manager ~~and in consultation with the Architect~~, the Construction Manager shall prepare a Control Estimate for the Owner's and Architect's review, and ~~acceptance~~the Owner's approval. The Control Estimate shall be the sum of the Construction Manager's estimate of the Cost of the Work and the Construction Manager's Fee ~~and shall include those items set forth in Section 2.2.4 below. When the Control Estimate is acceptable to the Owner, the Owner shall acknowledge it in writing~~. The Control Estimate shall be used to monitor actual costs and the timely performance of the Work. The Construction Manager shall update the Control Estimate with each Application for Payment as needed to reflect changes in the Work.

§ 3.2.2 The Control Estimate shall include:

.1 the documents enumerated in Article 15, including all Modifications thereto;

.2 a list of the assumptions made by the Construction Manager in the preparation of the Control Estimate, including assumptions under Section 3.2.4, to supplement the information provided by the Owner and contained in the Contract Documents;

.3 a statement of the estimated Cost of the Work organized by trade categories or systems, and the Construction Manager's Fee;

.4 a project schedule upon which the Control Estimate is based, indicating proposed Subcontractors, activity sequence and durations, milestone dates for receipt and approval of pertinent information, schedule of shop drawings and samples, procurement and delivery of materials or equipment, and the Owner's occupancy requirements;

.5 a date of Substantial Completion, if not established in accordance with Section 3.3.1.3; and

.6 contingencies for further development of design and construction, as required by Section 3.2.4.

§ 3.2.3 The Construction Manager shall meet with the Owner and Architect to review the Control Estimate. In the event that the Owner or Architect discovers any inconsistencies or inaccuracies in the information presented, they shall promptly notify the Construction Manager, who shall make appropriate adjustments to the Control Estimate. When the Control Estimate is approved by the Owner, the Owner shall acknowledge its approval in writing. The Owner's approval of the Control Estimate does not imply that the Control Estimate constitutes a Guaranteed Maximum Price.

§ 3.2.4 To the extent that the Contract Documents are anticipated to require further development, the Control Estimate shall include the costs attributable to such further development consistent with the Contract Documents and reasonably inferable therefrom. Such further development does not include changes in scope, systems, kinds and quality of materials, finishes, or equipment, all of which, if required, shall be incorporated in a revised Control Estimate by mutual agreement of the parties.

§ 3.2.5 The Construction Manager shall develop and implement a detailed system of cost control that will provide the Owner and Architect with timely information as to the anticipated total Cost of the Work. The cost control system shall compare the Control Estimate with the actual cost for activities in progress and estimates for uncompleted tasks and proposed changes. This information shall be reported to the Owner, in writing, no later than the Construction Manager's first Application for Payment and shall be revised and submitted with each Application for Payment.

~~**§ 2.3.1.3**~~ **§ 3.2.6** Prior to commencement of the Construction Phase, the Construction Manager shall not incur any cost to be reimbursed as part of the Cost of the Work, unless the Owner provides prior written authorization for such costs.

~~**§ 2.3.2.1** Those portions~~ **§ 3.2.7** The Owner shall authorize preparation of revisions to the ~~Work~~Contract Documents that incorporate the ~~Construction Manager does not customarily perform with the Construction Manager's own personnel shall be performed under subcontracts or by other appropriate agreements with~~agreed-upon assumptions contained in the Control Estimate. The Owner shall promptly furnish such revised Contract Documents to the Construction Manager. ~~The Owner may designate specific persons from whom, or entities from which, the Construction Manager shall obtain bids.~~ The Construction Manager shall ~~obtain bids from Subcontractors and from suppliers of materials or equipment fabricated especially for the Work and shall deliver such bids to the Architect. The Owner shall then determine, with the advice of the Construction Manager and the Architect, which bids will be accepted. The Construction Manager shall not be required to contract with anyone to whom the Construction Manager has reasonable objection.~~notify the Owner and Architect of any inconsistencies between the Control Estimate and the revised Contract Documents.

A134 SECTION 3.2 – CONTROL ESTIMATE

A134 Section 3.2 relates to the Control Estimate and received minor edits in the 2019 update. Section 3.2.1 was revised to require the architect to review the Control Estimate (previously, the construction manager was expected to consult with the architect in the preparation of the Control Estimate). Revisions to this section also clarify that the Control Estimate is used to monitor actual costs and timely progress of the Work and must be updated by the construction manager with each payment application.

Section 3.2.2 was previously included, in substantial form, in former Section 2.2.4.

Subsection .1 was modified to update the reference to the Contract Documents, consistent with the revisions to Article 15.

Subsection .2 was modified to delete the reference to "clarifications" contained within the Control Estimate, although the reference to "assumptions" remains.

Subsection .3 deleted "allowances," perhaps because allowances are already incorporated in the Cost of the Work. The authors recommend that the construction manager include allowances in the Control Estimate to better capture unknown costs at the time of preparing the Control Estimate.

Subsection .4 was heavily modified to more specifically set forth the schedule information that must be provided as part of the Control Estimate.

Subsection .5 requires the Control Estimate to include a date of Substantial Completion unless otherwise addressed in the Agreement.

And subsection .6 permits the Control Estimate to contain design and construction contingencies, subject to Section 3.2.4.

Section 3.2.3 is new and requires the construction manager to meet with the owner and architect to review the Control Estimate, and to make adjustments upon the discovery of inconsistencies. Additionally, the owner must approve the control estimate in writing for it to be effective, and such approval is not to be construed as establishing a GMP.

Finally, in Section 3.2.4, new language requires the Control Estimate to include costs attributable to further development of the Contract Documents if the parties anticipate at the time the Control Estimate is drafted that such further development will be necessary.

A133 SECTION 3.3 – CONSTRUCTION PHASE

§ ~~2~~3.3 Construction Phase

§ ~~2~~3.3.1 General

§ ~~2~~3.3.1.1 For purposes of Section 8.1.2 of A201–~~2007~~2017, the date of commencement of the Work shall mean the date of commencement of the Construction Phase.

§ 3.3.1.2 The Construction Phase shall commence upon the Owner's execution of the Guaranteed Maximum Price Amendment or, prior to acceptance of the Guaranteed Maximum Price proposal, by written agreement of the parties. The written agreement shall set forth a description of the Work to be performed by the Construction Manager, and any insurance and bond requirements for Work performed prior to execution of the Guaranteed Maximum Price Amendment ~~§ 2.3.1.2 The Construction Phase shall commence upon the Owner's acceptance of the Construction Manager's Guaranteed Maximum Price proposal or the Owner's issuance of a Notice to Proceed, whichever occurs earlier.~~

Section 3.3 addresses the construction manager's Construction Phase services. For the most part, the 2019 changes to this section are not material.

Revised Section 3.3.1.2 clarifies that the date of commencement of the construction phase begins upon the owner's execution of the GMP Amendment or earlier written agreement of the parties. Under the 2009 version, the construction phase commenced on execution of the GMP Amendment (A133) or approval of the Control Estimate (A134), or upon the owner's issuance of a notice to proceed. The notice to proceed concept has been replaced with the requirement that the parties agree, in writing, to proceed instead of allowing the owner to unilaterally order the construction manager to proceed. This provides an additional layer of protection for the construction manager, who may not be prepared to proceed with construction until a GMP Amendment (or Control Estimate) has been approved. This change was intended to allow some early construction phase activities to begin before execution of the GMP Amendment, a practice common in construction today. The change also accommodates the risk that other conditions not mentioned in the agreement, such as receipt of permits or evidence of project financing, could affect the actual start of construction.

A134 SECTION 3.3 – CONSTRUCTION PHASE

§ 3.3 Construction Phase

§ 3.3.1 General

§ 3.3.1.1 For purposes of Section 8.1.2 of A201–2017, the date of commencement of the Work shall mean the date of commencement of the Construction Phase.

§ 3.3.1.2 The Construction Phase shall commence upon the Owner's approval of the Control Estimate or, prior to acceptance of the Control Estimate, by written agreement of the parties. The written agreement shall set forth a description of the Work to be performed by the Construction Manager, and any insurance and bond requirements for Work performed prior to approval of the Control Estimate.

§ 3.3.1.3 Substantial Completion

§ 3.3.1.3.1 Subject to adjustments of the Contract Time as provided in the Contract Documents, the Construction Manager shall achieve Substantial Completion of the entire Work:

(Check one of the following boxes and complete the necessary information.)

[ ] Not later than ( ) calendar days from the date of commencement of the Work.
[ ] By the following date:
[ ] By the date to be established in the Control Estimate and approved by the Owner.

§ 3.3.1.3.2 Subject to adjustments of the Contract Time as provided in the Contract Documents, if portions of the Work are to be completed prior to Substantial Completion of the entire Work, the Construction Manager shall achieve Substantial Completion of such portions by the following dates:

Portion of Work	Substantial Completion Date

§ 3.3.1.3.3 If the Construction Manager fails to achieve Substantial Completion as provided in this Section 3.3.1.3, liquidated damages, if any, shall be assessed as set forth in Section 6.1.7.

The revisions to A134 Section 3.3.1.2 are similar to those in the A133 revision.

Section 3.3.1.3 is new and requires the parties to check a box as to whether substantial completion will be based on a number of calendar days from commencement, by a date certain, or by the date to be established (and agreed upon) by the owner in the Control Estimate. A similar provision is not included within the body of the A133 because the date of substantial completion is set forth in the GMP Amendment.

Section 3.3.1.3.2 inserts a provision where the parties can insert phased turnovers or substantial completion dates for certain project milestones. This concept is covered in the A133 through the GMP Amendment.

Section 3.3.1.3.3 provides that liquidated damages, if agreed to by the parties in Section 6.1.7, will apply if the construction manager fails to achieve Substantial Completion as required under Section 3.3.1.3. This concept is covered in the A133 through the GMP Amendment.

ARTICLE 4 OWNER'S RESPONSIBILITIES

A133 SECTION 4.1.2

§ 34.1.2 Prior to the execution of the Guaranteed Maximum Price Amendment, the Construction Manager may request in writing that the Owner provide reasonable evidence that the Owner has made financial arrangements to fulfill the Owner's obligations under the Contract. ~~Thereafter, the Construction Manager may only request such evidence if (1) the Owner fails to make payments to the Construction Manager as the Contract Documents require, (2) a change in the Work materially changes the Contract Sum, or (3) the Construction Manager identifies in writing a reasonable concern regarding the Owner's ability to make payment when due. The Owner shall furnish such evidence as a condition precedent to commencement or continuation of the Work or the portion of the Work affected by a material change. After the Owner furnishes the evidence, the Owner shall not materially vary such financial arrangements without prior notice to the Construction Manager and Architect.~~ After execution of the Guaranteed Maximum Price Amendment, the Construction Manager may request such information as set forth in A201–2017 Section 2.2.

Section 4.1.2 was modified to better align with Section 2.2 of the A201-2017 General Conditions. Now, the A133 and A134 clarify that the construction manager may seek financial assurances before executing the GMP Amendment (A133) or approving the Control Estimate (A134). Thereafter, the construction manager's right to seek financial assurances is governed by Section 2.2 of the A201. In addition, the 2009 versions of the A133 and A134 did not allow the construction manager to stop work if the owner fails to provide financial assurances, but the A201 did. Thus, the 2019 edits removed potentially inconsistent terms so the A133/A134 and the A201 read harmoniously.

A133/A134 SECTION 4.1.6

~~§ 3~~**§ 4.1.6** If the Owner identified a Sustainable Objective in Article 1, the Owner shall fulfill its responsibilities as required in AIA Document E234™–2019, Sustainable Projects Exhibit, Construction Manager as Constructor Edition, attached to this Agreement.

Section 4.1.6 added language regarding sustainability objectives. If sustainable objectives are required as part of Article 1, Initial Information, then the owner must fulfill the associated responsibilities.

A133/A134 SECTION 4.3 - ARCHITECT

§ 34.3 Architect

The Owner shall retain an Architect to provide services, duties and responsibilities as described in AIA Document B133™–20142019, Standard Form of Agreement Between Owner and Architect, Construction Manager as Constructor Edition., including any additional services requested by the Construction Manager that are necessary for the Preconstruction and Construction Phase services under this Agreement. The Owner shall provide the Construction Manager with a copy of the scope of services in the executed agreement between the Owner and the Architect, and any further modifications to the Architect's scope of services in the agreement.

Section 4.3 was modified to clarify that the owner's agreement with the architect will include any services of the architect that are required by the construction manager for the preconstruction phase or construction phase. It also clarifies that, if requested, the owner will provide the construction manager with a copy of the scope of services contained within the executed owner-architect agreement. The previous requirement that the owner provide the construction manager with a copy of the entire architect agreement was often stricken by owners to protect certain information from disclosure to the construction manager (architect's fee, payment terms, etc.). The 2019 revisions strike a fair balance between that interest of the owner and the construction manager's need to review and determine the scope of services to be provided by the architect.

ARTICLE 5 COMPENSATION AND PAYMENT FOR PRECONSTRUCTION PHASE SERVICES

A133 SECTION 5.1 – COMPENSATION

§ 45.1 Compensation

§ 45.1.1 For the Construction Manager's Preconstruction Phase services described in Sections 3.1 and 3.2, the Owner shall compensate the Construction Manager as follows:

~~§ 4.1.2 For the Construction Manager's Preconstruction Phase services described in Sections 2.1 and 2.2:~~

(Insert amount of, or basis for, compensation and include a list of reimbursable cost items, as applicable.)

~~§ 4~~**§ 5.1.2** The hourly billing rates for Preconstruction Phase services of the Construction Manager and the Construction Manager's Consultants and Subcontractors, if any, are set forth below.

(If applicable, attach an exhibit of hourly billing rates or insert them below.)

Individual or Position	Rate

§ 5.1.2.1 Hourly billing rates for Preconstruction Phase services include all costs to be paid or incurred by the Construction Manager, as required by law or collective bargaining agreements, for taxes, insurance, contributions, assessments and benefits and, for personnel not covered by collective bargaining agreements, customary benefits such as sick leave, medical and health benefits, holidays, vacations and pensions, and shall remain unchanged unless the parties execute a Modification.

§ 5.1.3 If the Preconstruction Phase services covered by this Agreement have not been completed within ( ) months of the date of this Agreement, through no fault of the Construction Manager, the Construction Manager's compensation for Preconstruction Phase services shall be equitably adjusted.

~~**§ 4.1.4** Compensation based on Direct Personnel Expense includes the direct salaries of the Construction Manager's personnel providing Preconstruction Phase services on the Project and the Construction Manager's costs for the mandatory and customary contributions and benefits related thereto, such as employment taxes and other statutory employee benefits, insurance, sick leave, holidays, vacations, employee retirement plans and similar contributions.~~

~~§ 4~~§ 5.2 Payments

§ ~~4~~5.2.1 Unless otherwise agreed, payments for services shall be made monthly in proportion to services performed.

§ ~~4~~5.2.2 Payments are due and payable upon presentation of the Construction Manager's invoice. Amounts unpaid ( ) days after the invoice date shall bear interest at the rate entered below, or in the absence thereof at the legal rate prevailing from time to time at the principal place of business of the Construction Manager.

(Insert rate of monthly or annual interest agreed upon.)

%

The changes made to the payment terms for preconstruction services in Article 5 reflect commonly made revisions by parties. Often, construction managers propose hourly billing rates for both the preconstruction and construction phase services. The former A133 and A134 did not have a streamlined way to account for such compensation structures. With the 2019 revisions, the construction manager and owner may agree to hourly billing rates by named individual or position.

Section 5.1.2.1 further stipulates that the hourly billing rates include all customary fringe benefits, which must remain unchanged through the project unless the parties agree to a Modification. When such fully burdened hourly rates are included in the contract, construction managers often seek a contractual agreement from the owner that the agreed-upon billing rates are not subject to Article 10's audit rights of owners.

ARTICLE 6 COMPENSATION FOR CONSTRUCTION PHASE SERVICES

A133 SECTION 6.1 – CONTRACT SUM

§ ~~5~~6.1 ~~For the Construction Manager's performance of the Work as described in Section 2.3, the~~Contract Sum

§ 6.1.1 The Owner shall pay the Construction Manager the Contract Sum in current funds. for the Construction Manager's performance of the Contract after execution of the Guaranteed Maximum Price Amendment. The Contract Sum is the Cost of the Work as defined in ~~Section 6.1.1~~ Article 7 plus the Construction Manager's Fee.

§ 56.1.12 The Construction Manager's Fee:

(State a lump sum, percentage of Cost of the Work or other provision for determining the Construction Manager's Fee.)

§ 56.1.23 The method of adjustment of the Construction Manager's Fee for changes in the Work:

§ 56.1.34 Limitations, if any, on a Subcontractor's overhead and profit for increases in the cost of its portion of the Work:

§ 56.1.45 Rental rates for Construction Manager-owned equipment shall not exceed percent (%) of the standard rental rate paid at the place of the Project.

§ 56.1.5 ~~Unit prices~~**6** Liquidated damages, if any:

(~~Identify~~Insert terms and ~~state the unit price; state the quantity limitations~~conditions for liquidated damages, if any,.)

§ 6.1.7 Other:

(Insert provisions for bonus, cost savings or other incentives, if any, that might result in a change to ~~which the unit price will be applicable~~the Contract Sum.)

~~**Item Units and Limitations Price per Unit ($0.00)**~~

A133 SECTION 6.2 – GUARANTEED MAXIMUM PRICE

~~§ 5~~§ 6.2 Guaranteed Maximum Price

~~**§ 5.2.1**~~ The Construction Manager guarantees that the Contract Sum shall not exceed the Guaranteed Maximum Price set forth in the Guaranteed Maximum Price Amendment, ~~as it is amended from time~~subject to ~~time. To~~ additions and deductions by Change Order as provided in the ~~extent the Cost of the Work exceeds~~Contract Documents. Costs which would cause the Guaranteed Maximum Price, to be exceeded shall be paid by the Construction Manager ~~shall bear such costs in excess of the Guaranteed Maximum Price~~ without reimbursement ~~or additional compensation from~~by the Owner.

~~*(Insert specific provisions if the Construction Manager is to participate in any savings.)*~~

~~**§ 5.2.2** The Guaranteed Maximum Price is subject to additions and deductions by Change Order as provided in the Contract Documents and the Date of Substantial Completion shall be subject to adjustment as provided in the Contract Documents.~~

A133 SECTION 6.3 – CHANGES IN THE WORK

~~§ 5~~§ 6.3 Changes in the Work

§ 56.3.1 The Owner may, without invalidating the Contract, order changes in the Work within the general scope of the Contract consisting of additions, deletions or other revisions. The Owner shall issue such changes in writing. ~~The Architect may make~~

~~minor changes in the Work as provided in Section 7.4 of AIA Document A201–2007, General Conditions of the Contract for Construction. The Construction Manager shall~~The Construction Manager may be entitled to an equitable adjustment in the Contract Time as a result of changes in the Work.

~~§ 5~~**§ 6.3.1.1** The Architect may order minor changes in the Work as provided in Article 7 of AIA Document A201– 2017, General Conditions of the Contract for Construction.

§ 6.3.2 Adjustments to the Guaranteed Maximum Price on account of changes in the Work subsequent to the execution of the Guaranteed Maximum Price Amendment may be determined by any of the methods listed in ~~Section~~Article 7~~.3.3~~ of AIA Document A201–~~2007~~2017, General Conditions of the Contract for Construction.

§ ~~5~~6.3.3 ~~In calculating adjustments~~Adjustments to subcontracts ~~(except those~~ awarded ~~with the Owner's prior consent~~ on the basis of ~~cost plus~~ a ~~fee), the terms~~ stipulated sum shall be determined in accordance with Article 7 of A201–2017, as they refer to "cost" and "fee~~" as used in Section 7.3.3.3 of AIA Document A201–2007~~," and ~~the term "costs" as used in Section 7.3.7 of AIA Document A201–2007 shall have the meanings assigned to them in AIA Document A201–2007 and shall~~ not ~~be modified~~ by ~~Sections 5.1 and 5.2, Sections 6.1 through~~Articles 6~~.7,~~ and ~~Section 6.8~~7 of this Agreement. Adjustments to subcontracts awarded with the Owner's prior written consent on the basis of cost plus a fee shall be calculated in accordance with the terms of those subcontracts.

§ ~~5~~6.3.4 In calculating adjustments to the Guaranteed Maximum Price, the terms "cost" and "costs" as used in ~~the above-referenced provisions~~Article 7 of AIA Document A201–~~2007~~2017 shall mean the Cost of the Work as defined in ~~Sections 6.1 to 6.~~Article 7 of this Agreement and the term "fee" shall mean the Construction Manager's Fee as defined in Section ~~5~~6.1.2 of this Agreement.

§ ~~5~~6.3.5 If no specific provision is made in Section ~~5~~6.1.~~2~~3 for adjustment of the Construction Manager's Fee in the case of changes in the Work, or if the extent of such changes is such, in the aggregate, that application of the adjustment provisions of Section ~~5~~6.1.~~2~~3 will cause substantial inequity to the Owner or Construction Manager, the Construction Manager's Fee shall be equitably adjusted on the same basis that was used to establish the Fee for the original Work, and the Guaranteed Maximum Price shall be adjusted accordingly.

Article 6, which handles the construction manager's compensation for construction phase services, was not heavily modified in 2019. Section 6.1.1 in both the A133 and A134 clarify that the construction manager is entitled to payment only after execution of the GMP Amendment (A133) or approval of the Control Estimate (A134).

Article 6 also now includes a fill-in-the-blank provision for liquidated damages (Section 6.1.6 of the A133 and Section 6.1.7 of the A134). The liquidated damages provision was included in the revisions made to the 2017 suite of AIA constructor forms. Consideration of a liquidated damages provision comports with industry norms. Interestingly, the liquidated damages provision in the revised A133 and A134 does not contain the typical qualifications for the application of liquidated damages. At a minimum, the parties should include such provisions as (1) time is of the essence; (2) the owner will suffer damages as a result of delayed completion; (3) the liquidated damages are a reasonable estimate of the owner's damages; and (4) such liquidated damages are not a penalty. Construction managers also would be wise to include language that the liquidated damages are the owner's sole remedy for delays.

Section 6.2 clarifies how the GMP may be adjusted. The previous versions of the A133 stated that the GMP could be adjusted "from time to time," which is vague. The 2019 revisions explain that the GMP can be adjusted by additions and deductions by Change Order, which more accurately captures how the GMP might be modified "from time to time." Additionally, the previous versions' language regarding the construction manager's obligation when the GMP is exceeded was imprecise. The 2019 revisions tighten this obligation by requiring the construction manager to pay costs in excess of the approved GMP.

ARTICLE 7 COST OF THE WORK FOR THE CONSTRUCTION PHASE

For the most part, the 2019 revisions are identical across both the A133 and the A134 agreements. With the addition of Article 1, former Article 6, Cost of the Work, is now Article 7.

A133 SECTION 7.1 – COSTS TO BE REIMBURSED

> **§ ~~6~~7.1 Costs to Be Reimbursed**
>
> **§ ~~6~~7.1.1** The term Cost of the Work shall mean costs necessarily incurred by the Construction Manager in the proper performance of the Work. ~~Such costs shall be at rates not higher than the standard paid at the place of the Project except with prior consent of the Owner.~~ The Cost of the Work shall include only the items set forth in Sections ~~6~~7.1 through ~~6~~7.7.
>
> **§ ~~6~~7.1.2** Where, pursuant to the Contract Documents, any cost is subject to the Owner's prior approval, the Construction Manager shall obtain ~~this~~such approval in writing prior to incurring the cost. ~~The parties~~
>
> **§ 7.1.3** Costs shall ~~endeavor to identify any such costs~~be at rates not higher than the standard rates paid at the place of the Project, except with prior ~~to executing Guaranteed Maximum Price Amendment~~approval of the Owner.

New Sections 7.1.1 and Section 7.1.3 separate out the language previously contained in former Section 6.1.

Revised Section 7.1.2 mandates that any owner approval of a cost required by the Contract Documents be provided in writing. This eliminates arguments over whether an oral direction from the owner or its representative constitutes approval of a Cost of the Work incurred by the construction manager.

A133 SECTION 7.2

> **§ ~~6~~7.2.1** Wages or salaries of construction workers directly employed by the Construction Manager to perform the construction of the Work at the site or, with the Owner's prior approval, at off-site workshops.

Labor costs were previously addressed in former Section 6.2 and are now addressed in Article 7.2. Section 7.2.1 added the concept that the construction manager's construction workers may be paid salaries instead of wages.

§ ~~6~~7.2.2 Wages or salaries of the Construction Manager's supervisory and administrative personnel when stationed at the site and performing Work, with the Owner's prior approval.

~~(If it is intended that the wages~~

§ 7.2.2.1 Wages or salaries of ~~certain personnel stationed at~~ the Construction Manager's ~~principal or~~supervisory and administrative personnel when performing Work and stationed at a location other ~~offices shall be included in the Cost~~than the site, but only for that portion of ~~the Work, identify in Section 11.5,~~time required for the Work, and limited to the personnel and activities listed below:

(Identify the personnel~~to be included, whether for all or only part~~, type of ~~their time, and~~ activity and, if applicable, any agreed upon percentage of time to be devoted to the ~~rates at which their time will be charged to the Work.)~~Work.)

Revised Section 7.2.2 clarifies that a construction manager could not station employees at the site solely to make them reimbursable under Article 7—they also must be performing Work for the project.

Moreover, one of the most often modified clauses of the Cost of the Work section of the A133/A134 is the clause concerning the reimbursement of the construction manager's principals when stationed off-site. A construction manager's supervisory personnel are often roving and not "stationed at the project site," and the construction manager wishes to include some portion of their compensation in the Cost of the Work. To accommodate the interests of both the construction manager and owner, the 2019 changes to 7.2.2.1 allow certain individuals to be reimbursed even if stationed elsewhere, provided they are actually performing certain identified services for the project.

Notably, former Section 6.2.5 (concerning the payment of bonuses) was deleted in its entirety and moved to new Section 7.9, Costs Not To Be Reimbursed. Construction managers should beware when using hourly billing rates for reimbursement under Section 7.2 that if those hourly rates include bonuses or incentive compensation, such inclusion should be disclosed to be completely transparent and contractually compliant.

§ 7.2.5 If agreed rates for labor costs, in lieu of actual costs, are provided in this Agreement, the rates shall remain unchanged throughout the duration of this Agreement, unless the parties execute a Modification.

New Section 7.2.5 states that when hourly billing rates are used, those rates must remain unchanged for the duration of the project. While such language may be reasonable for projects of short durations, most construction management at risk projects are large, complex, and multi-year projects. In such instances, the parties should consider including a preset rate escalation in Section 7.2.5.

A133 SECTION 7.5.2

> **§ ~~6~~7.5.2** Rental charges for temporary facilities, machinery, equipment, and hand tools not customarily owned by construction workers that are provided by the Construction Manager at the site, and the costs of transportation, installation, dismantling, minor repairs, ~~dismantling~~ and removal of such temporary facilities, machinery, equipment, and hand tools. Rates and quantities of equipment owned by the Construction Manager, or a related party as defined in Section 7.8, shall be subject to the Owner's prior approval. The total rental cost of any ~~Construction Manager-owned item~~such equipment may not exceed the purchase price of any comparable item. ~~Rates of Construction Manager-owned equipment and quantities of equipment shall be subject to the Owner's prior approval.~~

Section 7.5.2's revisions reflect the growing trend of construction managers owning their own equipment. Specifically, the drafters included language requiring that the cost of equipment owned by a party related to the construction manager be approved by the owner before being incurred. Owners likely were leery of construction managers using subsidiaries or other related parties (as defined in Section 7.8) as an additional profit center at the owners' expense. As such, owners wanted to be sure they had approval rights of such costs in the first instance.

A133 SECTION 7.6.1.2

> **§ 7.6.1.2** Costs for insurance through a captive insurer owned or controlled by the Construction Manager, with the Owner's prior approval.

A new Section 7.6.1.2 was added to allow costs of insurance through a captive insurer owned or controlled by the construction manager to be reimbursable.

A133 SECTION 7.8 – RELATED PARTY TRANSACTIONS

> **~~§ 6.10~~ § 7.8 Related Party Transactions**
>
> **§ ~~6.10~~7.8.1** For purposes of this Section ~~6.10~~7.8, the term "related party" shall mean (1) a parent, subsidiary, affiliate, or other entity having common ownership ~~or~~of, or sharing common management with, the Construction Manager; (2) any entity in which any stockholder in, or management employee of, the Construction Manager ~~owns any~~holds an equity interest in excess of ten percent in the aggregate; ~~or~~(3) any ~~person or~~ entity which has the right to control the business or affairs of the Construction Manager~~. The term "related party" includes~~; or (4) any person, or any member of the immediate family of any person ~~identified above.~~ , who has the right to control the business or affairs of the Construction Manager.

Section 7.8.1 concerns related party transactions and sets forth four separate scenarios under which a person or entity will be deemed a "related party" of the construction manager:

- A parent, subsidiary, affiliate, or other entity having common ownership of, or sharing common management with, the construction manager;

The modification here simply clarifies the original language.

- Any entity in which any stockholder in, or management employee of, the construction manager holds an equity interest in excess of ten percent in the aggregate;

The new language imparts a higher threshold for determining whether a management employee or shareholder of the construction manager holds more than a ten percent interest in another entity. By tying this definition to an equity interest, the drafters have limited the instances where a related party is defined to include shareholders of non-equity shares of another entity.

- Any entity which has the right to control the business or affairs of the construction manager; or,
- Any person, or any member of the immediate family of any person, who has the right to control the business or affairs of the construction manager.

The revisions to these last two clauses were not substantive—they merely split the definition to separately refer to entities or individuals (or immediate relatives of individuals) who control the business of the construction manager.

A133 SECTION 7.9 – COSTS NOT TO BE REIMBURSED

§ 7.9 Costs Not To Be Reimbursed

§ 7.9.1 The Cost of the Work shall not include the items listed below:

.1 Salaries and other compensation of the Construction Manager's personnel stationed at the Construction Manager's principal office or offices other than the site office, except as specifically provided in Section 7.2, or as may be provided in Article 14;
.2 Bonuses, profit sharing, incentive compensation, and any other discretionary payments, paid to anyone hired by the Construction Manager or paid to any Subcontractor or vendor, unless the Owner has provided prior approval;
.3 Expenses of the Construction Manager's principal office and offices other than the site office;
.4 Overhead and general expenses, except as may be expressly included in Sections 7.1 to 7.7;
.5 The Construction Manager's capital expenses, including interest on the Construction Manager's capital employed for the Work;
.6 Except as provided in Section 7.7.3 of this Agreement, costs due to the negligence of, or failure to fulfill a specific responsibility of the Contract by, the Construction Manager, Subcontractors, and suppliers, or anyone directly or indirectly employed by any of them or for whose acts any of them may be liable;
.7 Any cost not specifically and expressly described in Sections 7.1 to 7.7;
.8 Costs, other than costs included in Change Orders approved by the Owner, that would cause the Guaranteed Maximum Price to be exceeded; and
.9 Costs for services incurred during the Preconstruction Phase.

Section 7.9.1 concerns costs not to be reimbursed and previously existed as Section 6.8. Both the A133 and A134 have added Section 7.9.1.2, which excludes bonuses, incentives, and other discretionary compensation as reimbursable costs. This provision was previously expressly included in the definition of the Cost of the Work. Construction managers, therefore, should be mindful of this change when preparing their general conditions and labor costs under the 2019 agreements.

ARTICLE 8 DISCOUNTS, REBATES AND REFUNDS

The 2019 edits moved the provisions relating to discounts and rebates from former Sections 6.9.1 and 6.9.2 to standalone Article 8 without any material changes.

ARTICLE 9 SUBCONTRACTS AND OTHER AGREEMENTS

The new Article 9 consolidates several sections from Article 3 (originally, Article 2) covering construction manager responsibilities. The new Article 9 provisions in the A133 and A134 are largely the same except for the addition of Section 9.1.1 in the A133, discussed below.

A133 SECTION 9.1

> **§ 9.1** Those portions of the Work that the Construction Manager does not customarily perform with the Construction Manager's own personnel shall be performed under subcontracts or other appropriate agreements with the Construction Manager. The Owner may designate specific persons from whom, or entities from which, the Construction Manager shall obtain bids. The Construction Manager shall obtain bids from Subcontractors, and from suppliers of materials or equipment fabricated especially for the Work, who are qualified to perform that portion of the Work in accordance with the requirements of the Contract Documents. The Construction Manager shall deliver such bids to the Architect and Owner with an indication as to which bids the Construction Manager intends to accept. The Owner then has the right to review the Construction Manager's list of proposed subcontractors and suppliers in consultation with the Architect and, subject to Section 9.1.1, to object to any subcontractor or supplier. Any advice of the Architect, or approval or objection by the Owner, shall not relieve the Construction Manager of its responsibility to perform the Work in accordance with the Contract Documents. The Construction Manager shall not be required to contract with anyone to whom the Construction Manager has reasonable objection.

Section 9.1 contains a new requirement that the construction manager will solicit bids only from subcontractors or suppliers who are qualified to perform the solicited work. Although the language of the succeeding sentences has been slightly altered, the purpose of those sentences remains as originally drafted in the old Section 2.3.2.1: the construction manager will recommend bidders for subcontracts and the owner has the right to review and object to the proposed bidders.

Section 9.1 also adds exculpatory language clarifying that neither the owner's nor architect's approval of any recommended bidder or bid will relieve the construction manager of performing its work in accordance with the Contract Documents. This language discourages a construction manager from arguing that an owner's or architect's approval of a bid containing clarifications or exclusions implied acceptance of deviations from the Contract Documents.

> **§ 9.1.1** When a specific subcontractor or supplier (1) is recommended to the Owner by the Construction Manager; (2) is qualified to perform that portion of the Work; and (3) has submitted a bid that conforms to the requirements of the Contract Documents without reservations or exceptions, but the Owner requires that another bid be accepted, then the Construction Manager may require that a Change Order be issued to adjust the Guaranteed Maximum Price by the difference between the bid of the person or entity recommended

to the Owner by the Construction Manager and the amount of the subcontract or other agreement actually signed with the person or entity designated by the Owner.

Section 9.1.1 is the former Section 2.3.2.2 and concerns adjustments to the GMP when the owner rejects an otherwise qualified bidder. This section remains in the A133 and not in the A134, which does not include a GMP. The language was revised, however, to allow adjustments in the GMP regardless of whether the GMP has been established. Under the previous version, adjustments to the GMP on account of an owner rejection of a bidder could occur only after the GMP had been established. Additionally, the previous version permitted the construction manager to obtain an adjustment in the contract time if the owner-required bid had a longer performance time than the proposed bid from the construction manager.

ARTICLE 10 ACCOUNTING RECORDS

The Construction Manager shall keep full and detailed records and accounts related to the ~~cost~~Cost of the Work, and exercise such controls, as may be necessary for proper financial management under this Contract and to substantiate all costs incurred. The accounting and control systems shall be satisfactory to the Owner. The Owner and the Owner's auditors shall, during regular business hours and upon reasonable notice, be afforded access to, and shall be permitted to audit and copy, the Construction Manager's records and accounts, including complete documentation supporting accounting entries, books, job cost reports, correspondence, instructions, drawings, receipts, subcontracts, Subcontractor's proposals, Subcontractor's invoices, purchase orders, vouchers, memoranda, and other data relating to this Contract. The Construction Manager shall preserve these records for a period of three years after final payment, or for such longer period as may be required by law.

The 2019 revisions to Article 10 are minor. In the new version, the construction manager is now required to provide the owner with the construction manager's job cost reports, which are detailed reports that track all costs associated with a project and provide an in-depth look into the construction manager's costs and expenses. Construction managers also must provide owners with subcontractor invoices upon request.

ARTICLE 11 PAYMENTS FOR CONSTRUCTION PHASE SERVICES

The 2019 edits are similar between the A133 and A134. The discussion below relates to specific provisions in the A133 but it also applies to comparable provisions in the A134.

A133 SECTION 11.1 – PROGRESS PAYMENTS

§ ~~7~~11.1 Progress Payments

§ ~~7~~11.1.1 Based upon Applications for Payment submitted to the Architect by the Construction Manager, and Certificates for Payment issued by the Architect, the Owner shall make progress payments on account of the Contract Sum, to the Construction Manager, as provided below and elsewhere in the Contract Documents.

§ ~~7~~11.1.2 The period covered by each Application for Payment shall be one calendar month ending on the last day of the month, or as follows:

§ ~~7~~11.1.3 Provided that an Application for Payment is received by the Architect not later than the ___ day of a month, the Owner shall make payment of the amount certified ~~amount~~ to the Construction Manager not later than the ___ day of the _____month. If an Application for Payment is received by the Architect after the application date fixed above, payment of the amount certified shall be made by the Owner not later than ( ) days after the Architect receives the Application for Payment.

(Federal, state or local laws may require payment within a certain period of time.)

§ ~~7~~11.1.4 With each Application for Payment, the Construction Manager shall submit payrolls, petty cash accounts, receipted invoices or invoices with check vouchers attached, and any other evidence required by the Owner or Architect to demonstrate that ~~cash disbursements~~payments already made by the Construction Manager on account of the Cost of the Work equal or exceed progress payments already received by the Construction Manager, plus payrolls for the period covered by the present Application for Payment, less that portion of ~~those~~the progress payments attributable to the Construction Manager's Fee~~, plus payrolls for the period covered by the present Application for Payment~~.

§ ~~7~~11.1.5 Each Application for Payment shall be based on the most recent schedule of values submitted by the Construction Manager in accordance with the Contract Documents. The schedule of values shall allocate the entire Guaranteed Maximum Price among: (1) the various portions of the Work~~, except~~; (2) any contingency for costs that are included in the Guaranteed Maximum Price but not otherwise allocated to another line item or included in a Change Order; and (3) the Construction Manager's Fee ~~shall be shown as a single separate item.~~.

§ 11.1.5.1 The schedule of values shall be prepared in such form and supported by such data to substantiate its accuracy as the Architect may require. ~~This~~The schedule~~, unless objected to by the Architect,~~ of values shall be used as a basis for reviewing the Construction Manager's Applications for Payment.

~~§ 7~~**§ 11.1.5.2** The allocation of the Guaranteed Maximum Price under this Section 11.1.5 shall not constitute a separate guaranteed maximum price for the Cost of the Work of each individual line item in the schedule of values.

§ 11.1.5.3 When the Construction Manager allocates costs from a contingency to another line item in the schedule of values, the Construction Manager shall submit supporting documentation to the Architect.

§ 11.1.6 Applications for Payment shall show the percentage of completion of each portion of the Work as of the end of the period covered by the Application for Payment. The percentage of completion shall be the lesser of (1) the percentage of that portion of the Work which has actually been completed, or (2) the percentage obtained by dividing (a) the expense that has actually been incurred by the Construction Manager on account of that portion of the Work and for which the Construction Manager has made payment or intends to make ~~actual~~ payment prior to the next Application for Payment, by (b) the share of the Guaranteed Maximum Price allocated to that portion of the Work in the schedule of values.

~~§ 7.1.7 Subject~~**§ 11.1.7** In accordance with AIA Document A201–2017 and subject to other provisions of the Contract Documents, the amount of each progress payment shall be computed as follows:

~~.1~~ ~~Take that~~

§ 11.1.7.1 The amount of each progress payment shall first include:

.1 That portion of the Guaranteed Maximum Price properly allocable to completed Work as determined by multiplying the percentage of completion of each portion of the Work by the share of the Guaranteed Maximum Price allocated to that portion of the Work in the ~~schedule of values. Pending final determination of cost to the Owner of changes in the Work, amounts not in dispute shall be included as provided in Section 7.3.9 of AIA Document A201–2007~~most recent schedule of values;

.2 ~~Add that~~That portion of the Guaranteed Maximum Price properly allocable to materials and equipment delivered and suitably stored at the site for subsequent incorporation in the ~~Work,~~completed construction or, if approved in writing in advance by the Owner, suitably stored off the site at a location agreed upon in writing;

.3 ~~Add the~~ That portion of Construction ~~Manager's Fee, less retainage of percent (%).~~ Change Directives that the Architect determines, in the Architect's professional judgment, to be reasonably justified; and

.4 The Construction Manager's Fee ~~shall be~~, computed upon the Cost of the Work described in the preceding Sections 11.1.7.1.1 and 11.1.7.1.2 at the rate stated in Section ~~5~~6.1.2 or, if the Construction Manager's Fee is stated as a fixed sum in that Section, ~~shall be~~ an amount that bears the same ratio to that fixed-sum fee as the Cost of the Work included in Sections 11.1.7.1.1 and 11.1.7.1.2 bears to a reasonable estimate of the probable Cost of the Work upon its completion.

~~.4 Subtract retainage~~

§ 11.1.7.2 The amount of ~~percent (%) from that portion~~each progress payment shall then be reduced by:

.1 The aggregate of any amounts previously paid by the Owner;

.2 The amount, if any, for Work that remains uncorrected and for which the Architect has previously withheld a Certificate for Payment as provided in Article 9 of AIA Document A201–2017;

.3 Any amount for which the Construction Manager ~~self-performs~~does not intend to pay a Subcontractor or material supplier, unless the Work has been performed by others the Construction Manager intends to pay;

~~.5 Subtract the aggregate of previous payments made by the Owner;~~

~~.6 Subtract the~~**.4** For Work performed or defects discovered since the last payment application, any amount for which the Architect may withhold payment, or nullify a Certificate of Payment in whole or in part, as provided in Article 9 of AIA Document A201–2017;

.5 The shortfall, if any, indicated by the Construction Manager in the documentation required by Section ~~7~~11.1.4 to substantiate prior Applications for Payment, or resulting from errors subsequently discovered by the Owner's auditors in such documentation; and

~~.7 Subtract amounts, if any, for which the Architect has~~ **6** Retainage withheld ~~or nullified~~pursuant to Section 11.1.8.

§ 11.1.8 Retainage

§ 11.1.8.1 For each progress payment made prior to Substantial Completion of the Work, the Owner may withhold the following amount, as retainage, from the payment otherwise due:

(Insert a ~~Certificate~~percentage or amount to be withheld as retainage from each Application for Payment ~~as provided~~. The amount of retainage may be limited by governing law.)

§ 11.1.8.1.1 The following items are not subject to retainage:

(Insert any items not subject to the withholding of retainage, such as general conditions, insurance, etc.)

§ 11.1.8.2 Reduction or limitation of retainage, if any, shall be as follows:

(If the retainage established in Section ~~9.5~~11.1.8.1 is to be modified prior to Substantial Completion of the entire Work, insert provisions for such modification.)

§ 11.1.8.3 Except as set forth in this Section 11.1.8.3, upon Substantial Completion of the Work, the Construction Manager may submit an Application for Payment that includes the retainage withheld from prior Applications for Payment pursuant to this Section 11.1.8. The Application for Payment submitted at Substantial Completion shall not include retainage as follows:

(Insert any other conditions for release of retainage, such as upon completion of the Owner's audit and reconciliation, upon Substantial Completion.)

§ 11.1.9 If final completion of the Work is materially delayed through no fault of the Construction Manager, the Owner shall pay the Construction Manager any additional amounts in accordance with Article 9 of AIA Document A201–~~2007~~2017.

§ 11.1.10 Except with the Owner's prior written approval, the Construction Manager shall not make advance payments to suppliers for materials or equipment which have not been delivered and suitably stored at the site.

§ ~~§ 7.1.8~~ ~~The Owner and~~ **11.1.11** The Owner and the Construction Manager shall agree upon ~~(1)~~ a mutually acceptable procedure for review and approval of payments to Subcontractors, and ~~(2)~~ the percentage of retainage held on Subcontracts, and the Construction Manager shall execute subcontracts in accordance with those agreements.

§ ~~7~~11.1.~~9~~12 ~~Except with the Owner's prior approval, the Construction Manager shall not make advance payments to suppliers for materials or equipment which have not been delivered and stored at the site.~~

~~**§ 7.1.10**~~ In taking action on the Construction Manager's Applications for Payment, the Architect shall be entitled to rely on the accuracy and completeness of the information furnished by the Construction Manager, and such action shall not be deemed to ~~represent~~be a representation that (1) the Architect has made a detailed examination, audit, or arithmetic verification, of the documentation submitted in accordance with Section ~~7~~11.1.4 or other supporting data; (2) that the Architect has made exhaustive or continuous on-site inspections; or (3) that the Architect has made examinations to ascertain how or for what purposes the Construction Manager has used amounts previously paid on account of the Contract. Such examinations, audits, and verifications, if required by the Owner, will be performed by the Owner's auditors acting in the sole interest of the Owner.

Changes in Section 11.1.5 clarify that the construction manager's contingency must be represented in the schedule of values for the project.

Changes to Section 11.1.5.2 address a common concern among construction managers that when the owner requires them to allocate the GMP to specific line items, the owner is demanding a line-item guarantee for each item within the GMP. The new Section 11.1.5.2 states that such allocation is not a line-item GMP.

Section 11.1.5.3 was added to clarify that when the construction manager moves contingency funds to another line item in the schedule of values, it must also provide supporting documentation to the architect.

Section 11.1.7.1 vastly simplifies the process in calculating the amount of each progress payment. It also allows the construction manager to bill, and receive payment for, construction change directives in an amount the architect reasonably justifies. The previous version did not expressly contemplate inclusion of costs of construction change directives, but the parties routinely added it.

Section 11.1.7.2 now clearly delineates the deductions to be taken from progress payments. Previously, the deductions were stated in terms of retainage and previous payments from the owner.

Subsection .1 reduces the construction manager's progress payment by the aggregate amount previously paid to it by the owner.

Subsection .2 relates to remaining, uncorrected non-conforming work for which previous amounts have been withheld.

Subsection .3 permits the owner to reduce payments based on funds the construction manager does not intend to pay a subcontractor unless the construction manager intends to pay it to others who have performed the subcontractor's work. Construction managers typically object to this requirement because it interferes with the construction manager's management of its subcontractors and the risks of a subcontractor's nonperformance. The intent of subsection .3 likely is to prohibit unscrupulous construction managers from inappropriately withholding the owner's funds to the detriment of faultless subcontractors.

Subsection .4 allows the owner to reduce the progress payment for newly discovered non-conforming work.

Both the A133 and A134 contain revisions to the Retainage section (Section 11.1.8 of the A133 and Section 11.1.7 of the A134) and the Final Payment section (Section 11.2 of both agreements). Rather than stipulate the amount of retainage to be withheld and the timing for release of retainage, the 2019 revisions created fill-in-the-blank fields for the retainage provisions.

Section 11.1.8.1[6] allows the parties to stipulate the percentage to be withheld as retainage from each progress payment prior to the achievement of substantial completion.

Section 11.1.8.1.1[7] allows the parties to stipulate the items that should not be subject to retention. Common exclusions from retention include insurance, bonds, and general conditions.

Section 11.1.8.2[8] permits the parties to agree upon the reduction or early release of retention.

Section 11.1.8.3[9] permits the construction manager, once Substantial Completion has been achieved, to include prior retention amounts in a payment application,

6. *See* Section 11.1.7.1 of the A134.
7. *See* Section 11.1.7.1.1 of the A134.
8. *See* Section 11.1.7.2 of the A134.
9. *See* Section 11.1.7.3 of the A134.

subject to certain additional requirements for release of full retainage upon which the parties agree.

Section 11.1.9[10] allows the construction manager to claim additional payment if final completion is delayed due through no fault of its own. That claim would then be governed by Article 9 (Payments and Completion) of the A201.

A133 SECTION 11.2 – FINAL PAYMENT

§ ~~7~~11.2 Final Payment

§ ~~7~~11.2.1 Final payment, constituting the entire unpaid balance of the Contract Sum, shall be made by the Owner to the Construction Manager when

.1 the Construction Manager has fully performed the Contract, except for the Construction Manager's responsibility to correct Work as provided in ~~Section~~Article 12~~.2.2~~ of AIA Document A201–~~2007~~2017, and to satisfy other requirements, if any, which extend beyond final payment;

.2 the Construction Manager has submitted a final accounting for the Cost of the Work and a final Application for Payment; and

.3 a final Certificate for Payment has been issued by the Architect~~.~~ in accordance with Section 11.2.2.2.

~~The Owner's final payment to the Construction Manager shall be made no later than~~

§ 11.2.2 Within 30 days ~~after the issuance of the Architect's final Certificate for Payment, or as follows:~~

~~**§ 7.2.2** The Owner's auditors will review and report in writing on the~~ of the Owner's receipt of the Construction Manager's final accounting ~~within 30 days after delivery of the final accounting to~~for the Cost of the Work, the Owner shall conduct an audit of the Cost of the Work or notify the Architect ~~by~~that it will not conduct an audit.

§ 11.2.2.1 If the ~~Construction Manager. Based upon such~~ Owner conducts an audit of the Cost of the Work ~~as the Owner's auditors~~, the Owner shall, within 10 days after completion of the audit, submit a written report based upon the auditors' findings to ~~be substantiated by the Construction Manager's final accounting~~the Architect.

§ 11.2.2.2 Within seven days after receipt of the written report described in Section 11.2.2.1, or receipt of notice that the Owner will not conduct an audit, and provided that the other conditions of Section ~~7~~11.2.1 have been met, the Architect will~~, within seven days after receipt of the written report of the Owner's auditors,~~ either issue to the Owner a final Certificate for Payment with a copy to the Construction Manager, or notify the Construction Manager and Owner in writing of the Architect's reasons for withholding a certificate as provided in ~~Section~~Article 9~~.5.1~~ of ~~the~~ AIA Document A201–~~2007~~2017. The time periods stated in this Section 11.2.2 supersede those stated in ~~Section~~Article 9~~.4.1~~ of ~~the~~ AIA Document A201–~~2007~~2017. The Architect is not responsible for verifying the accuracy of the Construction Manager's final accounting.

§ ~~7~~11.2.2.3 If the Owner's ~~auditors~~auditors' report concludes that the Cost of the Work, as substantiated by the Construction Manager's final accounting ~~to be~~, is less than claimed by the Construction Manager, the Construction Manager shall be entitled to

10. *See* Section 11.1.8 of the A134.

> request mediation of the disputed amount without seeking an initial decision pursuant to ~~Section~~Article 15~~.2~~ of AIA Document A201–~~2007~~2017. A request for mediation shall be made by the Construction Manager within 30 days after the Construction Manager's receipt of a copy of the Architect's final Certificate for Payment. Failure to request mediation within this 30-day period shall result in the substantiated amount reported by the Owner's auditors becoming binding on the Construction Manager. Pending a final resolution of the disputed amount, the Owner shall pay the Construction Manager the amount certified in the Architect's final Certificate for Payment.
>
> **§ ~~7~~11.2.3** The Owner's final payment to the Construction Manager shall be made no later than 30 days after the issuance of the Architect's final Certificate for Payment, or as follows:
>
> **§ 11.2.4** If, subsequent to final payment, and at the Owner's request, the Construction Manager incurs costs, described in ~~Section 6~~Sections 7.1~~.1~~ through 7.7, and not excluded by Section ~~6.8~~7.9, to correct defective or nonconforming Work, the Owner shall reimburse the Construction Manager for such costs, and the Construction Manager's Fee applicable thereto, on the same basis as if such costs had been incurred prior to final payment, but not in excess of the Guaranteed Maximum Price. If ~~the Construction Manager has participated in savings as~~adjustments to the Contract Sum are provided for in Section ~~5.2~~6.1.7, the amount of ~~such savings~~those adjustments shall be recalculated ~~and appropriate credit given to the Owner~~, taking into account any reimbursements made pursuant to this Section 11.2.4 in determining the net amount to be paid by the Owner to the Construction Manager.

For the most part, the Final Payment section is identical in the A133 and A134. Section 11.2.2 requires the owner to undertake an audit of construction manager's final accounting within 30 days after receipt of the accounting information.

Alternatively, the owner may provide the architect with notice within that same 30-day period that it is electing not to perform an audit. If the owner does not perform an audit, it has 30 days after issuance of the architect's final certificate of payment to pay the construction manager.

Sections 11.2.2.1 and 11.2.2.2 establish deadlines for the parties' actions when the owner has required an audit. Once the audit is complete, the owner has 10 days to provide the construction manager with a written report of findings. The architect then has seven days after receipt of the owner's audit report (or seven days after owner's notice of election not to audit the project) to issue a final certificate of payment or notify the owner and construction manager of its reasons for withholding the final payment certificate.

Section 11.2.3 allows the parties to stipulate the timing of the final payment if 30 days after issuance of the architect's final certificate of payment is inappropriate.

Section 11.2.4 provides the construction manager with a mechanism to get paid for work performed after final payment so long as the costs incurred are reimbursable under Article 7. The A133 contains additional language where the parties' agreement contemplates shared savings or other incentives under Section 6.1.7 and the added language in Section 11.2.4 of the A133 addresses how the contract sum should be adjusted in that case.

A133/A134 SECTION 11.3 – INTEREST

~~ARTICLE 9~~§ 11.3 Interest

Payments due and unpaid under the Contract shall bear interest from the date payment is due at the rate stated below, or in the absence thereof, at the legal rate prevailing from time to time at the place where the Project is located.

(Insert rate of interest agreed upon, if any.)

%

Both the A133 and the A134 added language to allow the construction manager to receive interest on overdue payments. While owners often delete interest provisions, construction managers are wise to insist on being paid at least some interest for non-payment, particularly because timely payments are an owner's most significant obligation under the agreement, and without timely payments, the construction manager (and, more likely its subcontractors, vendors, and suppliers) is essentially financing the owner's project for the owner's benefit.

ARTICLE 12 DISPUTE RESOLUTION

A133 SECTION 12.1 – INITIAL DECISION MAKER

~~§ 9~~§ 12.1 Initial Decision Maker

§ 12.1.1 Any Claim between the Owner and Construction Manager shall be resolved in accordance with the provisions set forth in this Article ~~9~~12 and Article 15 of A201–~~2007~~2017. However, for Claims arising from or relating to the Construction Manager's Preconstruction Phase services, no decision by the Initial Decision Maker shall be required as a condition precedent to mediation or binding dispute resolution, and Section ~~9.3~~12.1.2 of this Agreement shall not apply.

~~§ 9.3 Initial Decision Maker~~

§ 12.1.2 The Architect will serve as the Initial Decision Maker pursuant to ~~Section~~Article 15~~.2~~ of AIA Document A201–~~2007~~2017 for Claims arising from or relating to the Construction Manager's Construction Phase services, unless the parties appoint below another individual, not a party to the Agreement, to serve as the Initial Decision Maker.

(If the parties mutually agree, insert the name, address and other contact information of the Initial Decision Maker, if other than the Architect.)

~~**§ 9.2** For any Claim subject to, but not resolved by mediation pursuant to Section 15.3 of AIA Document A201– 2007, the method of binding dispute resolution shall be as follows:~~

~~*(Check the appropriate box. If the Owner and Construction Manager do not select a method of binding dispute resolution below, or do not subsequently agree in writing to a binding dispute resolution method other than litigation, Claims will be resolved by litigation in a court of competent jurisdiction.)*~~

~~[ ] Arbitration pursuant to Section 15.4 of AIA Document A201–2007~~

~~[ ] Litigation in a court of competent jurisdiction~~

~~[ ] Other: *(Specify)*~~

§ 12.2 Binding Dispute Resolution

For any Claim subject to, but not resolved by mediation pursuant to Article 15 of AIA Document A201–2017, the method of binding dispute resolution shall be as follows:

(Check the appropriate box.)

[ ] Arbitration pursuant to Article 15 of AIA Document A201–2017

[ ] Litigation in a court of competent jurisdiction

[ ] Other: *(Specify)*

If the Owner and Construction Manager do not select a method of binding dispute resolution, or do not subsequently agree in writing to a binding dispute resolution method other than litigation, Claims will be resolved by litigation in a court of competent jurisdiction.

Changes to Article 12 are not substantive. The default Initial Decision Maker is still the architect (Sections 12.1.1 and 12.1.2) and the method of dispute resolution is still a check-the-box provision (Section 12.2). The only substantive change is the inclusion of the language at the end of Section 12.2 clarifying that, in the absence of full agreement, litigation is the default dispute resolution procedure. That language previously existed in the italicized instructions preceding the check-the-box dispute resolution provision. By moving this language out of the italicized instructions and into the actual text, the drafters acknowledge case law holding that disputes are subject to arbitration only when all parties specifically agree.

ARTICLE 13 TERMINATION OR SUSPENSION

A133 SECTION 13.1 – TERMINATION PRIOR TO EXECUTION OF THE GUARANTEED MAXIMUM PRICE AMENDMENT

§ ~~10~~13.1 Termination Prior to ~~Establishment~~Execution of the Guaranteed Maximum Price Amendment

~~**§ 10.1.1**~~**§ 13.1.1** If the Owner and the Construction Manager do not reach an agreement on the Guaranteed Maximum Price, the Owner may terminate this Agreement upon not less than seven days' written notice to the Construction Manager, and the Construction Manager may terminate this Agreement, upon not less than seven days' written notice to the Owner.

§ 13.1.2 In the event of termination of this Agreement pursuant to Section 13.1.1, the Construction Manager shall be compensated for Preconstruction Phase services and Work performed prior to receipt of a notice of termination, in accordance with the terms of this Agreement. In no event shall the Construction Manager's compensation under this Section exceed the compensation set forth in Section 5.1.

Section 13.1.1 is a new clause in the A133 (omitted from the A134) that allows both the owner and the construction manager to terminate the contract if they cannot reach agreement on the GMP. The party desiring termination must simply give the other party seven days' written notice.

Section 13.1.2 concerns compensation for termination of the contract when the parties cannot agree upon the GMP. In that case, the 2009 version of the A133, and both the 2009 and 2019 versions of the A134, provide that the construction manager is entitled to equitable compensation for preconstruction work and other services provided pre-termination. This new language, however, removes the concept of equitable compensation and instead ties compensation to what the construction manager is entitled to under the agreement.

A133 SECTION 13.2 – TERMINATION OR SUSPENSION FOLLOWING EXECUTION OF THE GUARANTEED MAXIMUM PRICE AMENDMENT

§ ~~10~~13.2 Termination ~~Subsequent to Establishing~~or Suspension Following Execution of the Guaranteed Maximum Price ~~Following execution of the Guaranteed Maximum Price~~ Amendment ~~and subject to the provisions of Section 10~~

§ 13.2.1 ~~and 10.2.2 below, the~~Termination

The Contract may be terminated by the Owner or the Construction Manager as provided in Article 14 of AIA Document A201–2017.

§ 13.2.2 Termination by the Owner for Cause

§ 13.2.2.1 If the Owner terminates the Contract for cause as provided in Article 14 of AIA Document A201–~~2007.~~

~~**§ 10.2.1** If the Owner terminates the Contract after execution of the Guaranteed Maximum Price Amendment~~2017, the amount ~~payable to the Construction Manager pursuant to Sections 14.2 and 14.4 of A201–2007 shall not exceed the amount the Construction Manager would otherwise have received pursuant to Sections 10.1.2 and 10.1.3 of this Agreement.~~, if any, to be paid

~~**§ 10.2.2** If the Construction Manager terminates the Contract after execution of the Guaranteed Maximum Price Amendment, the amount payable~~ to the Construction Manager under ~~Section~~Article 14~~.1.3~~ of AIA Document A201–~~2007~~2017 shall not cause the Guaranteed Maximum Price to be exceeded, nor shall ~~not exceed the amount the Construction Manager would otherwise have received under Sections 10.1.2 and 10.1.3 above, except that the Construction Manager's Fee shall be calculated as if the Work had been fully completed by the Construction Manager, utilizing as necessary a reasonable estimate of the Cost of the Work for Work not actually completed.~~it exceed an amount calculated as follows:

.1 Take the Cost of the Work incurred by the Construction Manager to the date of termination;

~~§ 10~~**.2** Add the Construction Manager's Fee, computed upon the Cost of the Work to the date of termination at the rate stated in Section 6.1 or, if the Construction Manager's Fee is stated as a fixed sum in that Section, an amount that bears the same ratio to that fixed-sum Fee as the Cost of the Work at the time of termination bears to a reasonable estimate of the probable Cost of the Work upon its completion;

.3 Subtract the aggregate of previous payments made by the Owner; and

.4 Subtract the costs and damages incurred, or to be incurred, by the Owner under Article 14 of AIA Document A201–2017.

§ 13.2.2.2 The Owner shall also pay the Construction Manager fair compensation, either by purchase or rental at the election of the Owner, for any equipment owned by the Construction Manager that the Owner elects to retain and that is not otherwise included in the Cost of the Work under Section 13.2.2.1.1. To the extent that the Owner elects to take legal assignment of subcontracts and purchase orders (including rental agreements), the Construction Manager shall, as a condition of receiving the payments referred to in this Article 13, execute and deliver all such papers and take all such steps, including the legal assignment of such subcontracts and other contractual rights of the Construction Manager, as the Owner may require for the purpose of fully vesting in the Owner the rights and benefits of the Construction Manager under such subcontracts or purchase orders.

§ 13.2.3 Termination by the Owner for Convenience

If the Owner terminates the Contract for convenience in accordance with Article 14 of AIA Document A201–2017, then the Owner shall pay the Construction Manager a termination fee as follows:

(Insert the amount of or method for determining the fee, if any, payable to the Construction Manager following a termination for the Owner's convenience.)

New Section 13.2.2.1 of the A133 tracks the termination for cause language that was previously included in the A134. However, both the A133 and A134 insert the previously glaring omission of the owner's right to deduct costs and damages incurred due to the construction manager's termination.

Section 13.2.2.2 in the A133 and A134 added language instructing the construction manager on the procedure upon a termination for cause. The first sentence permits the owner to pay the construction manager fair compensation (either purchase or rental) for the construction manager's owned equipment that the owner elects to retain. There are few scenarios, other than insolvency or bankruptcy, in which an owner should have the right to purchase a construction manager's equipment. For that reason, this provision is likely to be negotiated between owners and construction managers.

In the revised Section 13.2.3, the parties have the opportunity to negotiate a termination fee payable to the construction manager if the owner terminates the contract for convenience. The 2007 version of the A201 allowed the contractor (or construction manager) to receive overhead and profit on unperformed work when the owner terminated the contract for convenience. The 2017 version of the A201 and companion A101 agreement eliminated that requirement in favor of a negotiated "termination fee." This change in the A133 and A134 is consistent with the previous changes to the A201 and A101.

While it would be easy for the parties to skip over this section, the authors recommend that construction managers carefully consider the losses it might sustain if the owner terminates the contract for convenience. Construction managers often spend significant upfront costs associated with pursuing the award of the project, which is routinely a sunk cost. Additionally, construction managers will forecast staff based on project durations, which if truncated might impact overhead. And construction managers book expected profit at various points in the project. Instead of absorbing all of these costs, the construction manager should negotiate a fair preset fee to compensate for the potential financial loss caused by a termination for convenience.

ARTICLE 14 MISCELLANEOUS PROVISIONS

Article 14 moved a few provisions into the new Article 2.3.1, which incorporates reference of certain identified Sections from the A201 General Conditions, including Use and Ownership of Documents (old A133/A134 Section 11.2) and Governing Law (old A133/A134 Section 11.3). There were, however, several substantive changes to Article 14.

A133 SECTION 14.2 – SUCCESSORS AND ASSIGNS

§ 14.2 Successors and Assigns

§ 14.2.1~~.5 of A201–2007 shall apply to both the Preconstruction and Construction Phases~~.

~~**§ 11.3 Governing Law**~~

~~Section 13.1 of A201–2007 shall apply to both the Preconstruction and Construction Phases.~~

~~**§ 11.4 Assignment**~~

The Owner and Construction Manager, respectively, bind themselves, their ~~agents~~partners, successors, assigns and legal representatives to ~~this Agreement. Neither the Owner nor the Construction Manager shall assign this Agreement without the written consent of the other, except that the Owner may assign this Agreement to a lender providing financing for the Project if the lender agrees to assume the Owner's rights~~covenants, agreements, and obligations ~~under this Agreement.~~contained in the Contract Documents. Except as provided in Section 14.2.2 of this Agreement, and in Section 13.2.2 of A201–~~2007~~2017, neither party to the Contract shall assign the Contract as a whole without written consent of the other. If either party attempts to make ~~such~~ an assignment without such consent, that party shall nevertheless remain legally responsible for all obligations under the Contract.

~~§ 11~~**§ 14.2.2** The Owner may, without consent of the Construction Manager, assign the Contract to a lender providing construction financing for the Project, if the lender assumes the Owner's rights and obligations under the Contract Documents. The Construction Manager shall execute all consents reasonably required to facilitate the assignment.

The previous section regarding assignments was modified and separated into two distinct sections.

Section 14.2.1 is designed to bind both the owner and construction manager (and their respective legal representatives) to each other. Previously, this section referenced the parties' "agents," which could include the owner's separate contractors or the construction manager's subcontractors. Since such inclusion would be overly broad, the drafters substituted "partners" for "agents." This means that if either contracting entity has a partner (e.g., a limited partnership or joint venturer), then that partner would be equally bound to the other contracting entity.

Further, to clarify what the other entities (including successors, assigns, and partners) are bound to, the drafters included language that they are bound to the "covenants, agreements and obligations contained in the Contract Documents." This is broader than the earlier language, which tied those entities to the Agreement only.

Section 14.2.2 created a stand-alone clause that was previously captured in Section 14.2.1 (or, old A133/A134 Section 11.4). This language illustrates the concept that owners sometimes assign the contract to lenders as a condition of receiving financing for the project. Owners often require the construction manager to cooperate with its lender to provide the necessary consent required by the lender to effectuate the assignment. Section 14.2.2, therefore, addresses this issue by making the construction manager's cooperation a contractual requirement. Construction managers should know, in advance of contract execution, whether the owner will be financing the project in whole or in part through a lender. In that instance, the construction manager should obtain all lender-required documents as soon as possible to ensure that those documents do not expand its obligations or liabilities under the owner/construction manager agreement.

A133 SECTION 14.3 – INSURANCE AND BONDS

§ 14.3 Insurance and Bonds

§ 14.3.1 Preconstruction Phase

The Construction Manager shall maintain the following insurance for the duration of the Preconstruction Services performed under this Agreement. If any of the requirements set forth below exceed the types and limits the Construction Manager normally maintains, the Owner shall reimburse the Construction Manager for any additional cost.

§ 14.3.1.1 Commercial General Liability with policy limits of not less than ($) for each occurrence and ($) in the aggregate for bodily injury and property damage.

§ 14.3.1.2 Automobile Liability covering vehicles owned, and non-owned vehicles used, by the Construction Manager with policy limits of not less than ($) per accident for bodily injury, death of any person, and property damage arising out of the ownership, maintenance and use of those motor vehicles, along with any other statutorily required automobile coverage.

§ 14.3.1.3 The Construction Manager may achieve the required limits and coverage for Commercial General Liability and Automobile Liability through a combination of primary and excess or umbrella liability insurance, provided that such primary and excess or umbrella liability insurance policies result in the same or greater coverage as the coverages required under Sections 14.3.1.1 and 14.3.1.2, and in no event shall any excess or umbrella liability insurance provide narrower coverage than the primary policy. The excess policy shall not require the exhaustion of the underlying limits only through the actual payment by the underlying insurers.

§ 14.3.1.4 Workers' Compensation at statutory limits and Employers Liability with policy limits not less than ($) each accident, ($) each employee, and ($) policy limit.

§ 14.3.1.5 Professional Liability covering negligent acts, errors and omissions in the performance of professional services, with policy limits of not less than ($) per claim and ($) in the aggregate.

The majority of the insurance and bond provisions of the old A133 and A134 were moved into Exhibits A and B, respectively, which is consistent with one of the major changes to the A201 and A101 in 2017. The remaining references to insurance and bond requirements in the A133 and A134 concern requirements for the preconstruction phase, which mirror the insurance requirements set forth in the B133-2019.

Many owners desire certainty regarding the details of the general liability insurance to be provided by the construction manager. For this reason, owners may wish to modify Section 14.3.1.1 to specifically identify the types of general liability insurance required of the construction manager, such as contractual liability, completed operations and coverage for the construction manager's indemnification obligations.

Most significantly, Section 14.3.1.5 requires the construction manager to provide professional liability insurance for its preconstruction services. The express inclusion of this requirement clarifies the owner's expectation that the construction manager may be providing professional services as part of its preconstruction efforts. The contracting parties should be careful to understand the nature and extent of the construction manager's preconstruction services and to include, or exclude, the professional liability coverage required under Section 14.3.1.5, to align with their expectations and the provisions of Section 3.1.

ARTICLE 15 SCOPE OF THE AGREEMENT

A133 SECTION 15

§ ~~12~~15.1 This Agreement represents the entire and integrated agreement between the Owner and the Construction

Manager and supersedes all prior negotiations, representations or agreements, either written or oral. This Agreement may be amended only by written instrument signed by both Owner and Construction Manager.

§ ~~12~~**15.2** The following documents comprise the Agreement:

.1 AIA Document A133~~–2009~~™–2019, Standard Form of Agreement Between Owner and Construction Manager as Constructor where the basis of payment is the Cost of the Work Plus a Fee with a Guaranteed Maximum Price

.2 AIA Document A133™–2019, Exhibit A, Guaranteed Maximum Price Amendment, if executed

.3 AIA Document A133™–2019, Exhibit B, Insurance and Bonds

.4 AIA Document A201~~–2007~~™–2017, General Conditions of the Contract for Construction

.~~3~~5 AIA Document ~~E201™–2007, Digital Data Protocol Exhibit, if completed, or the following:~~

~~.4 AIA Document E202™–2008~~E203™–2013, Building Information Modeling ~~Protocol~~and Digital Data Exhibit, ~~if completed, or the following~~dated as indicated below:

~~.5~~*(Insert the date of the E203-2013 incorporated into this Agreement.)*

.6 Other Exhibits:

(Check all boxes that apply.)

[ ] AIA Document E234™–2019, Sustainable Projects Exhibit, Construction Manager as Constructor Edition, dated as indicated below:

(Insert the date of the E234-2019 incorporated into this Agreement.)

Article 15 enumerates the exhibits that comprise the Contract Documents. Section 15.2 specifies the exhibits that comprise the Agreement between the owner and the construction manager.[11]

Both the A133 and A134 removed the Insurance Article from the agreement itself and moved it into a separate exhibit to the base contract (Exhibit B to the A133 and Exhibit A to the A134). All other documents that form part of the Contract Documents must be listed in this Article. Indeed, Section 2.1 states that all Contract Documents are listed in Article 15. Accordingly, plans, specifications, addenda, the construction manager's proposal, and the like need to be expressly included in Section 15.2.7 to be considered a Contract Document.

A133 EXHIBIT A – GUARANTEED MAXIMUM PRICE AMENDMENT

Exhibit A to the A133 is the Guaranteed Maximum Price Amendment. It sets forth the GMP, the required date of Substantial Completion, and other terms, and is generally executed toward or at the end of the design phase. The 2019 revisions to the GMP Amendment are relatively minor.

A133 ARTICLE A.1 GUARANTEED MAXIMUM PRICE

§ A.1.1 Guaranteed Maximum Price

Pursuant to Section ~~2~~3.2.6 of the Agreement, the Owner and Construction Manager hereby amend the Agreement to establish a Guaranteed Maximum Price. As agreed by the Owner and Construction Manager, the Guaranteed Maximum Price is an amount that the Contract Sum shall not exceed. The Contract Sum consists of the Construction Manager's Fee plus the Cost of the Work, as that term is defined in Article 6 of ~~this~~the Agreement.

§ A.1.1.1 The Contract Sum is guaranteed by the Construction Manager not to exceed ________ ($), subject to additions and deductions by Change Order as provided in the Contract Documents.

§ A.1.1.2 Itemized Statement of the Guaranteed Maximum Price. Provided below is an itemized statement of the Guaranteed Maximum Price organized by trade categories, including allowances~~, contingencies,~~; the Construction Manager's contingency; alternates,; the Construction Manager's Fee,; and other items that comprise the Guaranteed Maximum Price as defined in Section 3.2.1 of the Agreement.

(Provide itemized statement below or reference an attachment.)

§ A.1.1.3 The ~~Guaranteed Maximum Price~~Construction Manager's Fee is ~~based on the following alternates, if any, which are described~~set forth in ~~the Contract Documents and are hereby accepted by the Owner:~~

~~(State the numbers or other identification~~Section 6.1.2 of ~~accepted alternates. If the Contract Documents permit the Owner to accept other alternates subsequent to the execution of this Amendment, attach a schedule of such other alternates showing the amount for each and the date when the amount expires.)~~the Agreement.

11. Section 15.2 of the A134 is identical to the A133 except for reference to the A133 Exhibit A, which is the Guaranteed Maximum Price Amendment. Since the A134 is not subject to a guaranteed maximum price, it will not have a GMP Amendment. Exhibit A to the A134 is the Insurance and Bonds exhibit, which is Exhibit B to the A133.

§ A.1.1.4 ~~Allowances~~ The method of adjustment of the Construction Manager's Fee for changes in the Work is set forth in Section 6.1.3 of the Agreement.

§ A.1.1.5 Alternates

§ A.1.1.5.1 Alternates, if any, included in the Guaranteed Maximum Price~~, if any~~:

~~*(Identify allowance and state exclusions, if any, from the allowance price.)*~~

Item **Price** ~~**($0.00)**~~

§ A.1.1.5.2 ~~Assumptions~~ Subject to the conditions noted below, the following alternates may be accepted by the Owner following execution of this Exhibit A. Upon acceptance, the Owner shall issue a Modification to the Agreement.

(Insert below each alternate and the conditions that must be met for the Owner to accept the alternate.)

Item	Price	Conditions for Acceptance

§ A.1.1.6 Unit prices, if any~~, on~~ :

(Identify the item and state the unit price and quantity limitations, if any, to which the unit price will be applicable.)

Item	Units and Limitations	Price per Unit ($0.00)

Section A.1.1.2 sets forth the itemized statement of the GMP and has been revised to include a specific reference to the construction contingency. It also provides a mechanism for the parties to refer to an attachment, as GMPs are typically lengthy documents.

Sections A.1.1.3 and A.1.1.4 relate to construction manager's base fee and fee on changes, which reference back to Sections 6.1.2 and 6.1.3 of the A133.

Sections A.1.1.5.1 and A.1.1.5.2 refer to alternates and separate alternates that are contained within the GMP and alternates that the owner may accept post-GMP by change order. Unit prices were removed from the A133 and inserted into Section A.1.1.6.

A133 ARTICLE A.2 DATE OF COMMENCEMENT AND SUBSTANTIAL COMPLETION

§ A.2.1 The date of commencement of the Work shall be:

(Check one of the following boxes.)

[ ] The date of execution of this Amendment.

[ ] Established as follows:

(Insert a date or a means to determine the date of commencement of the Work.)

If a date of commencement of the Work is not selected, then the date of commencement shall be the date of execution of this Amendment.

§ A.2.2 Unless otherwise provided, the Contract Time is the period of time, including authorized adjustments, allotted in the Contract Documents for Substantial Completion of the Work. The Contract Time shall be measured from the date of commencement of the Work.

§ A.2.3 Substantial Completion

§ A.2.3.1 Subject to adjustments of the Contract Time as provided in the Contract Documents, the Construction Manager shall achieve Substantial Completion of the entire Work:

(Check one of the following boxes and complete the necessary information.)

[ ] Not later than ( ) calendar days from the date of commencement of the Work.
[ ] By the following date:

§ A.2.3.2 Subject to adjustments of the Contract Time as provided in the Contract Documents, if portions of the Work are to be completed prior to Substantial Completion of the entire Work, the Construction Manager shall achieve Substantial Completion of such portions by the following dates:

Portion of Work	Substantial Completion Date

§ A.2.3.3 If the Construction Manager fails to achieve Substantial Completion as provided in this Section A.2.3, liquidated damages, if any, shall be assessed as set forth in Section 6.1.6 of the Agreement.

Article A.2 is a new section regarding construction commencement and substantial completion. Section A.2.1 provides a check-the-box option for the date of commencement, which is either the date of execution of the GMP Amendment or as otherwise agreed. If neither box is checked, the default date of commencement is the execution of the GMP Amendment.

Section A.2.2 provides a definition of the Contract Time.

Section A.2.3 inserts language regarding Substantial Completion. Section A.2.3.1 provides a check-the-box approach for Substantial Completion either as a number of days after commencement or as a date certain.

If the construction is phased, or there are other substantial completion dates for specific milestones, the parties can enumerate them in Section A.2.3.2.

Section A.2.3.3 provides that liquidated damages set forth in Section 6.1.6 (if agreed upon by the parties) will apply if the construction manager fails to achieve Substantial Completion as required under Section A.2.3.3.

A133 ARTICLE A.3 INFORMATION ON WHICH AMENDMENT IS BASED

§ A.3.1 The Guaranteed Maximum Price ~~is~~ and Contract Time set forth in this Amendment are based on the Contract

Documents and the following:

§ A.3.1.1~~.6~~ The ~~Guaranteed Maximum Price is based upon the~~ following Supplementary and other Conditions of the Contract:

Document	Title Date	Pages

§ A.3.1.~~1.7~~**2** The ~~Guaranteed Maximum Price is based upon the~~ following Specifications:

(Either list the Specifications here, or refer to an exhibit attached to this ~~Agreement~~Amendment.)

Section **Title** **Date** **Pages**

§ A.3.1.1.83 The ~~Guaranteed Maximum Price is based upon the~~ following Drawings:

(Either list the Drawings here, or refer to an exhibit attached to this ~~Agreement~~Amendment.)

Number **Title** **Date**

§ A.3.1.4 The Sustainability Plan, if any:

(If the Owner identified a Sustainable Objective in the Owner's Criteria, identify the document or documents that comprise the Sustainability Plan by title, date and number of pages, and include other identifying information. The Sustainability Plan identifies and describes the Sustainable Objective; the targeted Sustainable Measures; implementation strategies selected to achieve the Sustainable Measures; the Owner's and Construction Manager's roles and responsibilities associated with achieving the Sustainable Measures; the specific details about design reviews, testing or metrics to verify achievement of each Sustainable Measure; and the Sustainability Documentation required for the Project, as those terms are defined in Exhibit C to the Agreement.)

Title **Date** **Pages**

Other identifying information:

§ A.3.1.95 Allowances, if any, included in the Guaranteed Maximum Price:

(Identify each allowance.)

Item **Price**

§ A.3.1.6 Assumptions and clarifications, if any, upon which the Guaranteed Maximum Price is based:

(Identify each assumption and clarification.)

§ A.3.1.7 The Guaranteed Maximum Price is based upon the following other documents and information:

(List any other documents or information here, or refer to an exhibit attached to this ~~Agreement~~Amendment.)

Article A.3 enumerates the information on which the GMP is based and includes a listing of the Contract Documents, including supplementary conditions, specifications, drawings, sustainability plan, allowances, assumptions, and any other listed documents or information.

A133 ARTICLE A.4 CONSTRUCTION MANAGER'S CONSULTANTS, CONTRACTORS, DESIGN PROFESSIONALS, AND SUPPLIERS

§ A.24.1 The ~~anticipated date of Substantial Completion established by this~~Construction Manager shall retain the consultants, contractors, design professionals, and suppliers, identified below:

(List name, discipline, address, and other information.)

Article A.4 requires the construction manager to identify all parties it will retain.

A133 EXHIBIT B – INSURANCE AND BONDS

A134 EXHIBIT A – INSURANCE AND BONDS

As discussed above in connection with Section 14.3, the majority of the insurance and bond provisions of the old A133 and A134 were moved into Exhibits B and A, respectively, which is consistent with one of the major changes to the A201 and A101 in 2017. Specifically, before the 2017 changes to the A201 and associated agreements, the insurance and bond provisions required for the project were contained in Article 11 of the A201. To facilitate review of the project's insurance requirements and minimize project-specific edits to the A201, those provisions were removed from the A201 and placed into exhibits to the agreements. Accordingly, insurance provisions for projects delivered using a construction manager are now contained in separate exhibits to the A133 and A134. These exhibits are generally identical to the A101 insurance exhibit.

B133–2019: Standard Form of Agreement between Owner and Architect, Construction Manager as Constructor Edition

ARTICLE 1 INITIAL INFORMATION

Article 1, Initial Information generally sets forth the basic project-related information (e.g., project milestones, budget information, identification of the parties' representatives, and identification of consultants). For the most part, the 2019 revisions to Article 1 are not substantive.

§ 1.1 This Agreement is based on the Initial Information set forth in this Section 1.1.

(~~Note the disposition for the following items by inserting the requested~~For each item in this section, insert the information or a statement such as "not applicable~~,"~~" or "unknown at time of execution~~," or "to be determined later by mutual agreement~~.")

§ 1.1.1 The Owner's program for the Project:

(~~Identify~~Insert the Owner's program, identify documentation that establishes the Owner's program, or state the manner in which the program will be developed.)

§ 1.1.2 The Project's physical characteristics:

(Identify or describe~~, if appropriate, size, location, dimensions, or other~~ pertinent information about the Project's physical characteristics, such as size; location; dimensions; geotechnical reports; site~~, boundary and~~ boundaries; topographic surveys; traffic and utility studies; availability of public and private utilities and services; legal description of the site; etc.)

§ 1.1.3 The Owner's budget for the Cost of the Work, as defined in Section 6.1:

(Provide total and, if known, a line item breakdown.)

§ 1.1.4 The Owner's anticipated design and construction ~~schedule~~milestone dates:

.1 Design phase milestone dates, if any:
.2 ~~Commencement of construction~~Construction commencement date:
.3 Substantial Completion date or dates:
.4 Other milestone dates:
~~**.4** Other:~~

§ 1.1.5 The Owner intends to retain a Construction Manager pursuant to the following agreement:

(Indicate agreement type.)

[ ] AIA Document A133–~~2009~~2019, Standard Form of Agreement Between Owner and Construction Manager as Constructor where the basis of payment is the Cost of the Work Plus a Fee with a Guaranteed Maximum Price.

[ ] AIA Document A134–~~2009~~2019, Standard Form of Agreement Between Owner and Construction Manager as Constructor where the basis of payment is the Cost of the Work Plus a Fee without a Guaranteed Maximum Price.

§ 1.1.6 The Owner's requirements for accelerated or fast-track ~~scheduling~~design and construction, or phased construction are set forth below:

(List number and type of bid/procurement packages.)

§ 1.1.7 ~~Other Project information:~~

~~(Identify special characteristics or needs of~~The Owner's anticipated Sustainable Objective for the Project ~~not provided elsewhere, such as the Owner's sustainable objective, if any, or historic preservation requirements.)~~:

(Identify and describe the Owner's Sustainable Objective for the Project, if any.)

However, the 2019 revisions did add three new clauses worth noting: (1) the addition of a sustainable objective provision; (2) revisions to the reliance on Initial Information provision; and (3) incorporation of AIA Document E203-2013, Building Information Modeling and Digital Data Exhibit. All of these revisions were made in the 2017 A201 family documents and carried forward into the construction manager family documents.

1. SUSTAINABLE OBJECTIVES

> **§ 1.1.7.1** If the Owner identifies a Sustainable Objective, the Owner and Architect shall complete and incorporate AIA Document E234™–2019, Sustainable Projects Exhibit, Construction Manager as Constructor Edition, into this Agreement to define the terms, conditions and services related to the Owner's Sustainable Objective. If E234–2019 is incorporated into this Agreement, the Owner and Architect shall incorporate the completed E234–2019 into the agreements with the consultants and contractors performing services or Work in any way associated with the Sustainable Objective.

Sustainable objectives are increasingly becoming industry standard. This provision references the newly revised Sustainable Projects Exhibit to be used with the Construction Manager as Constructor suite of AIA documents. By including this exhibit in the owner-architect agreement, the parties agree upfront to roles, responsibilities, and requirements for achieving sustainability metrics. In addition, if the Exhibit is used as required in Section 1.1.7.1, both the owner and the architect are obligated to incorporate the Exhibit in their downstream agreements. In other words, the owner will be required to incorporate the Exhibit in its agreement with the construction manager, which will bind the construction manager to the terms agreed to between the owner and architect. Undoubtedly, inclusion of this Exhibit will require coordination like that employed on a design-build project, where the construction manager must ensure that the architect will accept the flow-down provisions of its agreement with the owner. The owner and architect should be careful to review the Exhibit and integrate it with how digital data will be transmitted and used on the project or strike the new language from this agreement.

2. RELIANCE ON INITIAL INFORMATION

> **§ 1.2** The Owner and Architect may rely on the Initial Information. Both parties, however, recognize that ~~such information~~ the Initial Information may materially change and, in that event, the Owner and the Architect shall appropriately adjust the Architect's services, schedule for the Architect's services, and the Architect's compensation. The Owner shall adjust the Owner's budget for the Cost of the Work and the Owner's anticipated design and construction milestones, as necessary, to accommodate material changes in the Initial Information.

The revisions to Section 1.2 are straightforward. Previously, if the Initial Information was materially changed, the parties agreed to adjust the architect's schedule and compensation. The prior provision, however, did not anticipate that the actual scope of the architect's services may also require adjustment if a material change occurred in the Initial Information. As such, this provision was modified to allow for an adjustment to the architect's services when a material change in the Initial

Information occurs. Further, if a material change in the Initial Information changes the project budget or time for design and/or construction, then the owner is required to make such adjustments. Obviously, if the material change does not impact the cost of the work or the time for completion, then no adjustment will be required.

3. DIGITAL PROTOCOLS

§ 1.3 The parties shall agree upon protocols governing the transmission and use of Instruments of Service or any other information or documentation in digital form. The parties will use AIA Document E203™–2013, Building Information Modeling and Digital Data Exhibit, to establish the protocols for the development, use, transmission, and exchange of digital data.

As technology continues to advance, parties routinely rely on electronic means for transmitting information. The incorporation of AIA Document E20–2013, Building Information Modeling and Digital Data Exhibit, in this Agreement reflects the growing need to, and increasing focus on, protecting digitally transmitted data and the architect's intellectual property in particular. The owner and architect should be careful to review the Exhibit and integrate it with how digital data will be transmitted and used on the project or strike the new language from this agreement.

§ 1.3.1 Any use of, or reliance on, all or a portion of a building information model without agreement to protocols governing the use of, and reliance on, the information contained in the model and without having those protocols set forth in AIA Document E203™–2013, Building Information Modeling and Digital Data Exhibit, and the requisite AIA Document G202™–2013, Project Building Information Modeling Protocol Form, shall be at the using or relying party's sole risk and without liability to the other party and its contractors or consultants, the authors of, or contributors to, the building information model, and each of their agents and employees.

Routinely, the owner or construction manager will ask for the architect's electronic drawing files to prepare building information modeling (BIM), constructability reviews, coordination or conflict reports, or other digital representations. The intent is to be able to use this information to more efficiently plan, coordinate, and construct the project. The architect, however, needs to protect its intellectual property and must have control over the electronic files. It also does not want to assume liability for any assumptions made by the construction manager or its subcontractors in their use of the electronic files that may result in additional costs to the project or, for that matter, any changes these entities may have made to the electronic files. The intent of this additional language, therefore, is to ensure that the ground rules for the use and reliance of the architect's BIM are agreed-to upfront and that, in the absence of such an agreement, the architect will be relieved of liability for the improper use of or reliance on those files.

Like the newly added Sustainability Objective Exhibit, the owner will have to negotiate the terms of these electronic data exhibits with both the architect and construction manager (who may be at odds over the terms) simultaneously or run the risk of liability gaps between their contract documents.

ARTICLE 2 ARCHITECT'S RESPONSIBILITIES

The most noteworthy addition to Article 2 is the inclusion of a representation from the architect that it is licensed in the jurisdiction where the project is located:

> **§ 2.1** The Architect shall provide ~~the~~ professional services as set forth in this Agreement. The Architect represents that it is properly licensed in the jurisdiction where the Project is located to provide the services required by this Agreement, or shall cause such services to be performed by appropriately licensed design professionals.

Undoubtedly, this representation was previously inferred in prior owner-architect agreements, but, for the avoidance of doubt, has now been added as an express representation from the architect. It was also part of the 2017 revisions to the A201 family of documents. Additional revisions in Article 2 relate to the insurance required to be provided by the architect, with the most substantive change to the requirement being that the owner be named an additional insured on the architect's Commercial General Liability and Automobile Liability for claims caused in whole or in part by the architect's negligent acts or omissions.[1] The addition of this carve-out language is indicative of the architect's continued focus on limiting its liability for issues that do not arise out of its negligence.

ARTICLE 3 SCOPE OF ARCHITECT'S BASIC SERVICES

The purpose of Article 3 is to set forth the basic services the architect agrees to provide in exchange for the compensation outlined in Article 11. Most of the revisions in Article 3 are stylistic. Some changes, however, more clearly delineate the architect's responsibilities with certain obligations that overlap with or otherwise involve the construction manager, such as the project schedule, the architect's construction phase services, and the architect's certification of payment to the construction manager. In addition, there were a few changes made to the architect's own obligations.

1. PROJECT SCHEDULE

Under the B133-2014, the architect was required to submit to the owner and construction manager for their respective review the architect's schedule for the performance of its services (including design reviews) to be included in the overall project construction schedule. The B133-2019 clarifies that the submission to the construction manager is for the construction manager's *review* while the submission to the owner is for the owner's *approval*:

> **§ 3.1.3** As soon as practicable after the date of this Agreement, the Architect shall submit ~~to~~, for the ~~Owner~~ Construction Manager's review and the ~~Construction Manager~~ Owner's approval, a schedule for the performance of the Architect's services ~~for inclusion in the Project schedule prepared by the Construction Manager.~~ The schedule ~~of the Architect's services~~ shall include design phase milestone dates, as well as the anticipated dates ~~when cost estimates or design reviews may occur, and~~ for the commencement of construction and for Substantial Completion of the Work as set forth in the Initial Information. The schedule shall include allowances for periods of time required ~~(1)~~ for the Owner's review, ~~(2) for the Construction Manager's review~~, ~~(3)~~for the Construction Manager's review, for

1. *See* B133™–2019, § 2.6.7.

> the performance of the Construction Manager's Preconstruction Phase services, ~~(4)~~ for the performance of the Owner's consultants, and ~~(5)~~ for approval of submissions by authorities having jurisdiction over the Project. Once approved by the Owner, time limits established by the schedule shall not, except for reasonable cause, be exceeded by the Architect or Owner. With the Owner's approval, the Architect shall adjust the schedule, if necessary, as the Project proceeds until the commencement of construction.

In addition, Section 3.1.3 removes references to design review dates in the architect's schedule but adds references to the commencement of construction and Substantial Completion as identified in Article 1, Initial Information. The editors also moved the language from old Section 3.1.5 to the penultimate sentence in Section 3.1.3. Further, the architect can amend its schedule of services, with agreement by the owner, until construction commences.

2. ARCHITECT'S OBLIGATIONS

This section was modified to ensure that the owner obtains the architect's consent for certain actions. For example, the architect will not be responsible for any direction given, or substitution made, by the owner without the architect's written approval:

> ~~§ 3.1.6~~**§ 3.1.5** The Architect shall not be responsible for an Owner's directive or substitution, or for the Owner's acceptance of non-conforming work, made or given without the Architect's written approval.

Such written approval also extends to the owner's agreement to accept non-conforming work.[2] This requirement places the burden squarely on the owner to ensure it has the architect's written concurrence with its directions given, or acceptances made, without which it cannot later seek to hold the architect accountable.

3. ARCHITECT'S CONSTRUCTION PHASE SERVICES

Section 3.6.2.1 was revised to require the architect to "promptly" provide information to the owner regarding deviations uncovered during its site inspection.

> **§ 3.6.2.1** The Architect shall visit the site at intervals appropriate to the stage of construction, or as otherwise required in Section 4.~~3~~2.3, to become generally familiar with the progress and quality of the portion of the Work completed, and to determine, in general, if the Work observed is being performed in a manner indicating that the Work, when fully completed, will be in accordance with the Contract Documents. However, the Architect shall not be required to make exhaustive or continuous on-site inspections to check the quality or quantity of the Work. On the basis of the site visits, the Architect shall keep the Owner reasonably informed about the progress and quality of the portion of the Work completed, and promptly report to the Owner (1) known deviations from the Contract Documents ~~and~~ , (2) known deviations from the most recent construction schedule submitted by the Construction Manager, and (~~2~~3) defects and deficiencies observed in the Work.

2. *See* B133™–2019, § 3.1.5.

Previously, there was no time component to the architect's obligation to report non-conformances and, obviously, timely reporting of such issues is critically important to the owner. Additionally, the 2019 revisions make clear that the architect is obligated to report only *known* deviations from the construction manager's most recent construction schedule, relieving the architect from any implied requirement to discover those deviations.

There also were changes to the architect's submittal review obligations. Curiously, although the architect must still review and approve the construction manager's submittal schedule, its affirmative obligation to review submittals within the times provided in the approved schedule was removed.

> **§ 3.6.4.2** ~~In accordance with the Architect-approved submittal schedule, the~~The Architect shall review and approve, or take other appropriate action upon, the Construction Manager's submittals such as Shop Drawings, Product Data and Samples, but only for the limited purpose of checking for conformance with information given and the design concept expressed in the Contract Documents. Review of such submittals is not for the purpose of determining the accuracy and completeness of other information such as dimensions, quantities, and installation or performance of equipment or systems, which are the Construction Manager's responsibility. The Architect's review shall not constitute approval of safety precautions or~~, unless otherwise specifically stated by the Architect, of any~~ construction means, methods, techniques, sequences or procedures. The Architect's approval of a specific item shall not indicate approval of an assembly of which the item is a component.

This language may have been deleted to limit redundancy, as Section 3.6.4.1 requires the architect to act on submittals within the approved submittal schedule.[3] The revisions also eliminate the responsibility of the architect to approve safety precautions or construction means or methods, which are within the construction manager's domain.

Further, changes were made to the provision regarding submittals or shop drawings that were certified by a design professional retained by the construction manager.[4]

> **§ 3.6.4.3** If the Contract Documents specifically require the Construction Manager to provide professional design services or certifications by a design professional related to systems, materials, or equipment, the Architect shall specify the appropriate performance and design criteria that such services must satisfy. The Architect shall review ~~shop drawings~~and take appropriate action on Shop Drawings and other submittals related to the Work designed or certified by the Construction Manager's design professional ~~retained by~~, provided the ~~Construction Manager that~~submittals bear such professional's seal and signature when submitted to the Architect. The Architect's review shall be for the limited purpose of checking for conformance with information given and the design concept expressed in the Contract Documents. The Architect shall be entitled to rely upon, and shall not be responsible for, the adequacy, and accuracy ~~and completeness~~ of the services, certifications, and approvals performed or provided by such design professionals.

3. *See* B133™–2019, § 3.6.4.1.
4. *See* B133™–2019, § 3.6.4.2.

Particularly, exculpatory language was added to clarify that the architect's review of other design professionals' submittals is for limited purposes of conformance with information given and the design concept contained in the contract documents. The exculpatory language goes further and provides that the architect will not be responsible for the adequacy and accuracy of the information supplied by the construction manager. Notably, however, the concept of "completeness" was deleted, which arguably has the effect of placing liability for incomplete submittals or shop drawings with the architect. This change was part of the 2017 revisions to the A201 family of documents. The drafters reasoned that the concept of "completeness" is included within "adequacy." For example, if a shop drawing is not complete, it would not be adequate.

4. ARCHITECT'S CERTIFICATE OF PAYMENT TO CONSTRUCTION MANAGER

The architect is required to certify the amounts due to the construction manager, and those certificates are representations on which the owner is entitled to rely.[5] Perhaps most significantly missing from the B133–2009 was the obligation of the architect to represent to the owner that the construction manager is actually entitled to payment in the amount certified by the architect. The 2019 revisions take care of that omission.

> **§ 3.6.3.1** The Architect shall review and certify the amounts due the Construction Manager and shall issue certificates in such amounts. The Architect's certification for payment shall constitute a representation to the Owner, based on the Architect's evaluation of the Work as provided in Section 3.6.2 and on the data comprising the Construction Manager's Application for Payment, that, to the best of the Architect's knowledge, information and belief, the Work has progressed to the point indicated ~~and that~~, the quality of the Work is in accordance with the Contract Documents., and that the Construction Manager is entitled to payment in the amount certified. The foregoing representations are subject to (1) ~~to~~ an evaluation of the Work for conformance with the Contract Documents upon Substantial Completion, (2) ~~to~~ results of subsequent tests and inspections, (3) ~~to~~ correction of minor deviations from the Contract Documents prior to completion, and (4) ~~to~~ specific qualifications expressed by the Architect.

ARTICLE 4 SUPPLEMENTAL AND ADDITIONAL SERVICES

The 2019 revisions to Article 4 make a distinction between "supplemental" services and "additional" services, a distinction also made by the 2017 revisions to the A201 family of documents. The intent of this distinction is to clarify that "Supplemental Services" are services that are beyond the architect's basic services but are agreed upon at the time of the signing of the contract. "Additional Services" also are beyond the architect's basic services but are added after the contract is signed and may increase the architect's compensation.

1. SUPPLEMENTAL SERVICES (SECTION 4.1)

Section 4.1 enumerates a table of services that functions like a checklist of Supplemental Services, which are expressly assigned to either the owner or the architect. If neither the owner nor the architect is identified as providing the supplemental service, then that service is not being provided.

5. *See* B133™–2019, § 3.6.3.1.

§ 4.1 ~~Additional~~ Supplemental Services

§ 4.1.1 The services listed below are not included in Basic Services but may be required for the Project. The Architect shall provide the listed ~~Additional~~Supplemental Services only if specifically designated in the table below as the Architect's responsibility, and the Owner shall compensate the Architect as provided in Section 11.2. Unless otherwise specifically addressed in this Agreement, if neither the Owner nor the Architect is designated, the parties agree that the listed Supplemental Service is not being provided for the Project.

(Designate the ~~Additional~~Architect's Supplemental Services and the Owner's Supplemental Services required for the Project by indicating whether the Architect or Owner shall ~~provide in the second column of the table below. In~~be responsible for providing the ~~third column indicate whether the service~~identified Supplemental Service. Insert a description ~~is located~~of the Supplemental Services in Section 4.~~2 or in~~1.2 below or attach the description of services as an ~~attached~~ exhibit~~. If in an exhibit, identify the exhibit~~ to this Agreement.)

The table of supplemental services in Section 4.1.1 also was modified to delete the "location of service description" as it is not necessary and was often left blank.[6] Additionally, if either the architect or the owner is identified as providing a supplemental service, then additional details regarding the description of each supplemental service is now required to be provided in Sections 4.1.2.1 and 4.1.2.2, respectively:

§ 4.1.2 Description of Supplemental Services

§ 4.1.2 ~~Insert a~~**.1** A description of each ~~Additional~~Supplemental Service ~~designated~~identified in Section 4.1.1 as the Architect's responsibility is provided below.

(Describe in detail the Architect's Supplemental Services identified in Section 4.1.1 or, if ~~not further described~~set forth in an exhibit, identify the exhibit. The AIA publishes a number of Standard Form of Architect's Services documents that can be included as an exhibit to describe the Architect's Supplemental Services.)

§ 4.1.2.2 A description of each Supplemental Service identified in Section 4.1.1 as the Owner's responsibility is provided below.

(Describe in detail the Owner's Supplemental Services identified in Section 4.1.1 or, if set forth in an exhibit, identify the exhibit.)

If a sustainable objective is identified in Article 1, the new B133 makes clear that such services associated with the sustainable objective are to be paid for as a supplemental service:

§ 4.1.3 If the Owner identified a Sustainable Objective in Article 1, the Architect shall provide, as a Supplemental Service, the Sustainability Services required in AIA Document E234™–2019, Sustainable Projects Exhibit, Construction Manager as Constructor Edition, attached to this ~~document~~Agreement. The Owner shall compensate the Architect as provided in Section 11.2.

6. *See* B133™–2019, § 4.1.

The benefit of delineating sustainable objectives as a supplemental service is to clarify that costs associated with obtaining sustainable certifications are not included in the cost of architect's basic services, as such costs are routinely not included in the architect's standard design fee proposals and may vary depending on the level of certification, or certifying agency, the owner requires.

2. ADDITIONAL SERVICES (SECTION 4.2)

Several changes were made to the services the architect may be required to perform as a changed, or additional, service to the basic services contemplated under the agreement.

§ 4.~~3~~2.1 Upon recognizing the need to perform the following Additional Services, the Architect shall notify the Owner with reasonable promptness and explain the facts and circumstances giving rise to the need. The Architect shall not proceed to provide the following ~~services~~Additional Services until the Architect receives the Owner's written authorization:

.1 Services necessitated by a change in the Initial Information, previous instructions or recommendations given by the Construction Manager or the Owner, approvals given by the Owner, or a material change in the Project including~~, but not limited to,~~ size, quality, complexity, the Owner's schedule or budget for Cost of the Work, or bid packages in addition to those listed in Section 1.1.6;

.2 Making revisions in Drawings, Specifications, or other documents (as required pursuant to Section 6.7), when such revisions are required because the Construction Manager's estimate of the Cost of the Work, Guaranteed Maximum Price proposal, or Control Estimate exceeds the Owner's budget, except where such excess is due to changes initiated by the Architect in scope, capacities of basic systems, or the kinds and quality of materials, finishes, or equipment;

.3 Services necessitated by the ~~Owner's request for extensive sustainable design alternatives, such as unique system designs, in-depth material research, energy modeling, or LEED® certification~~enactment or revision of codes, laws, or regulations, including changing or editing previously prepared Instruments of Service;

.4 Changing or editing previously prepared Instruments of Service necessitated by ~~the enactment or revision~~official interpretations of applicable codes, laws or regulations~~, or official interpretations~~ that are either (a) contrary to specific interpretations by the applicable authorities having jurisdiction made prior to the issuance of the building permit, or (b) contrary to requirements of the Instruments of Service when those Instruments of Service were prepared in accordance with the applicable standard of care;

.5 Services necessitated by decisions of the Owner or Construction Manager not rendered in a timely manner or any other failure of performance on the part of the Owner or the Owner's consultants or contractors;

.6 Preparing digital ~~data~~models or other design documentation for transmission to the Owner's consultants and contractors, or to other Owner-authorized recipients;

.7 Preparation of design and documentation for alternate bid or proposal requests proposed by the Owner or Construction Manager;

.8 Preparation for, and attendance at, a public presentation, meeting or hearing;

.9 Preparation for, and attendance at, a dispute resolution proceeding or legal proceeding, except where the Architect is party thereto;

.10 ~~Evaluation of the qualifications of bidders or persons providing proposals;~~

~~.11~~**.10** Consultation concerning replacement of Work resulting from fire or other cause during construction; or

.~~12~~11 Assistance to the Initial Decision Maker, if other than the Architect;

.~~13~~12 Services necessitated by replacement of the Construction Manager or conversion of the Construction Manager as constructor project delivery method to an alternative project delivery method;

.~~14~~13 Services necessitated by the Owner's delay in engaging the Construction Manager; ~~and~~

.14 Making revisions to the Drawings, Specifications, and other documents resulting from agreed-upon assumptions and clarifications included in the Guaranteed Maximum Price Amendment or Control Estimate; and

.15 Making revisions ~~in~~to the Drawings, Specifications, and other documents resulting from substitutions included in the ~~agreed to assumptions and clarifications contained in the~~ Guaranteed Maximum Price Amendment or Control Estimate.

The list of additional services has two notable changes: the deletion of the reference to services associated with extensive sustainable design alternatives[7] (likely because this was specifically added as a supplemental service under Section 4.1.3), and the services associated with design revisions to capture the agreed-upon clarifications and exclusions in the construction manager's Guaranteed Maximum Price or Control Estimate.[8] The latter was presumably added because owners and architects could not agree as to whether such revisions were included in the architect's base compensation. Obviously, if the owner believes such revisions should be covered as part of the architect's basic compensation, it should be careful to strike subparagraph 14 from the enumeration of additional services. (The same can be said for any of the other services listed in Section 4.2.1.)

This Section also clarified that "Additional Services" include services required due to the enactment or revision of laws or codes after the Instruments of Service were prepared[9] or due to official interpretation of applicable codes that are either contrary to interpretations made prior to the building permit's issuance or where the Instruments of Services were prepared in accordance with the applicable standard of care.[10] These sections attempt to balance the diverging interests between the owner and the architect—the owner expects that the design documents provided by the architect will comply with all applicable laws and codes and the architect can design only to those laws and codes in effect at the time it prepares its Instruments of Service *and* cannot accept liability for code official interpretations, as those interpretations can vary and are not under the architect's knowledge or control. As such, the additional language seeks to establish a baseline of code compliance expected to be included in the architect's basic services, with reasonable allowances for unexpected changes or unreasonable interpretations of code officials to be compensated for as an additional service.

7. *See* B133™–2019, § 4.2.1.3.
8. *See* B133™–2019, § 4.2.1.14.
9. *See* B133™–2019, § 4.2.1.3.
10. *See* B133™–2019, § 4.2.1.4.

Additional changes were made to clarify the owner's liability to pay for certain additional services undertaken by the architect to avoid delay during the construction phase:

> **§ 4.~~3~~2.2** To avoid delay in the Construction Phase, the Architect shall provide the following Additional Services, notify the Owner with reasonable promptness, and explain the facts and circumstances giving rise to the need. If, upon receipt of the Architect's notice, the Owner ~~subsequently~~ determines that all or parts of ~~those~~the services are not required, the Owner shall give prompt written notice to the Architect~~, and the~~ of the Owner's determination. The Owner shall ~~have no further obligation to~~ compensate the Architect for ~~those~~the services provided prior to the Architect's receipt of the Owner's notice:
>
> **.1** Reviewing a Construction Manager's submittal out of sequence from the submittal schedule ~~agreed to~~approved by the Architect;
> **.2** Responding to the Construction Manager's requests for information that are not prepared in accordance with the Contract Documents or where such information is available to the Construction Manager from a careful study and comparison of the Contract Documents, field conditions, other Owner-provided information, Construction Manager-prepared coordination drawings, or prior Project correspondence or documentation;
> **.3** Preparing Change Orders, and Construction Change Directives that require evaluation of the Construction Manager's proposals and supporting data, or the preparation or revision of Instruments of Service;
> **.4** Evaluating an extensive number of Claims as the Initial Decision Maker; or
> **.5** Evaluating substitutions proposed by the Owner or Construction Manager and making subsequent revisions to Instruments of Service resulting therefrom~~; or~~.
> **.6** ~~To the extent the Architect's Basic Services are affected, providing Construction Phase Services 60 days after (1) the date of Substantial Completion of the Work or (2) the anticipated date of Substantial Completion, identified in Initial Information, whichever is earlier.~~

Prior to the 2019 edits, if the owner determined that the architect's additional services listed in Section 4.2.2 were not needed, the owner could provide written notice to that effect and avoid further payment obligations for those services. The 2019 changes provide that the architect will be paid for these additional services up to the point when the owner provides notice that it does not want these services. This change clarifies that the architect will be paid for these services until notified otherwise by the owner. This clearly places a responsibility on the owner to react to the architect's notice and to give prompt notice of whether it desires to have the architect perform those additional services; once it does, the owner will not be responsible to pay for services performed after the owner declines them.

ARTICLE 5 OWNER'S RESPONSIBILITIES

For the most part, the revisions made to Article 5 are minor. For example, the last sentence in Section 5.1 was moved to a standalone provision in Section 5.16:

> **§ 5.16** Within 15 days after receipt of a written request from the Architect, the Owner shall furnish the requested information as necessary and relevant for the Architect to evaluate, give notice of, or enforce lien rights.

Interestingly, the 2019 revisions included the deletion of Section 5.3, which required the owner to engage the construction manager to create the overall project schedule. Perhaps this section was deleted because the obligation is contained in the owner-construction manager agreement or may be contracted to a separate scheduling consultant.

Further, in order to remain consistent with other parts of the agreement, Section 5.7 (regarding owner's supplemental services) and Section 5.8 (regarding sustainable objectives) were reiterated in Article 5. Finally, and perhaps most significantly, Section 5.13 as revised requires the owner to include the architect on all communications with the construction manager that relate to the architect's services or responsibilities:

> **§ 5.~~12~~13** The Owner shall ~~contemporaneously provide~~include the Architect ~~with any~~in all communications ~~provided to~~with the Construction Manager ~~about matters arising out~~that relate to or affect the Architect's services or professional responsibilities. The Owner shall promptly notify the Architect of ~~or~~ the substance of any direct communications between the Owner and the Construction Manager otherwise relating to the ~~Contract Documents.~~Project. Communications by and with the Architect's consultants shall be through the Architect.

Previously, the owner had a lesser obligation to contemporaneously provide the architect with any correspondence to the construction manager relating to the construction documents. Now, the owner has an affirmative obligation to include the architect on a broader range of correspondence with the construction manager.

The intent of the revisions to the communications section, which was revised in the 2017 agreements, is to permit the owner and the construction manager to have discussions that do not need to contemporaneously include the architect. This Section 5.13 should be read in conjunction with section 4.2.4 of A201-2017, which is more permissive of direct communications between the owner and contractor (or, here, the construction manager).

These revisions reflect the AIA's response to criticism before the 2017 A201 edits for requiring all communications between the contractor and owner to go through the architect. With the 2017 edits, the AIA recognized that in some circumstances there was not a need for the architect to be involved in owner/contractor communications while balancing the need to include the architect in discussions regarding project design that impact the architect's services.

ARTICLE 6 COST OF THE WORK

The Cost of the Work article in the B133 does *not* relate to the architect's compensation relative to the architect's services. That is handled in Article 11. Rather, Article 6's coverage of Cost of the Work explains the architect's design (and re-design) obligations vis-à-vis the owner's budget and the construction manager's Cost of the Work as set forth in the construction management agreement. This Article was not significantly modified. Particularly noteworthy are the changes in Sections 6.1, 6.3 and 6.5:

> **§ 6.1** For purposes of this Agreement, the Cost of the Work shall be the total cost to the Owner to construct all elements of the Project designed or specified by the Architect and shall include the Construction ~~Managers'~~Manager's general conditions costs,

overhead, and profit. The Cost of the Work also includes the reasonable value of labor, materials, and equipment, donated to, or otherwise furnished by, the Owner. The Cost of the Work does not include the compensation of the Architect,; the compensation of the Construction Manager for Preconstruction Phase services,; the costs of the land, rights-of-way, financing, or contingencies for changes in the Work; or other costs that are the responsibility of the Owner.

This change clarifies that if items are donated to the owner, or otherwise furnished by the owner, those items are included in the B133's definition of Cost of the Work for purposes of calculating the architect's fee. These types of costs generally are *not* included in the definition of Cost of the Work in the construction management agreement because the construction manager should not earn a fee on owner-furnished items unless the construction manager has contractual responsibility for installing those items. The architect, however, may be responsible for design services relative to the owner-furnished items (such as specifying fixtures or equipment), which is the probable justification for this added language.

§ 6.3 The Owner shall require the Construction Manager to include appropriate contingencies for design, bidding or negotiating, price escalation, and market conditions in estimates of the Cost of the Work. The Architect shall be entitled to rely on the accuracy and completeness of estimates of the Cost of the Work the Construction Manager prepares as the Architect progresses with its Basic Services. The Architect shall prepare, as an Additional Service, revisions to the Drawings, Specifications or other documents required due to the Construction Manager's inaccuracies or incompleteness in preparing cost estimates, or due to market conditions the Architect could not reasonably anticipate. The Architect may review the Construction Manager's estimates solely for the Architect's guidance in completion of its services, however, the Architect shall report to the Owner any material inaccuracies and inconsistencies noted during any such review.

§ 6.3.1 If the Architect is providing ~~detailed~~ cost estimating services as ~~an Additional~~a Supplemental Service, and a discrepancy exists between the Construction Manager's cost estimates and the Architect's cost estimates, the Architect ~~shall work cooperatively with~~and the Construction Manager shall work together to ~~conform~~reconcile the cost estimates ~~to one another~~.

~~**§ 6.3.2** Subject to Section 4.3, if the Owner engages a Cost Consultant and a discrepancy exists between the Construction Manager's estimate and the Cost Consultant's estimate, the Architect shall assist the Cost Consultant and Construction Manager as necessary to conform the estimates to one another.~~

Section 6.3 added a provision entitling the architect to compensation as a Supplemental Service for revisions to its documents required due to market conditions that were not reasonably foreseeable. Previously, the architect would be entitled to additional compensation only if the revisions were necessitated due to inaccuracies or incompleteness in the construction manager's cost estimates. Previous Sections 6.3.1 and 6.3.2 were merged into one provision, with the obligation to reconcile cost estimates placed on the architect and construction manager equally. As Section 6.3.1 was written previously, the onus was, instead, on the architect to cooperate with the construction manager to reconcile the estimates.

§ 6.5 If the Construction Manager's estimate of the Cost of the Work at the conclusion of the Design Development Phase exceeds the Owner's budget for the Cost of the Work, the Owner shall

.1 give written approval of an increase in the budget for the Cost of the Work;
.2 terminate in accordance with Section 9.5;
.3 in consultation with the Architect and Construction Manager, revise the Project program, scope, or quality as required to reduce the Cost of the Work; or
.~~3~~4 implement any other mutually acceptable alternative.

If the construction manager's Cost of the Work at the end of the design development stage exceeds the owner's budget, the owner can now terminate the owner-architect agreement for convenience. Previously, the owner's options included increasing its budget, reducing the project criteria to meet the budget, or any other mutually acceptable alternative. Notably, there was no specific obligation on the architect to produce a design that could meet the owner's budget and the construction manager's Cost of the Work. Now, the architect may be faced with a termination of its services if it does not produce a design that meets these requirements.

§ 6.6 If the Owner chooses to proceed under Section 6.5.~~2~~3, the Architect, without additional compensation, shall incorporate the ~~required modifications~~revisions in the Construction Documents Phase as necessary to comply with the Owner's budget for the Cost of the Work at the conclusion of the Design Development Phase Services, or the budget as adjusted under Section 6.5.1. The Architect's ~~modification of~~revisions in the Construction Documents Phase shall be the limit of the Architect's responsibility ~~as a Basic Service~~ under this Article 6.

ARTICLE 7 COPYRIGHTS AND LICENSES

The revisions to Article 7 reflect the incorporation of the digital data protocols in Articles 1 and 13 by removing reference to the need to establish digital protocols and clarifying that the reproduction of the Instruments of Service will be subject to the protocols established in Article 1.

§ 7.1 The Architect and the Owner warrant that in transmitting Instruments of Service, or any other information, the transmitting party is the copyright owner of such information or has permission from the copyright owner to transmit such information for its use on the Project. ~~If the Owner and Architect intend to transmit Instruments of Service or any other information or documentation in digital form, they shall endeavor to establish necessary protocols governing such transmissions.~~

. . .

§ 7.3 ~~Upon execution of this Agreement, the~~The Architect grants to the Owner a nonexclusive license to use the Architect's Instruments of Service solely and exclusively for purposes of constructing, using, maintaining, altering and adding to the Project, provided that the Owner substantially performs its obligations under this Agreement, including prompt payment of all sums ~~when~~ due, ~~under this Agreement~~pursuant to Article 9 and Article 11. The Architect shall obtain similar nonexclusive licenses from the Architect's consultants consistent with this Agreement. The license granted under this section permits the Owner to authorize the Construction Manager, Subcontractors, Sub-subcontractors, and ~~material or equipment~~ suppliers, as well as the Owner's consultants and separate contractors, to reproduce applicable portions of the Instruments of Service, subject to any protocols established pursuant to Section 1.3, solely and exclusively for use in performing services or construction for the Project. If the Architect rightfully terminates this Agreement for cause as provided in Section 9.4, the license granted in this Section 7.3 shall terminate.

Further, for the avoidance of any doubt, the drafters included express language that Article 7 survives termination of the agreement.

§ 7.5 Except as otherwise stated in Section 7.3, the provisions of this Article 7 shall survive the termination of this Agreement.

ARTICLE 8 CLAIMS AND DISPUTES

Article 8, Claims and Disputes, was lightly modified for 2019—mostly to remove the architect's duty to defend the owner and to clarify that disputes will be resolved by arbitration only if the parties expressly agree.

Non-substantive changes include:

§ 8.1 General

§ 8.1.1 The Owner and Architect shall commence all claims and causes of action~~, whether in contract, tort, or otherwise,~~ against the other and arising out of or related to this Agreement , whether in contract, tort, or otherwise, in accordance with the requirements of the ~~method of~~ binding dispute resolution method selected in this Agreement and within the period specified by applicable law, but in any case not more than 10 years after the date of Substantial Completion of the Work. The Owner and Architect waive all claims and causes of action not commenced in accordance with this Section 8.1.1.

§ 8.2.4 If the parties do not resolve a dispute through mediation pursuant to this Section 8.2, the method of binding dispute resolution shall be the following:

(Check the appropriate box.)

[ ] Arbitration pursuant to Section 8.3 of this Agreement
[ ] Litigation in a court of competent jurisdiction
[ ] Other: *(Specify)*

~~:~~ If the Owner and Architect do not select a method of binding dispute resolution ~~below~~, or do not subsequently agree in writing to a binding dispute resolution method other than litigation, the dispute will be resolved in a court of competent jurisdiction~~.)~~.

~~[ ] Arbitration pursuant to Section 8.3 of this Agreement~~
~~[ ] Litigation in a court of competent jurisdiction~~
~~[ ] Other: *(Specify)*~~

Substantively, however, the indemnification provision contains additional language:

> **§ 8.1.3** The Architect shall indemnify and hold the Owner and the Owner's officers and employees harmless from and against damages, losses and judgments arising from claims by third parties, including reasonable attorneys' fees and expenses recoverable under applicable law, but only to the extent they are caused by the negligent acts or omissions of the Architect, its employees and its consultants in the performance of professional services under this Agreement. The Architect's obligation to indemnify and hold the Owner and the Owner's officers and employees harmless does not include a duty to defend. The Architect's duty to indemnify the Owner under this ~~provision~~Section 8.1.3 shall be limited to the available proceeds of the insurance coverage required by this Agreement.

Architects generally will not accept a duty to defend contained within an indemnity provision because the costs of defense are not covered by its insurance program, and architects are generally unwilling to accept any liability in excess of what is insurable. Rather than rely on the simple omission from the indemnity obligation (e.g., "The Architect shall indemnify and hold the Owner... harmless"), the new language clearly excludes the duty to defend from the architect's obligations under this Section. As such, there can be no argument that a duty to defend is implied by this provision. Attorneys representing an owner would be wise to insert additional language requiring the architect to reimburse its costs of defense if it is ultimately determined that the architect is liable for indemnity under Section 8.1.3. Additionally, the language added at the end of Section 8.1.3 clarifies that the architect's liability under the indemnification provision is limited to the available proceeds of the insurance required by this Agreement. As previously drafted, it could be inferred that the architect's liability was limited to the coverage of its entire insurance program, which may be much greater than the limits prescribed by the agreement.

Finally, for the avoidance of any doubt, the drafters included express language that Article 8 survives termination of the agreement.

> **§ 8.4** The provisions of this Article 8 shall survive the termination of this Agreement.

ARTICLE 9 TERMINATION OR SUSPENSION

Other than a minor grammatical tweak in Section 9.1, the substantive change to Article 9 relates to the architect's entitlement to certain payment upon a termination for convenience.

> **§ 9.1** If the Owner fails to make payments to the Architect in accordance with this Agreement, such failure shall be considered substantial nonperformance and cause for termination or, at the Architect's option, cause for suspension of performance of services under this Agreement. If the Architect elects to suspend services, the Architect shall give seven days' written notice to the Owner before suspending services. In the event of a suspension of services, the Architect shall have no liability to the Owner for delay or damage caused the Owner because of such suspension of services. Before resuming services, the Owner shall pay the Architect ~~shall be paid~~ all sums due prior to suspension and any expenses incurred in the interruption and resumption of the Architect's services. The Architect's fees for the remaining services and the time schedules shall be equitably adjusted.

. . .

§ 9.6 ~~In~~If the ~~event of termination not the fault of~~ Owner terminates this Agreement for its convenience pursuant to Section 9.5, or the Architect, terminates this Agreement pursuant to Section 9.3, the Owner shall compensate the Architect ~~shall be compensated~~ for services performed prior to termination, ~~together with~~ Reimbursable Expenses ~~then due~~incurred, and ~~all Termination Expenses as defined in Section 9.7.~~

~~**§ 9.7** Termination Expenses are in addition to compensation for the Architect's services and include expenses directly~~costs attributable to termination ~~for which~~, including the ~~Architect is not otherwise compensated, plus an amount for~~costs attributable to the Architect's ~~anticipated profit on the value~~termination of ~~the services not performed by the Architect~~consultant agreements.

§ 9.7 In addition to any amounts paid under Section 9.6, if the Owner terminates this Agreement for its convenience pursuant to Section 9.5, or the Architect terminates this Agreement pursuant to Section 9.3, the Owner shall pay to the Architect the following fees:

(Set forth below the amount of any termination or licensing fee, or the method of determining any termination or licensing fee.)

.1 Termination Fee:

.2 Licensing Fee of the Owner intends to continue using the Architect's Instruments of Service:

Accordingly, if the owner terminates the agreement for convenience, or if the architect terminates the agreement for non-payment, the architect is entitled to recover: (1) payment for services rendered before termination; (2) reimbursable expenses incurred; (3) costs associated with termination of the architect's consultant agreements; (4) a termination fee; and (5) a licensing fee if the owner plans to use the architect's Instruments of Service post-termination.[11] While the licensing fee was previously contemplated in Section 11.9 of the previous B133, the termination fee is new. Both construction managers and architects are wise to include a termination fee in a termination for convenience clause so that the owner will give pause before simply terminating the agreement. Some savvy owners may obtain the desired services from the architect and, once the design has progressed to a certain point, may decide to manage the construction administration on its own. In such case, under the prior version of this agreement, all the owner had to pay for were the services and expenses incurred to date. The architect, however, may have priced the agreement based on projected staff costs, projected profit, and other projected costs. While it will be made "whole" for the costs incurred through the date of the termination, there may be a real cost to the architect for lost anticipated profit and overhead. As such, a termination fee can attempt to place the architect in a more equitable financial position if the owner decides to terminate for convenience. And, if appropriately sized, the termination fee can serve as a disincentive for the owner to terminate for convenience (which can be done at any stage in the project).

Finally, Section 9.8 inserts an automatic termination provision, which clarifies the expected duration of the architect's services under the agreement to one year after Substantial Completion:

11. *See* B133™–2019, §§ 9.6 and 9.7.

> **§ 9.8** Except as otherwise expressly provided herein, this Agreement shall terminate one year from the date of Substantial Completion.

Architects routinely stay engaged on a project longer than originally anticipated under their agreement with the owner. And, in some cases, architects are not adequately reimbursed for those extended services. By including this new language, the parties are clearly setting forth expectations for the duration of the agreement. Obviously, if the architect's services are required beyond the year post-Substantial Completion, the parties may execute a change order to extend the duration of the agreement, which will provide the architect an opportunity to obtain appropriate compensation for such extension.

ARTICLE 10 MISCELLANEOUS PROVISIONS

Article 10 compiles miscellaneous provisions, and the 2019 version amended several of those provisions. Section 10.1, the choice of law provision, was amended to make clear that the jurisdiction's choice of law rules are excluded:

> **§ 10.1** This Agreement shall be governed by the law of the place where the Project is located, ~~except that if~~excluding that jurisdiction's choice of law rules. If the parties have selected arbitration as the method of binding dispute resolution, the Federal Arbitration Act shall govern Section 8.3.

In other words, if choice of law rules of the jurisdiction would apply the laws of another jurisdiction, the parties, by contract, agree to overrule that choice of law and, instead, apply the law where the project is located.

> **§ 10.3** The Owner and Architect, respectively, bind themselves, their agents, successors, assigns, and legal representatives to this Agreement. Neither the Owner nor the Architect shall assign this Agreement without the written consent of the other, except that the Owner may assign this Agreement to a lender providing financing for the Project if the lender agrees to assume the Owner's rights and obligations under this Agreement, including any payments due to the Architect by the Owner prior to the assignment.

Section 10.3, the assignment provision, added language to make clear that the owner could assign the architect's agreement to its lender without the architect's consent *provided the lender agrees to make any payments that were due prior to the assignment*.

> **§ 10.7** The Architect shall have the right to include photographic or artistic representations of the design of the Project among the Architect's promotional and professional materials. The Architect shall be given reasonable access to the completed Project to make such representations. However, the Architect's materials shall not include the Owner's confidential or proprietary information if the Owner has previously advised the Architect in writing of the specific information considered by the Owner to be confidential or proprietary. The Owner shall provide professional credit for the Architect in the Owner's promotional materials for the Project. This Section 10.7 shall survive the termination of this Agreement unless the Owner terminates this Agreement for cause pursuant to Section 9.4.

Section 10.7, which permits the architect to use photographs or artistic representations of the project, was modified to specify that such right survives termination of the agreement unless the architect is terminated for cause.

> **§ 10.8** If the Architect or Owner receives information specifically designated ~~by the other party~~ as "confidential" or "business proprietary," the receiving party shall keep such information strictly confidential and shall not disclose it to any other person except ~~to (1) its employees, (2) those who need to know the content of such information in order to perform services or construction solely and exclusively for the Project, or (3) its consultants and contractors whose contracts include similar restrictions on the use of confidential information~~as set forth in Section 10.8.1. This Section 10.8 shall survive the termination of this Agreement.
>
> **§ 10.8.1.** The receiving party may disclose "confidential" or "business proprietary" information after 7 days' notice to the other party, when required by law, arbitrator's order, or court order, including a subpoena of other form of compulsory legal process issued by a court or governmental entity, or to the extent such information is reasonably necessary for the receiving party to defend itself in any dispute. The receiving paty may also disclose such information to its employees, consultants, or contractors in order to perform services or work solely and exclusively for the Project, provided those employees, consultants and contractors are subject to the restrictions on the disclosure and use of such information as set forth in this Section 10.8.

The confidentiality clause in Section 10.8 was expanded in 10.8.1 to permit disclosure of such information after seven days' notice when required by law, court order, or subpoena. Additionally, the receiving party can disclose confidential information after seven days' notice if necessary to defend itself in a dispute. Section 10.8 also states that the confidentiality restriction survives termination of the Agreement.

> **§ 10.9** The invalidity of any provision of the Agreement shall not invalidate the Agreement or its remaining provisions. If it is determined that any provision of the Agreement violates any law, or is otherwise invalid or unenforceable, then that provision shall be revised to the extent necessary to make that provision legal and enforceable. In such case the Agreement shall be construed, to the fullest extent permitted by law, to give effect to the parties' intentions and purposes in executing the Agreement.

Finally, consistent with revisions made to the 2017 suite of AIA forms, a savings clause was added in Section 10.9 to provide that any provisions of the agreement that are invalid or unenforceable will be revised to the extent necessary to allow them to be enforced.

ARTICLE 11 COMPENSATION

Several changes were made to the Compensation article. Specifically, Section 11.1 provides three options for the architect's basis of payment: (1) stipulated sum; (2) percentage basis of the owner's budget for the Cost of the Work; or (3) another basis to be described. For percentage-based compensation, the 2019 changes are quite different:

§ 11.6 When compensation identified in Section 11.1 is ~~based~~ on a percentage basis, progress payments for each phase of Basic Services shall be calculated by multiplying the percentages identified in this Article by the Owner's most recent budget for the Cost of the Work. Compensation paid in previous progress payments shall not be adjusted based on subsequent updates to the Owner's budget for the Cost of the Work.

§ 11.6.1 When compensation is on a percentage basis and any portions of the Project are deleted or otherwise not constructed, compensation for those portions of the Project shall be payable to the extent services are performed on those portions~~, in accordance with the schedule set forth in Section 11.5 based on (1) the Owner-accepted Guaranteed Maximum Price Amendment or Control Estimate, as applicable, or (2) if the Guaranteed Maximum Price proposal or Control Estimate has not been accepted by the Owner, the most recent estimate of the Cost of the Work prepared by the Construction Manager for such portions of the Project.~~. The Architect shall be entitled to compensation in accordance with this Agreement for all services performed whether or not the Construction Phase is commenced.

Section 11.6 provides for compensation based on a percentage of the owner's *current* budget for the cost of the work, which can be subject to change. If a subsequent budget is downwardly adjusted, the architect is not required to reimburse, or otherwise deduct from its current payment application, the amount it was previously paid based on the higher budget. Although this likely makes sense from an accounting perspective, the practical result is that the architect may receive a windfall. Further, if work is deleted, the owner must still pay the architect on a percentage basis as though the value of the work was not deducted from the budget but only if the architect performed services for the deleted work. The architect is neither required to adjust an invoice or reimburse in the case of a reduction in scope, nor allowed to retroactively adjust billings for prior invoices when the budget is increased. These changes are consistent with the 2017 edits to the A201.

Changes were also made to align with Article 4, which now includes references to both "Supplemental" and "Additional Services"; such references were carried through to Article 11 to make sure that the architect's compensation for both types of services are captured.[12] Several revisions were also made to the reimbursable expenses provision:

§ 11.8 Compensation for Reimbursable Expenses

§ 11.8.1 Reimbursable Expenses are in addition to compensation for Basic, Supplemental, and Additional Services and include expenses incurred by the Architect and the Architect's consultants directly related to the Project, as follows:

.1 Transportation and authorized out-of-town travel and subsistence;
.2 Long distance services, dedicated data and communication services, teleconferences, Project ~~Web~~ web sites, and extranets;
.3 ~~Fees paid for securing approval of~~ Permitting and other fees required by authorities having jurisdiction over the Project;
.4 Printing, reproductions, plots, and standard form documents;
.5 Postage, handling, and delivery;

12. *See* B133™–2019, §§11.2, 11.4 and 11.10.2.3.

.6 Expense of overtime work requiring higher than regular rates, if authorized in advance by the Owner;
.7 Renderings, <u>physical</u> models, mock-ups, professional photography, and presentation materials requested by the Owner <u>or required for the Project</u>;
.8 <u>If required by the Owner, and with the Owner's prior written approval, the</u> Architect's consultants' ~~expense~~ <u>expenses</u> of professional liability insurance dedicated exclusively to this Project, or the expense of additional insurance coverage or limits ~~if the Owner requests such insurance~~ in excess of that normally ~~carried~~ <u>maintained</u> by the Architect's consultants;
.9 All taxes levied on professional services and on reimbursable expenses;
.10 Site office expenses; ~~and~~
~~.11~~ <u>**.11**</u> <u>Registration fees and any other fees charged by the Certifying Authority or by other entities as necessary to achieve the Sustainable Objective; and</u>
<u>**.12**</u> Other similar Project-related expenditures.

Section 11.8.1.3 is an interesting change in that the intent of the original provision was to provide permitting fees to be paid to the architect as a reimbursable expense; however, it also implied responsibility for the architect to "secure" the permits, which may have other implications for the architect's liability. And, the prior language could have also been read to exclude reimbursement for fees that were incurred if the architect did not actually receive approvals. The revisions remove these possibilities and make clear that permitting fees are reimbursable expenses.

Section 11.8.1.8 also clears up confusion regarding project-specific professional liability insurance, which is typically not maintained by architects as part of the insurance program and can be expensive to procure. So that there is no confusion as to whether this is required (and therefore, a reimbursable expense), the owner must require project-specific professional liability insurance and agree to reimburse those costs. Similarly, if the owner requires (and approves the reimbursement for) insurance over what the architect ordinarily maintains as part of its insurance program, then such expenses also are reimbursable.[13]

Finally, if a sustainability certification is required by the agreement (e.g., LEED certification), an upfront payment will be made to the architect for registration fees with the certifying authority. (Section 11.10.1.2.) Additional fees charged by the sustainable certifying authority are also reimbursable expenses. (Section 11.8.1.11.)

ARTICLE 12 SPECIAL TERMS AND CONDITIONS

No substantive changes.

ARTICLE 13 SCOPE OF THE AGREEMENT

Section 13.2 specifically includes the Sustainability Exhibit (AIA E234–2019) and BIM and Digital Data Exhibit (AIA E203–2013) as referenced in the Article 1 revisions. The owner and architect should be careful to review the Exhibit and integrate it with how digital data will be transmitted and used on the project or strike the inclusion of this document in the enumeration of Exhibits in Section 13.2.

13. *See* B133™–2019, §11.9.

§ 13.1 This Agreement represents the entire and integrated agreement between the Owner and the Architect and supersedes all prior negotiations, representations or agreements, either written or oral. This Agreement may be amended only by written instrument signed by both the Owner and Architect.

§ 13.2 This Agreement is comprised of the following documents ~~listed~~identified below:

.1 AIA Document B133™–~~2014~~2019, Standard Form Agreement Between Owner and Architect, Construction Manager as Constructor Edition

.2 AIA Document E203™–2013, Building Information Modeling and Digital Data Exhibit, dated as indicated below, if completed, or the following:
(Insert the date of the E203-2013 incorporated into this agreement.)

.3 Exhibits:
(Check the appropriate box for any exhibits incorporated into this Agreement.)

[ ] AIA Document E234™–2019, Sustainable Projects Exhibit, Construction Manager as Constructor Edition dated as indicated below.

(Insert the date of the E234–2019 incorporated into this agreement.)

[ ] Other Exhibits incorporated into this Agreement:

(Clearly identify any other exhibits incorporated into this Agreement, including any exhibits and scopes of services identified as exhibits in Section 4.1.2.)

.4 Other documents:
(List other documents, if any, ~~including additional scopes of service~~ forming part of the Agreement.)

APPENDIX:
AIA® Document Comparative

AIA® Document Comparative

A232™ – 2019 Compared to A232™ – 2009

Additions to A232–2009 are underlined. Deletions from A232–2009 are in ~~strikethrough~~ text.

Title

General Conditions of the Contract for Construction, Construction Manager as Adviser Edition

Cover Page

for the following PROJECT:
(Name, and location or address)

THE CONSTRUCTION MANAGER:
(Name, legal status, and address)

THE OWNER:
(Name, legal status, and address)

THE ARCHITECT:
(Name, legal status, and address)

Table of Articles

1 GENERAL PROVISIONS
2 OWNER
3 CONTRACTOR
4 ARCHITECT AND CONSTRUCTION MANAGER
5 SUBCONTRACTORS
6 CONSTRUCTION BY OWNER OR BY ~~OTHER~~SEPARATE CONTRACTORS
7 CHANGES IN THE WORK
8 TIME
9 PAYMENTS AND COMPLETION
10 PROTECTION OF PERSONS AND PROPERTY
11 INSURANCE AND BONDS
12 UNCOVERING AND CORRECTION OF WORK
13 MISCELLANEOUS PROVISIONS
14 TERMINATION OR SUSPENSION OF THE CONTRACT
15 CLAIMS AND DISPUTES

Article 1 General Provisions

§ 1.1 Basic Definitions
§ 1.1.1 The Contract Documents. The Contract Documents are enumerated in the Agreement between the Owner and Contractor (hereinafter the Agreement~~),~~) and consist of the Agreement, Conditions of the Contract (General, Supplementary and other Conditions), Drawings, Specifications, Addenda issued prior to execution of the Contract, other documents listed in the Agreement, and Modifications issued after execution of the Contract. A Modification is (1) a written amendment to the Contract signed by both parties, (2) a Change Order, (3) a Construction Change Directive, or (4) a written order for a minor change in the Work issued by the Architect. Unless specifically enumerated in the Agreement, the Contract Documents do not include the advertisement or invitation to bid, Instructions to Bidders, sample forms, other information furnished by the Owner in anticipation of receiving bids or

proposals, the Contractor's bid or proposal, or portions of addenda relating to bidding or proposal requirements).

§ 1.1.2 The Contract. The Contract Documents form the Contract for Construction. The Contract represents the entire and integrated agreement between the parties hereto and supersedes prior negotiations, representations, or agreements, either written or oral. The Contract may be amended or modified only by a Modification. The Contract Documents shall not be construed to create a contractual relationship of any kind (1) between the Contractor and the Architect or the Architect's consultants, (2) between the Owner and the Construction Manager or the Construction Manager's consultants, (3) between the Owner and the Architect or the Architect's consultants, (4) between the Contractor and the Construction Manager or the Construction Manager's consultants, (5) between the Owner and a Subcontractor or Sub-subcontractor (6) between the Construction Manager and the Architect, or (7) between any persons or entities other than the Owner and Contractor. The Construction Manager and Architect shall, however, be entitled to performance and enforcement of obligations under the Contract intended to facilitate performance of their duties.

§ 1.1.3 The Work. The term "Work" means the construction and services required by the Contract Documents, whether completed or partially completed, and includes all other labor, materials, equipment, and services provided or to be provided by the Contractor to fulfill the Contractor's obligations. The Work may constitute the whole or a part of the Project.

§ 1.1.4 The Project. The Project is the total construction of which the Work performed under the Contract Documents may be the whole or a part and which may include construction by other Multiple Prime Contractors, and by the Owner's own forces, including persons or entities under separate contracts not administered by the Construction Manager and Separate Contractors.

§ 1.1.5 The Drawings.§ 1.1.5 Contractors. Contractors are persons or entities, other than the Contractor or Separate Contractors, who perform Work under contracts with the Owner that are administered by the Architect and Construction Manager.

> ***Note:** The definition of Separate Contractors in new Section 1.1.6 is derived from language that formerly appeared in Section 6.1.1.*

§ 1.1.6 Separate Contractors. Separate Contractors are persons or entities who perform construction under separate contracts with the Owner not administered by the Architect and Construction Manager.

§ 1.1.7 The Drawings. The Drawings are the graphic and pictorial portions of the Contract Documents showing the design, location and dimensions of the Work, generally including plans, elevations, sections, details, schedules, and diagrams.

§ 1.1.68 The Specifications. The Specifications are that portion of the Contract Documents consisting of the written requirements for materials, equipment, systems, standards and workmanship for the Work, and performance of related services.

§ 1.1.79 Instruments of Service. Instruments of Service are representations, in any medium of expression now known or later developed, of the tangible and intangible creative work performed by the Architect and the Architect's consultants under their respective professional services agreements. Instruments of Service may include, without limitation, studies, surveys, models, sketches, drawings, specifications, and other similar materials.

§ 1.1.810 Initial Decision Maker. The Initial Decision Maker is the person identified in the Agreement to render initial decisions on Claims in accordance with Section 15.2 and certify termination of the Agreement under Section 14.2.2. The Initial Decision Maker shall not show partiality to the Owner or Contractor and shall not be liable for results of interpretations or decisions rendered in good faith.

§ 1.2 Correlation and Intent of the Contract Documents

§ 1.2.1 The intent of the Contract Documents is to include all items necessary for the proper execution and completion of the Work by the Contractor. The Contract Documents are complementary, and what is required by one shall be as binding as if required by all; performance by the Contractor shall be required only to the extent consistent with the Contract Documents and reasonably inferable from them as being necessary to produce the indicated results.

§ 1.2.1.1 The invalidity of any provision of the Contract Documents shall not invalidate the Contract or its remaining provisions. If it is determined that any provision of the Contract Documents violates any law, or is otherwise invalid or unenforceable, then that provision shall be revised to the extent necessary to make that provision legal and enforceable. In such case the Contract Documents shall be construed, to the fullest extent permitted by law, to give effect to the parties' intentions and purposes in executing the Contract.

§ 1.2.2 Organization of the Specifications into divisions, sections and articles, and arrangement of Drawings shall not control the Contractor in dividing the Work among Subcontractors or in establishing the extent of Work to be performed by any trade.

§ 1.2.3 Unless otherwise stated in the Contract Documents, words that have well-known technical or construction industry meanings are used in the Contract Documents in accordance with such recognized meanings.

§ 1.3 Capitalization
Terms capitalized in these General Conditions include those that are (1) specifically defined, (2) the titles of numbered articles, or (3) the titles of other documents published by the American Institute of Architects.

§ 1.4 Interpretation
In the interest of brevity the Contract Documents frequently omit modifying words such as "all" and "any" and articles such as "the" and "an," but the fact that a modifier or an article is absent from one statement and appears in another is not intended to affect the interpretation of either statement.

§ 1.5 Ownership and Use of Drawings, Specifications, and Other Instruments of Service
§ 1.5.1 The Architect and the Architect's consultants shall be deemed the authors and owners of their respective Instruments of Service, including the Drawings and Specifications, and ~~will~~ retain all common law, statutory, and other reserved rights in their Instruments of Service, including copyrights. The Contractor, Subcontractors, sub-subcontractors, and ~~material or equipment~~ suppliers shall not own or claim a copyright in the Instruments of Service. Submittal or distribution to meet official regulatory requirements or for other purposes in connection with ~~this~~the Project is not to be construed as publication in derogation of the ~~Architect,~~Architect's or Architect's consultants' reserved rights.

§ 1.5.2 The Contractor, Subcontractors, Sub-subcontractors, and ~~material or equipment~~ suppliers are authorized to use and reproduce the Instruments of Service provided to them, subject to any protocols established pursuant to Sections 1.7 and 1.8, solely and exclusively for execution of the Work. All copies made under this authorization shall bear the copyright notice, if any, shown on the Instruments of Service. The Contractor, Subcontractors, Sub-subcontractors, and ~~material or equipment~~ suppliers may not use the Instruments of Service on other projects or for additions to ~~this~~the Project outside the scope of the Work without the specific written consent of the Owner, Architect, and the Architect's consultants.

Note: *Section 1.6 formerly appeared at Section 13.3.*

§ 1.6 Notice
§ 1.6.1 Except as otherwise provided in Section 1.6.2, where the Contract Documents require one party to notify or give notice to the other party, such notice shall be provided in writing to the designated representative of the party to whom the notice is addressed and shall be deemed to have been duly served if delivered in person, by mail, by courier, or by electronic transmission if a method for electronic transmission is set forth in the Agreement.

§ 1.6.2 Notice of Claims as provided in Section 15.1.3 shall be provided in writing and shall be deemed to have been duly served only if delivered to the designated representative of the party to whom the notice is addressed by certified or registered mail, or by courier providing proof of delivery.

§ 1.7 Digital Data Use and Transmission ~~of Data in Digital Form~~
~~If the~~The parties ~~intend to transmit~~shall agree upon protocols governing the transmission and use of Instruments of Service or any other information or documentation in digital form~~, they shall endeavor~~. The parties will use AIA Document E203™–2013, Building Information Modeling and Digital Data Exhibit, to establish ~~necessary protocols governing such transmissions, unless otherwise already provided in the Agreement or the Contract Documents~~the protocols for the development, use, transmission, and exchange of digital data.

§ 1.8 Building Information Models Use and Reliance
Any use of, or reliance on, all or a portion of a building information model without agreement to protocols governing the use of, and reliance on, the information contained in the model and without having those protocols set forth in AIA Document E203™–2013, Building Information Modeling and Digital Data Exhibit, and the requisite AIA Document G202™–2013, Project Building Information Modeling Protocol Form, shall be at the using or relying party's sole risk and without liability to the other party and its contractors or consultants, the authors of, or contributors to, the building information model, and each of their agents and employees.

Article 2 Owner

§ 2.1 General
§ 2.1.1 The Owner is the person or entity identified as such in the Agreement and is referred to throughout the Contract Documents as if singular in number. The Owner shall designate in writing a representative who shall have express authority to bind the Owner with respect to all matters requiring the Owner's approval or authorization. Except as otherwise provided in ~~Article~~Section 4.2.1, the Construction Manager and the Architect do not have such authority. The term "Owner" means the Owner or the Owner's authorized representative.

§ 2.1.2 The Owner shall furnish to the Contractor, within fifteen days after receipt of a written request, information necessary and relevant for the Contractor to evaluate, give notice of, or enforce mechanic's lien rights. Such information shall include a correct statement of the record legal title to the property on which the Project is located, usually referred to as the site, and the Owner's interest therein.

§ 2.2 ~~Information and Services Required~~Evidence of the ~~Owner~~Owner's Financial Arrangements
§ 2.2.1 Prior to commencement of the Work, and upon written request by the Contractor ~~may request in writing that~~, the Owner ~~provide~~shall furnish to the Contractor reasonable evidence that the Owner has made financial arrangements to fulfill the Owner's obligations under the Contract. ~~Thereafter, the~~The Contractor ~~may only request~~ shall have no obligation to commence the Work until the Owner provides such evidence. If commencement of the Work is delayed under this Section 2.2.1, the Contract Time shall be extended appropriately.

§ 2.2.2 Following commencement of the Work and upon written request by the Contractor, the Owner shall furnish to the Contractor reasonable evidence that the Owner has made financial arrangements to fulfill the Owner's obligations under the Contract only if (1) the Owner fails to make payments to the Contractor as the Contract Documents require; (2~~) a change in the Work materially changes the Contract Sum; or (3~~) the Contractor identifies in writing a reasonable concern regarding the Owner's ability to make payment when due~~. The Owner shall furnish such evidence as a condition precedent to commencement or continuation of the Work or the portion of the Work affected by a material change. After the Owner furnishes the evidence~~; or (3) a change in the Work materially changes the Contract Sum. If the Owner fails to provide such evidence, as required, within fourteen days of the Contractor's request, the Contractor may immediately stop the Work and, in that event, shall notify the Owner that the Work has stopped. However, if the request is made because a change in the Work materially changes the Contract Sum under (3) above, the Contractor may immediately stop only that portion of the Work affected by the change until reasonable evidence is provided. If the Work is stopped under this Section 2.2.2, the Contract Time shall be extended appropriately and the Contract Sum shall be increased by the amount of the Contractor's reasonable costs of shutdown, delay and start-up, plus interest as provided in the Contract Documents.

§ 2.2.3 After the Owner furnishes evidence of financial arrangements under this Section 2.2, the Owner shall not materially vary such financial arrangements without prior notice to the Contractor.

~~**§ 2.2.2**~~**§ 2.2.4** Where the Owner has designated information furnished under this Section 2.2 as "confidential," the Contractor shall keep the information confidential and shall not disclose it to any other person. However, the Contractor may disclose "confidential" information, after seven (7) days' notice to the Owner, where disclosure is required by law, including a subpoena or other form of compulsory legal process issued by a court or governmental entity, or by court or arbitrator(s) order. The Contractor may also disclose "confidential" information to its employees, consultants, sureties, Subcontractors and their employees, Sub-subcontractors, and others who need to know the content of such information solely and exclusively for the Project and who agree to maintain the confidentiality of such information.

§ 2.3 Information and Services Required of the Owner

§ 2.3.1 Except for permits and fees that are the responsibility of the Contractor under the Contract Documents, including those required under Section 3.7.1, the Owner shall secure and pay for necessary approvals, easements, assessments and charges required for construction, use or occupancy of permanent structures or for permanent changes in existing facilities. Unless otherwise provided under the Contract Documents, the Owner, ~~through~~assisted by the Construction Manager, shall secure and pay for the building permit.

> ***Note:*** *Portions of Section 2.3.2 formerly appeared at Section 4.1.1.*

§ 2.3.2 The Owner shall retain an architect lawfully licensed to practice architecture, or an entity lawfully practicing architecture, in the jurisdiction where the Project is located. That person or entity is identified as the Architect in the Agreement and is referred to throughout the Contract Documents as if singular in number.

§ 2.3.3 The Owner shall retain a construction manager adviser lawfully practicing construction management in the jurisdiction where the Project is located. That person or entity is identified as the Construction Manager in the Agreement and is referred to throughout the Contract Documents as if singular in number.

> ***Note:*** *Portions of Section 2.3.4 formerly appeared at Section 4.1.4.*

~~§ 2.2.3~~§ 2.3.4 If the employment of the Construction Manager or Architect terminates, the Owner shall employ a successor construction manager or architect to whom the Contractor has no reasonable objection and whose status under the Contract Documents shall be that of the Construction Manager or Architect, respectively.

§ 2.3.5 The Owner shall furnish surveys describing physical characteristics, legal limitations and utility locations for the site of the Project, and a legal description of the site. The Contractor shall be entitled to rely on the accuracy of information furnished by the Owner but shall exercise proper precautions relating to the safe performance of the Work.

§ 2.~~2.4~~3.6 The Owner shall furnish information or services required of the Owner by the Contract Documents with reasonable promptness. The Owner shall also furnish any other information or services under the Owner's control and relevant to the Contractor's performance of the Work with reasonable promptness after receiving the Contractor's written request for such information or services.

§ 2.~~2.5~~3.7 Unless otherwise provided in the Contract Documents, the Owner shall furnish to the Contractor one copy of the Contract Documents for purposes of making reproductions pursuant to Section 1.5.2.

§ 2.~~2.6~~3.8 The Owner shall ~~endeavor to~~ forward all communications to the Contractor through the Construction Manager~~ and~~. Other communication shall ~~contemporaneously provide the same communications to the Architect about matters arising out of or relating to the Contract Documents~~be made as set forth in Section 4.2.6.

§ 2.~~3~~4 Owner's Right to Stop the Work

If the Contractor fails to correct Work that is not in accordance with the requirements of the Contract Documents as required by Section 12.2 or repeatedly fails to carry out Work in accordance with the Contract Documents, the Owner may issue a written order to the Contractor to stop the Work, or any portion thereof, until the cause for such order has been eliminated; however, the right of the Owner to stop the Work shall not give rise to a duty on the part of the Owner to exercise this right for the benefit of the Contractor or any other person or entity, except to the extent required by Section 6.1.3.

§ 2.~~4~~5 Owner's Right to Carry Out the Work

If the Contractor defaults or neglects to carry out the Work in accordance with the Contract Documents and fails within a ten-day period after receipt of ~~written~~ notice from the Owner to commence and continue correction of such default or neglect with diligence and promptness, the Owner may, without prejudice to other remedies the Owner may have, correct such ~~deficiencies. In such case an appropriate Change Order shall be issued deducting from payments then or thereafter due the Contractor~~default or neglect. Such action by the Owner and amounts charged to the Contractor are both subject to review by the Construction Manager and prior approval of the Architect, and the Construction Manager or Architect may, pursuant to Section 9.5.1, withhold or nullify a Certificate for Payment in whole or in part, to the extent reasonably necessary to reimburse the Owner for the reasonable cost of correcting such deficiencies, including Owner's expenses and compensation for the Construction Manager's and Architect's and their respective consultants' additional services made necessary by such default, neglect, or failure. ~~Such action by the Owner~~If current and ~~amounts charged to the Contractor are both subject to prior approval of the Architect, after consultation with the Construction Manager. If~~ future payments ~~then or thereafter due the Contractor~~ are not sufficient to cover such amounts, the Contractor shall pay the difference to the Owner. If the Contractor disagrees with the actions of the Owner or the Architect, or the amounts claimed as costs to the Owner, the Contractor may file a Claim pursuant to Article 15.

Article 3 Contractor

§ 3.1 General
§ 3.1.1 The Contractor is the person or entity identified as such in the Agreement and is referred to throughout the Contract Documents as if singular in number. The Contractor shall be lawfully licensed, if required in the jurisdiction where the Project is located. The Contractor shall designate in writing a representative who shall have express authority to bind the Contractor with respect to all matters under this Contract. The term "Contractor" means the Contractor or the Contractor's authorized representative.

§ 3.1.2 The ~~plural term "Multiple Prime Contractors" refers to persons or entities who perform construction under contracts with the Owner that are administered by the Construction Manager. The term does not include the Owner's own forces, including persons or entities under separate contracts not administered by the Construction Manager.~~

~~**§ 3.1.3** The~~ Contractor shall perform the Work in accordance with the Contract Documents.

§ 3.1.~~4~~3 The Contractor shall not be relieved of its obligations to perform the Work in accordance with the Contract Documents either by activities or duties of the Construction Manager or Architect in their administration of the Contract, or by tests, inspections or approvals required or performed by persons or entities other than the Contractor.

§ 3.2 Review of Contract Documents and Field Conditions by Contractor
§ 3.2.1 Execution of the Contract by the Contractor is a representation that the Contractor has visited the site, become generally familiar with local conditions under which the Work is to be performed, and correlated personal observations with requirements of the Contract Documents.

§ 3.2.2 Because the Contract Documents are complementary, the Contractor shall, before starting each portion of the Work, carefully study and compare the various Contract Documents relative to that portion of the Work, as well as the information furnished by the Owner pursuant to Section 2.~~2.~~3.5, shall take field measurements of any existing conditions related to that portion of the Work, and shall observe any conditions at the site affecting it. These obligations are for the purpose of facilitating coordination and construction by the Contractor and are not for the purpose of discovering errors, omissions, or inconsistencies in the Contract Documents; however, the Contractor shall promptly report to the Construction Manager and Architect any errors, inconsistencies or omissions discovered by or made known to the Contractor as a request for information submitted to the Construction Manager in such form as the Construction Manager and Architect may require. It is recognized that the Contractor's review is made in the Contractor's capacity as a contractor and not as a licensed design professional, unless otherwise specifically provided in the Contract Documents.

§ 3.2.3 The Contractor is not required to ascertain that the Contract Documents are in accordance with applicable laws, statutes, ordinances, codes, rules and regulations, or lawful orders of public authorities, but the Contractor shall promptly report to the Construction Manager and Architect any nonconformity discovered by or made known to the Contractor as a request for information submitted to Construction Manager in such form as the Construction Manager and Architect may require.

§ 3.2.4 If the Contractor believes that additional cost or time is involved because of clarifications or instructions the Architect issues in response to the Contractor's notices or requests for information pursuant to Sections 3.2.2 or 3.2.3, the Contractor shall ~~make~~submit Claims as provided in Article 15. If the Contractor fails to perform the obligations of Sections 3.2.2 or 3.2.3, the Contractor shall pay such costs and damages to the Owner, subject to section 15.1.7, as would have been avoided if the Contractor had performed such obligations. If the Contractor performs those obligations, the Contractor shall not be liable to the Owner or Architect for damages resulting from errors, inconsistencies or omissions in the Contract Documents, for differences between field measurements or conditions and the Contract Documents, or for nonconformities of the Contract Documents to applicable laws, statutes, ordinances, codes, rules and regulations, and lawful orders of public authorities.

§ 3.3 Supervision and Construction Procedures
§ 3.3.1 The Contractor shall supervise and direct the Work, using the Contractor's best skill and attention. The Contractor shall be solely responsible for, and have control over, construction means, methods, techniques, sequences, and procedures, and for coordinating all portions of the Work under the Contract, unless the Contract Documents give other specific instruction concerning these matters. If the Contract Documents give specific instructions concerning construction means, methods, techniques, sequences, or procedures, the Contractor shall evaluate the jobsite safety thereof and, except as stated below, shall be fully and solely responsible for the jobsite safety of such means, methods, techniques, sequences, or procedures. If the Contractor determines that such means, methods, techniques, sequences or procedures may not be safe, the Contractor shall give timely written notice to the Owner, the Construction Manager, and the Architect, and shall not proceed with that portion of the Work without further written instructions from the Architect, through the Construction Manager. If the Contractor is then instructed to proceed with the requiredpropose alternative means, methods, techniques, sequences, or procedures without acceptance of changes . The Architect shall evaluate the proposed by the Contractor, the Owner shall bealternative solely responsible for any lossconformance with the design intent for the completed construction. The Construction Manager shall review the proposed alternative for sequencing, constructability, and coordination impacts on the other Contractors. Unless the Architect or damage arising solely from those Owner-requiredthe Construction Manager objects to the Contractor's proposed alternative, the Contractor shall perform the Work using its alternative means, methods, techniques, sequences, or procedures.

§ 3.3.2 The Contractor shall be responsible to the Owner for acts and omissions of the Contractor's employees, Subcontractors and their agents and employees, and other persons or entities performing portions of the Work for, or on behalf of, the Contractor or any of its Subcontractors.

§ 3.3.3 The Contractor shall be responsible for inspection of portions of the Project already performed to determine that such portions are in proper condition to receive subsequent Work.

§ 3.4 Labor and Materials
§ 3.4.1 Unless otherwise provided in the Contract Documents, the Contractor shall provide and pay for labor, materials, equipment, tools, construction equipment and machinery, water, heat, utilities, transportation, and other facilities and services necessary for proper execution and completion of the Work, whether temporary or permanent and whether or not incorporated or to be incorporated in the Work.

§ 3.4.2 Except in the case of minor changes in the Work authorizedapproved by the Architect in accordance with Sections Section 3.12.8 or ordered by the Architect in accordance with Section 7.4, the Contractor may make substitutions only with the consent of the Owner, after evaluation by the Architect, in consultation with the Construction Manager, and in accordance with a Change Order or Construction Change Directive.

§ 3.4.3 The Contractor shall enforce strict discipline and good order among the Contractor's employees and other persons carrying out the Work. The Contractor shall not permit employment of unfit persons or persons not properly skilled in tasks assigned to them.

§ 3.5 Warranty
§ 3.5.1 The Contractor warrants to the Owner, Construction Manager, and Architect that materials and equipment furnished under the Contract will be of good quality and new unless the Contract Documents require or permit otherwise. The Contractor further warrants that the Work will conform withto the requirements of the Contract Documents and will be free from defects, except for those inherent in the quality of the Work the Contract Documents require or permit. Work, materials, or equipment not conforming to these requirements may be considered defective. The Contractor's warranty excludes remedy for damage or defect caused by abuse, alterations to the Work not executed by the Contractor, improper or insufficient maintenance, improper operation, or normal wear and tear and normal usage. If required by the Construction Manager or Architect, the Contractor shall furnish satisfactory evidence as to the kind and quality of materials and equipment.

§ 3.5.2 All material, equipment, or other special warranties required by the Contract Documents shall be issued in the name of the Owner, or shall be transferable to the Owner, and shall commence in accordance with Section 9.8.4.

§ 3.6 Taxes
The Contractor shall pay sales, consumer, use and similar taxes for the Work or portions thereof provided by the Contractor that are legally enacted when bids are received or negotiations concluded, whether or not yet effective or

merely scheduled to go into effect.

§ 3.7 Permits, Fees, Notices, and Compliance with Laws

§ 3.7.1 Unless otherwise provided in the Contract Documents, the Owner, ~~through~~assisted by the Construction Manager, shall secure and pay for the building permit. The Contractor shall secure and pay for other permits, fees, licenses, and inspections by government agencies necessary for proper execution and completion of the Work that are customarily secured after execution of the Contract and legally required at the time bids are received or negotiations concluded.

§ 3.7.2 The Contractor shall comply with and give notices required by applicable laws, statutes, ordinances, codes, rules and regulations, and lawful orders of public authorities applicable to performance of the Work.

§ 3.7.3 If the Contractor performs Work knowing it to be contrary to applicable laws, statutes, ordinances, codes, rules and regulations, or lawful orders of public authorities, the Contractor shall assume appropriate responsibility for such Work and shall bear the costs attributable to correction.

§ 3.7.4 Concealed or Unknown Conditions. If the Contractor encounters conditions at the site that are (1) subsurface or otherwise concealed physical conditions that differ materially from those indicated in the Contract Documents or (2)~~-~~ unknown physical conditions of an unusual nature that differ materially from those ordinarily found to exist and generally recognized as inherent in construction activities of the character provided for in the Contract Documents, the Contractor shall promptly provide notice to the Owner, Construction Manager, and the Architect before conditions are disturbed and in no event later than ~~21~~14 days after first observance of the conditions. The Architect and Construction Manager will promptly investigate such conditions and, if the Architect, in consultation with the Construction Manager, determines that they differ materially and cause an increase or decrease in the Contractor's cost of, or time required for, performance of any part of the Work, will recommend that an equitable adjustment be made in the Contract Sum or Contract Time, or both. If the Architect, in consultation with the Construction Manager, determines that the conditions at the site are not materially different from those indicated in the Contract Documents and that no change in the terms of the Contract is justified, the Architect shall promptly notify the Owner, Construction Manager, and Contractor~~ in writing~~, stating the reasons. If the Owner or Contractor disputes the Architect's determination or recommendation, either party may ~~proceed~~submit a Claim as provided in Article 15.

§ 3.7.5 If, in the course of the Work, the Contractor encounters human remains or recognizes the existence of burial markers, archaeological sites or wetlands not indicated in the Contract Documents, the Contractor shall immediately suspend any operations that would affect them and shall notify the Owner, Construction Manager, and Architect. Upon receipt of such notice, the Owner shall promptly take any action necessary to obtain governmental authorization required to resume the operations. The Contractor shall continue to suspend such operations until otherwise instructed by the Owner but shall continue with all other operations that do not affect those remains or features. Requests for adjustments in the Contract Sum and Contract Time arising from the existence of such remains or features may be made as provided in Article 15.

§ 3.8 Allowances

§ 3.8.1 The Contractor shall include in the Contract Sum all allowances stated in the Contract Documents. Items covered by allowances shall be supplied for such amounts and by such persons or entities as the Owner may direct, but the Contractor shall not be required to employ persons or entities to whom the Contractor has reasonable objection.

§ 3.8.2 Unless otherwise provided in the Contract Documents:

- **.1** ~~Allowances~~allowances shall cover the cost to the Contractor of materials and equipment delivered at the site and all required taxes, less applicable trade discounts;
- **.2** Contractor's costs for unloading and handling at the site, labor, installation costs, overhead, profit, and other expenses contemplated for stated allowance amounts shall be included in the Contract Sum but not in the allowances; and
- **.3** ~~Whenever~~whenever costs are more than or less than allowances, the Contract Sum shall be adjusted accordingly by Change Order. The amount of the Change Order shall reflect (1) the difference between actual costs and the allowances under Section 3.8.2.1 and (2) changes in Contractor's costs under Section 3.8.2.2.

§ 3.8.3 Materials and equipment under an allowance shall be selected by the Owner with reasonable promptness.

§ 3.9 Superintendent
§ 3.9.1 The Contractor shall employ a competent superintendent and necessary assistants who shall be in attendance at the Project site during performance of the Work. The superintendent shall represent the Contractor, and communications given to the superintendent shall be as binding as if given to the Contractor.

§ 3.9.2 The Contractor, as soon as practicable after award of the Contract, shall ~~furnish in writing to~~notify the Owner and Architect, through the Construction Manager, of the name and qualifications of a proposed superintendent. ~~The~~ Within 14 days of receipt of the information, the Construction Manager may ~~reply within 14 days to~~notify the Contractor~~ in writing~~, stating ~~(1)~~ whether the Owner, the Construction Manager, or the Architect (1) has reasonable objection to the proposed superintendent or (2) ~~that any of them~~ require additional time ~~to~~for review. Failure of the Construction Manager to ~~reply~~ provide notice within the 14-‑day period shall constitute notice of no reasonable objection.

§ 3.9.3 The Contractor shall not employ a proposed superintendent to whom the Owner, Construction Manager, or Architect has made reasonable and timely objection. The Contractor shall not change the superintendent without the Owner's consent, which shall not unreasonably be withheld or delayed.

§ 3.10 Contractor's Construction and Submittal Schedules
§ 3.10.1 The Contractor, promptly after being awarded the Contract, shall ~~prepare and~~ submit for the Owner's and Architect's information, and the Construction Manager's ~~approval~~use in developing the Project schedule, a Contractor's construction schedule for the Work. The schedule shall contain detail appropriate for the Project, including (1) the date of commencement of the Work, interim schedule milestone dates, and the date of Substantial Completion; (2) an apportionment of the Work by construction activity; and (3) the time required for completion of each portion of the Work. The schedule shall provide for the orderly progression of the Work to completion and shall not exceed time limits current under the Contract Documents~~,~~. The schedule shall be revised at appropriate intervals as required by the conditions of the Work and Project~~, shall be related to the entire Project schedule to the extent required by the Contract Documents, and shall provide for expeditious and practicable execution of the Work~~. The Contractor shall cooperate with the Construction Manager in scheduling and performing the Contractor's Work to avoid conflict with, and as to cause no delay in, the work or activities of other ~~Multiple Prime~~ Contractors, or the construction or operations of the Owner's own forces~~.~~ or Separate Contractors.

§ 3.10.2 The Contractor~~ shall prepare a submittal schedule~~, promptly after being awarded the Contract and thereafter ~~update it~~ as necessary to maintain a current submittal schedule, ~~and~~ shall submit ~~the~~a submittal schedule~~(s)~~ for the Construction Manager's and Architect's approval. The Architect and Construction Manager's approval shall not be unreasonably~~ be~~ delayed or withheld. The submittal schedule shall (1) be coordinated with the Contractor's construction schedule, and (2) allow the Construction Manager and Architect reasonable time to review submittals. If the Contractor fails to submit a submittal schedule, or fails to provide submittals in accordance with the approved submittal schedule, the Contractor shall not be entitled to any increase in Contract Sum or extension of Contract Time based on the time required for review of submittals.

§ 3.10.3 The Contractor shall participate with -other Contractors, the Construction Manager, and the Owner in reviewing and coordinating all- schedules for incorporation into the Project schedule that is prepared by the Construction Manager. The Contractor shall make revisions to the construction schedule and submittal schedule as deemed necessary by the Construction Manager to conform to the Project schedule.

§ 3.10.4 The Contractor shall perform the Work in general accordance with the most recent schedules submitted to the Owner, Construction Manager, and Architect, and incorporated into the approved Project schedule.

§ 3.11 Documents and Samples at the Site
The Contractor shall ~~maintain~~make available, at the Project site~~ for~~, the ~~Owner one copy of the Drawings, Specifications, Addenda,~~Contract Documents, including Change Orders, Construction Change Directives, and other Modifications, in good order and marked currently to indicate field changes and selections made during construction, and ~~one copy of~~the approved Shop Drawings, Product Data, Samples, and similar required submittals. These ~~documents~~ shall be in electronic form or paper copy, available to the Construction Manager, Architect, and Owner, and delivered to the Construction Manager for submittal to the Owner upon completion of the Work as a record of the Work as constructed.

§ 3.12 Shop Drawings, Product Data, and Samples
§ 3.12.1 Shop Drawings are drawings, diagrams, schedules, and other data specially prepared for the Work by the

Contractor or a Subcontractor, Sub-subcontractor, manufacturer, supplier, or distributor to illustrate some portion of the Work.

§ 3.12.2 Product Data are illustrations, standard schedules, performance charts, instructions, brochures, diagrams, and other information furnished by the Contractor to illustrate materials or equipment for some portion of the Work.

§ 3.12.3 Samples are physical examples that illustrate materials, equipment, or workmanship, and establish standards by which the Work will be judged.

§ 3.12.4 Shop Drawings, Product Data, Samples, and similar submittals are not Contract Documents. Their purpose is to demonstrate ~~the way by which~~how the Contractor proposes to conform to the information given and the design concept expressed in the Contract Documents for those portions of the Work for which the Contract Documents require submittals. Review by the Architect and Construction Manager is subject to the limitations of Sections 4.2.~~9~~10 through ~~-~~4.2.~~11~~12. Informational submittals upon which the Construction Manager and Architect are not expected to take responsive action may be so identified in the Contract Documents. Submittals that are not required by the Contract Documents may be returned by the Construction Manager or Architect without action.

§ 3.12.5 The Contractor shall review for compliance with the Contract Documents, approve, and submit to the Construction Manager, Shop Drawings, Product Data, Samples, and similar submittals required by the Contract Documents, in accordance with the Project submittal schedule approved by the Construction Manager and Architect~~,~~ or, in the absence of an approved Project submittal schedule, with reasonable promptness and in such sequence as to cause no delay in the Work or in the activities of other ~~Multiple Prime~~ Contractors, Separate Contractors, or the Owner's own forces. The Contractor shall cooperate with the Construction Manager in the coordination of the Contractor's Shop Drawings, Product Data, Samples, and similar submittals with related documents submitted by other ~~Multiple Prime~~ Contractors.

§ 3.12.6 By submitting Shop Drawings, Product Data, Samples, and similar submittals, the Contractor represents to the Owner, Construction Manager, and Architect, that the Contractor has (1) reviewed and approved them, (2) determined and verified materials, field measurements and field construction criteria related thereto, or will do so, and (3) checked and coordinated the information contained within such submittals with the requirements of the Work and of the Contract Documents.

§ 3.12.7 The Contractor shall perform no portion of the Work for which the Contract Documents require submittal and review of Shop Drawings, Product Data, Samples, or similar submittals, until the respective submittal has been reviewed and approved by the Architect.

§ 3.12.8 The Work shall be in accordance with approved submittals except that the Contractor shall not be relieved of responsibility for deviations from the requirements of the Contract Documents by the Architect's approval of Shop Drawings, Product Data, Samples, or similar submittals, unless the Contractor has specifically ~~informed~~notified the Construction Manager and Architect ~~in writing~~ of such deviation at the time of submittal and (1) the Architect has given written approval to the specific deviation as a minor change in the Work, or (2) a Change Order or Construction Change Directive has been issued authorizing the deviation. The Contractor shall not be relieved of responsibility for errors or omissions in Shop Drawings, Product Data, Samples, or similar submittals, by the Architect's approval thereof.

§ 3.12.9 The Contractor shall direct specific attention, in writing or on resubmitted Shop Drawings, Product Data, Samples, or similar submittals, to revisions other than those requested by the Construction Manager and Architect on previous submittals. In the absence of such ~~written~~ notice, the Architect's approval of a resubmission shall not apply to such revisions.

§ 3.12.10 The Contractor shall not be required to provide professional services that constitute the practice of architecture or engineering unless such services are specifically required by the Contract Documents for a portion of the Work or unless the Contractor needs to provide such services in order to carry out the Contractor's responsibilities for construction means, methods, techniques, sequences, and procedures. The Contractor shall not be required to provide professional services in violation of applicable law.

§ 3.12.10.1 If professional design services or certifications by a design professional related to systems, materials, or equipment are specifically required of the Contractor by the Contract Documents, the Owner and the Architect will specify all performance and design criteria that such services must satisfy. The Contractor shall be entitled to rely upon the adequacy and accuracy of the performance and design criteria provided in the Contract Documents. The Contractor shall cause such services or certifications to be provided by a properlyan appropriately licensed design professional, whose signature and seal shall appear on all drawings, calculations, specifications, certifications, Shop Drawings, and other submittals prepared by such professional. Shop Drawings, and other submittals related to the Work, designed or certified by such professional, if prepared by others, shall bear such professional's written approval when submitted to the Architect. The Owner, the Architect, and the ArchitectConstruction Manager shall be entitled to rely upon the adequacy, and accuracy and completeness of the services, certifications, and approvals performed or provided by such design professionals, provided the Owner and Architect have specified to the Contractor allthe performance and design criteria that such services must satisfy. Pursuant to this Section 3.12.10, the Architect will review, and approve or take other appropriate action on submittals only for the limited purpose of checking for conformance with information given and the design concept expressed in the Contract Documents. The ContractorConstruction Manager shall not be responsiblereview submittals for the adequacy of the performancesequencing, constructability, and design criteria specified in the Contract Documentscoordination impacts on other Contractors.

§ 3.12.10.2 If the Contract Documents require the Contractor's design professional to certify that the Work has been performed in accordance with the design criteria, the Contractor shall furnish such certifications to the Construction Manager and Architect at the time and in the form specified by the Architect.

§ 3.13 Use of Site
§ 3.13.1 The Contractor shall confine operations at the site to areas permitted by applicable laws, statutes, ordinances, codes, rules and regulations, and lawful orders of public authorities, and the Contract Documents and shall not unreasonably encumber the site with materials or equipment.

§ 3.13.2 The Contractor shall coordinate the Contractor's operations with, and secure the approval of, the Construction Manager before using any portion of the site.

§ 3.14 Cutting and Patching
§ 3.14.1 The Contractor shall be responsible for cutting, fitting, or patching required to complete the Work or to make its parts fit together properly. All areas requiring cutting, fitting and, or patching shall be restored to the condition existing prior to the cutting, fitting and, or patching, unless otherwise required by the Contract Documents.

§ 3.14.2 The Contractor shall not damage or endanger a portion of the Work or fully or partially completed construction of the Owner's own forcesOwner, Separate Contractors, or of other Multiple Prime Contractors by cutting, patching, or otherwise altering such construction, or by excavation. The Contractor shall not cut or otherwise alter such construction by the Owner's own forcesOwner, Separate Contractors, or by other Multiple Prime Contractors except with written consent of the Construction Manager, Owner, and such other Multiple Prime Contractors; such consent or Separate Contractors. Consent shall not be unreasonably withheld. The Contractor shall not unreasonably withhold, from the Separate Contractors, other Multiple Prime Contractors, or the Owner the Contractor's, its consent to cutting or otherwise altering the Work.

§ 3.15 Cleaning Up
§ 3.15.1 The Contractor shall keep the premises and surrounding area free from accumulation of waste materials orand rubbish caused by operations under the Contract. At completion of the Work, the Contractor shall remove waste materials, rubbish, the Contractor's tools, construction equipment, machinery, and surplus materials from and about the Project.

§ 3.15.2 If the Contractor fails to clean up as provided in the Contract Documents, the Owner, or Construction Manager with the Owner's approval, may do so and the Owner shall be entitled to reimbursement from the Contractor.

§ 3.16 Access to Work
The Contractor shall provide the Owner, Construction Manager, and Architect with access to the Work in preparation and progress wherever located.

§ 3.17 Royalties, Patents and Copyrights
The Contractor shall pay all royalties and license fees. The Contractor shall defend suits or claims for infringement of copyrights and patent rights and shall hold the Owner, Construction Manager, and Architect harmless from loss on account thereof, but shall not be responsible for such defense or loss when a particular design, process, or product

of a particular manufacturer or manufacturers is required by the Contract Documents, or where the copyright violations are contained in Drawings, Specifications, or other documents prepared by the Owner, Architect, or Construction Manager. However, if ~~the Contractor has reason to believe that the required design, process or product is~~ an infringement of a copyright or ~~a~~ patent is discovered by, or made known to, the Contractor, the Contractor shall be responsible for ~~such~~the loss unless ~~such~~the information is promptly furnished to the Architect through the Construction Manager.

§ 3.18 Indemnification
§ 3.18.1 To the fullest extent permitted by law, the Contractor shall indemnify and hold harmless the Owner, Construction Manager, Architect, Construction Manager's and Architect's consultants, and agents and employees of any of them from and against claims, damages, losses, and expenses, including but not limited to attorneys' fees, arising out of or resulting from performance of the Work, provided that such claim, damage, loss, or expense is attributable to bodily injury, sickness, disease or death, or to injury to or destruction of tangible property (other than the Work itself)), but only to the extent caused by the negligent acts or omissions of the Contractor, a Subcontractor, anyone directly or indirectly employed by them, or anyone for whose acts they may be liable, regardless of whether or not such claim, damage, loss, or expense is caused in part by a party indemnified hereunder. Such obligation shall not be construed to negate, abridge, or reduce other rights or obligations of indemnity that would otherwise exist as to a party or person described in this Section 3.18.

§ 3.18.2 In claims against any person or entity indemnified under this Section 3.18 by an employee of the Contractor, a Subcontractor, anyone directly or indirectly employed by them, or anyone for whose acts they may be liable, the indemnification obligation under Section 3.18.1 shall not be limited by a limitation on amount or type of damages, compensation, or benefits payable by or for the Contractor or a Subcontractor under workers' compensation acts, disability benefit acts, or other employee benefit acts.

Article 4 Architect and Construction Manager

§ 4.1 General
~~**§ 4.1.1** The Owner shall retain an architect lawfully licensed to practice architecture or an entity lawfully practicing architecture in the jurisdiction where the Project is located. That person or entity is identified as the Architect in the Agreement and is referred to throughout the Contract Documents as if singular in number.~~

~~**§ 4.1.2** The Owner shall retain a construction manager lawfully licensed to practice construction management or an entity lawfully practicing construction management in the jurisdiction where the Project is located. That person or entity is identified as the Construction Manager in the Agreement and is referred to throughout the Contract Documents as if singular in number.~~

§ 4.1.1 The Architect is the person or entity retained by the Owner pursuant to Section 2.3.2 and identified as such in the Agreement.

§ 4.1.2 The Construction Manager is the person or entity retained by the Owner pursuant to Section 2.3.3 and identified as such in the Agreement.

§ 4.1.3 Duties, responsibilities, and limitations of authority of the Construction Manager and Architect as set forth in the Contract Documents shall not be restricted, modified, or extended without written consent of the Owner, Construction Manager, Architect, and Contractor. Consent shall not be unreasonably withheld.

~~**§ 4.1.4** If the employment of the Construction Manager or Architect is terminated, the Owner shall employ a successor construction manager or architect as to whom the Contractor has no reasonable objection and whose status under the Contract Documents shall be that of the Construction Manager or Architect, respectively.~~

§ 4.2 Administration of the Contract
§ 4.2.1 The Construction Manager and Architect will provide administration of the Contract as described in the Contract Documents and will be the Owner's representatives during construction until the date the Architect issues the final Certificate for Payment. The Construction Manager and Architect will have authority to act on behalf of the Owner only to the extent provided in the Contract Documents.

§ 4.2.2 The Architect will visit the site at intervals appropriate to the stage of construction, or as otherwise agreed with the Owner, to become generally familiar with the progress and quality of the portion of the Work completed, and to determine in general if the Work observed is being performed in a manner indicating that the Work, when fully completed, will be in accordance with the Contract Documents. However, the Architect will not be required to make exhaustive or continuous on-site inspections to check the quality or quantity of the Work. On the basis of the site visits, the Architect will keep the Owner and the Construction Manager reasonably informed about the progress and quality of the portion of the Work completed, and promptly report to the Owner and Construction Manager ~~(1)~~ known deviations from the Contract Documents and ~~from the most recent Project schedule prepared by the Construction Manager, and (2)~~ defects and deficiencies observed in the Work.

§ 4.2.3 The Construction Manager shall provide~~ a staffing plan to include~~ one or more representatives who shall be in attendance at the Project site whenever the Work is being performed. The Construction Manager will determine in general if the Work observed is being performed in accordance with the Contract Documents, will keep the Owner and Architect reasonably informed of the progress of the Work, and will promptly report to the Owner and Architect ~~(1)~~ known deviations from the Contract Documents and the most recent Project schedule, and~~ (2)~~ defects and deficiencies observed in the Work.

§ 4.2.4 The Construction Manager will schedule and coordinate the activities of the Contractor and other ~~Multiple Prime~~ Contractors in accordance with the latest approved Project schedule.

§ 4.2.5 The Construction Manager, except to the extent required by Section 4.2.4, and Architect will not have control over, ~~or~~ charge of, or responsibility for, the construction means, methods, techniques, sequences or procedures, or for the safety precautions and programs in connection with the Work, since these are solely the Contractor's rights and responsibilities under the Contract Documents, ~~except as provided in Section 3.3.1,~~ and neither will be responsible for the Contractor's failure to perform the Work in accordance with the requirements of the Contract Documents. Neither the Construction Manager nor the Architect will have control over or charge of, or be responsible for acts or omissions of, the Contractor, Subcontractors, or their agents or employees, or of any other persons or entities performing portions of the Work.

§ 4.2.6 Communications~~ Facilitating Contract Administration~~. ~~Except as otherwise provided in the Contract Documents or when direct communications have been specially authorized, the~~. The Owner ~~and Contractor~~ shall ~~endeavor to~~ communicate with ~~each other through~~ the Contractor and the Construction ~~Manager, and shall contemporaneously provide the same communications to the Architect~~ Manager's consultants through the Construction Manager about matters arising out of or relating to the Contract Documents. The Owner and Construction Manager shall include the Architect in all communications that relate to or affect the Architect's services or professional responsibilities. The Owner shall promptly notify the Architect of the substance of any direct communications between the Owner and the Construction Manager otherwise relating to the Project. Communications by and with the Architect's consultants shall be through the Architect. Communications by and with Subcontractors and ~~material~~ suppliers shall be through the Contractor. Communications by and with other ~~Multiple Prime~~ Contractors shall be through the Construction Manager~~ and shall be contemporaneously provided to the Architect if those communications are about matters arising out of or related to the Contract Documents.~~. Communications by and with the Owner's own forces and Separate Contractors shall be through the Owner. The Contract Documents may specify other communication protocols.

§ 4.2.7 The Construction Manager and Architect will review and certify all Applications for Payment by the Contractor, in accordance with the provisions of Article 9.

§ 4.2.8 The Architect and Construction Manager have authority to reject Work that does not conform to the Contract Documents, and will notify each other about the rejection.~~ The Construction Manager shall determine in general whether the Work of the Contractor is being performed in accordance with the requirements of the Contract Documents and notify the Owner, Contractor and Architect of defects and deficiencies in the Work.~~ Whenever the Construction Manager considers it necessary or advisable, the Construction Manager will have authority to require ~~additional~~ inspection or testing of the Work in accordance with Sections 13.~~5~~4.2 and 13.~~5~~4.3, upon written authorization of the Owner, whether or not ~~such~~the Work is fabricated, installed or completed. The foregoing authority of the Construction Manager will be subject to the provisions of Sections 4.2.18 through 4.2.20 inclusive, with respect to interpretations and decisions of the Architect. However, neither the Architect's nor the Construction Manager's authority to act under this Section 4.2.8 nor a decision made by either of them in good faith either to exercise or not to exercise such authority shall give rise to a duty or responsibility of the Architect or the Construction Manager to the Contractor, Subcontractors, ~~material and equipment~~ suppliers, their agents or employees, or other persons performing any of the Work.

§ ~~4.2.9~~§ 4.2.9 Utilizing the submittal schedule provided by the Contractor, the Construction Manager shall prepare, and revise as necessary, a Project submittal schedule incorporating information from other Contractors, the Owner, Owner's consultants, Owner's Separate Contractors and vendors, governmental agencies, and participants in the Project under the management of the Construction Manager. The Project submittal schedule and any revisions shall be submitted to the Architect for approval.

§ 4.2.10 The Construction Manager will receive and promptly review for conformance with the submittal requirements of the Contract Documents, all submittals from the Contractor such as Shop Drawings, Product Data, and Samples. Where there are ~~Multiple Prime~~other Contractors, the Construction Manager will also check and coordinate the information contained within each submittal received from the Contractor and other ~~Multiple Prime~~ Contractors, and transmit to the Architect those recommended for approval. By submitting Shop Drawings, Product Data, Samples, and similar submittals, the Construction Manager represents to the Owner and Architect that the Construction Manager has reviewed and recommended them for approval. The Construction Manager's actions will be taken in accordance with the Project submittal schedule approved by the Architect or, in the absence of an approved Project submittal schedule, with reasonable promptness while allowing sufficient time to permit adequate review by the Architect.

§ 4.2.~~10~~11 The Architect will review and approve, or take other appropriate action upon, the Contractor's submittals such as Shop Drawings, Product Data, and Samples, but only for the limited purpose of checking for conformance with information given and the design concept expressed in the Contract Documents. The Architect's action will be taken in accordance with the submittal schedule approved by the Architect or, in the absence of an approved submittal schedule, with reasonable promptness while allowing sufficient time in the Architect's professional judgment to permit adequate review. Upon the Architect's completed review, the Architect shall transmit its submittal review to the Construction Manager.

§ 4.2.~~11~~12 Review of the Contractor's submittals by the Construction Manager and Architect is not conducted for the purpose of determining the accuracy and completeness of other details such as dimensions and quantities, or for substantiating instructions for installation or performance of equipment or systems, all of which remain the responsibility of the Contractor as required by the Contract Documents. The Construction Manager and Architect's review of the Contractor's submittals shall not relieve the Contractor of the obligations under Sections 3.3, 3.5, and 3.12. The Construction Manager and Architect's review shall not constitute approval of safety precautions or~~,~~ ~~unless otherwise specifically stated by the Construction Manager and Architect,~~ of any construction means, methods, techniques, sequences, or procedures. The Architect's approval of a specific item shall not indicate approval of an assembly of which the item is a component.

§ 4.2.~~12~~13 The Construction Manager will prepare Change Orders and Construction Change Directives.

§ 4.2.~~13~~14 The Construction Manager and the Architect will take appropriate action on Change Orders or Construction Change Directives in accordance with Article 7~~.~~, and the Architect will have authority to order minor changes in the Work as provided in Section 7.4. The Architect, in consultation with the Construction Manager, will investigate and make determinations and recommendations regarding concealed and unknown conditions as provided in Section 3.7.4.

§ 4.2.~~14~~15 Utilizing the documents provided by the Contractor, the Construction Manager will maintain at the site for the Owner one copy of all Contract Documents, approved Shop Drawings, Product Data, Samples, and similar required submittals, in good order and marked currently to record all changes and selections made during construction. These will be available to the Architect and the Contractor, and will be delivered to the Owner upon completion of the Project.

§ 4.2.~~15~~16 The Construction Manager will assist the Architect in conducting inspections to determine the date or dates of Substantial Completion and the date of final completion; issue Certificates of Substantial Completion in conjunction with the Architect pursuant to Section 9.8; and receive and forward to the Owner written warranties and related documents required by the Contract and assembled by the Contractor pursuant to Section 9.10. The Construction Manager will forward to the Architect a final Application and Certificate for Payment or final Project Application and Project Certificate for Payment upon the Contractor's compliance with the requirements of the Contract Documents.

§ 4.2.~~16~~17 If the Owner and Architect agree, the Architect will provide one or more ~~project~~Project representatives to assist in carrying out the Architect's responsibilities at the site. TheThe Owner shall notify the Construction Manager of any change in the duties, responsibilities and limitations of authority of such projectthe Project representatives shall be as set forth in an exhibit to be incorporated in the Contract Documents.

§ 4.2.1718 The Architect will interpret and decide matters concerning performance under, and requirements of, the Contract Documents on written request of the Construction Manager, Owner, or Contractor through the Construction Manager. The Architect's response to such requests will be made in writing within any time limits agreed upon or otherwise with reasonable promptness.

§ 4.2.1819 Interpretations and decisions of the Architect will be consistent with the intent of, and reasonably inferable from, the Contract Documents and will be in writing or in the form of drawings. When making such interpretations and decisions, the Architect will endeavor to secure faithful performance by both Owner and Contractor, will not show partiality to either, and will not be liable for results of interpretations or decisions so rendered in good faith.

§ 4.2.1920 The Architect's decisions on matters relating to aesthetic effect will be final if consistent with the intent expressed in the Contract Documents.

§ 4.2.2021 The Construction Manager will receive and review requests for information from the Contractor, and forward each request for information to the Architect, with the Construction Manager's recommendation. The Architect will review and respond in writing to, through the Construction Manager, to requests for information about the Contract Documents. The Construction Manager's recommendation and the Architect's response to each request will be made in writing within any time limits agreed upon or otherwise with reasonable promptness. If appropriate, the Architect will prepare and issue supplemental Drawings and Specifications in response to the requests for information.

Article 5 Subcontractors

§ 5.1 Definitions

§ 5.1.1 A Subcontractor is a person or entity who has a direct contract with the Contractor to perform a portion of the Work at the site. The term "Subcontractor" is referred to throughout the Contract Documents as if singular in number and means a Subcontractor or an authorized representative of the Subcontractor. The term "Subcontractor" does not include other Multiple Prime Contractors or Separate Contractors or the subcontractors of other Multiple PrimeContractors or Separate Contractors.

§ 5.1.2 A Sub-subcontractor is a person or entity who has a direct or indirect contract with a Subcontractor to perform a portion of the Work at the site. The term "Sub-subcontractor" is referred to throughout the Contract Documents as if singular in number and means a Sub-subcontractor or an authorized representative of the Sub-subcontractor.

§ 5.2 Award of Subcontracts and Other Contracts for Portions of the Work

§ 5.2.1 Unless otherwise stated in the Contract Documents or the bidding requirements, the Contractor, as soon as practicable after award of the Contract, shall furnish in writing tonotify the Construction Manager, for review by the Owner, Construction Manager and Architect the names, of the persons or entities (proposed for each principal portion of the Work, including those who are to furnish materials or equipment fabricated to a special design) proposed for each principal portion. Within 14 days of receipt of the Work. Theinformation, the Construction Manager may reply within 14 days to notify the Contractor in writing stating (1) whether the Owner, the Construction Manager or the Architect (1) has reasonable objection to any such proposed person or entity or, (2) that the Construction Manager, Architect or Owner requires additional time for review. Failure of the Construction Manager, Owner, or Architect to replyprovide notice within the 14-day period shall constitute notice of no reasonable objection.

§ 5.2.2 The Contractor shall not contract with a proposed person or entity to whom the Owner, Construction Manager or Architect has made reasonable and timely objection. The Contractor shall not be required to contract with anyone to whom the Contractor has made reasonable objection.

§ 5.2.3 If the Owner, Construction Manager or Architect has reasonable objection to a person or entity proposed by the Contractor, the Contractor shall propose another to whom the Owner, Construction Manager or Architect has no reasonable objection. If the proposed but rejected Subcontractor was reasonably capable of performing the Work, the Contract Sum and Contract Time shall be increased or decreased by the difference, if any, occasioned by such change, and an appropriate Change Order shall be issued before commencement of the substitute Subcontractor's Work. However, no increase in the Contract Sum or Contract Time shall be allowed for such change unless the Contractor has acted promptly and responsively in submitting names as required.

§ 5.2.4 The Contractor shall not substitute a Subcontractor, person, or entity for one previously selected if the Owner, Construction Manager or Architect makes reasonable objection to such substitution.

§ 5.3 Subcontractual Relations
By appropriate written agreement~~, written where legally required for validity~~, the Contractor shall require each Subcontractor, to the extent of the Work to be performed by the Subcontractor, to be bound to the Contractor by terms of the Contract Documents, and to assume toward the Contractor all the obligations and responsibilities, including the responsibility for safety of the Subcontractor's Work, ~~which~~that the Contractor, by these Contract Documents, assumes toward the Owner, Construction Manager and Architect. Each subcontract agreement shall preserve and protect the rights of the Owner, Construction Manager and Architect under the Contract Documents with respect to the Work to be performed by the Subcontractor so that subcontracting thereof will not prejudice such rights, and shall allow to the Subcontractor, unless specifically provided otherwise in the subcontract agreement, the benefit of all rights, remedies, and redress against the Contractor that the Contractor, by the Contract Documents, has against the Owner. Where appropriate, the Contractor shall require each Subcontractor to enter into similar agreements with Sub-subcontractors. The Contractor shall make available to each proposed Subcontractor, prior to the execution of the subcontract agreement, copies of the Contract Documents to which the Subcontractor will be bound, and, upon written request of the Subcontractor, identify to the Subcontractor terms and conditions of the proposed subcontract agreement that may be at variance with the Contract Documents. Subcontractors will similarly make copies of applicable portions of such documents available to their respective proposed Sub-subcontractors.

§ 5.4 Contingent Assignment of Subcontracts
§ 5.4.1 Each subcontract agreement for a portion of the Work is assigned by the Contractor to the Owner, provided that

.1 assignment is effective only after termination of the Contract by the Owner for cause pursuant to Section 14.2 and only for those subcontract agreements that the Owner accepts by notifying the Subcontractor and Contractor~~ in writing~~; and

.2 assignment is subject to the prior rights of the surety, if any, obligated under bond relating to the Contract.

When the Owner accepts the assignment of a subcontract agreement, the Owner assumes the Contractor's rights and obligations under the subcontract.

§ 5.4.2 Upon such assignment, if the Work has been suspended for more than 30 days, the Subcontractor's compensation shall be equitably adjusted for increases in cost resulting from the suspension.

§ 5.4.3 Upon~~ such~~ assignment to the Owner under this Section 5.4, the Owner may further assign the subcontract to a successor Contractor or other entity. If the Owner assigns the subcontract to a successor Contractor or other entity, the Owner shall nevertheless remain legally responsible for all of the successor Contractor's obligations under the subcontract.

Article 6 Construction by Owner or by ~~Other~~ Separate Contractors

§ 6.1 Owner's Right to Perform Construction with Own Forces and to Award Other Contracts
§ 6.1.1 The Owner reserves the right to perform construction or operations related to the Project with the Owner's own forces, ~~which include persons or entities under separate contracts not administered by the Construction Manager,~~ and ~~to award other contracts in connection~~ with ~~other portions of the Project or other construction or operations on the site~~Separate Contractors retained under Conditions of the Contract ~~identical or~~ substantially similar to ~~these~~those of this Contract, including those ~~portions~~provisions of the Conditions of the Contract related to insurance and waiver of subrogation~~. If the Contractor claims that delay or additional cost is involved because of such action by the Owner, the Contractor shall make such Claim as provided in Article 15~~.

§ 6.1.2 When the Owner performs construction or operations with the Owner's own forces ~~including persons or entities under separate contracts not administered by the Construction Manager~~or Separate Contractors, the Owner shall provide for coordination of such forces and Separate Contractors with the Work of the Contractor, who shall cooperate with them.

§ 6.1.3 Unless otherwise provided in the Contract Documents, when the Owner performs construction or operations related to the Project with the Owner's own forces or with Separate Contractors, the Owner or its Separate Contractors shall ~~be deemed to be subject to~~have the same obligations and ~~to have the same~~ rights that ~~apply to~~ the Contractor has under the Conditions of the Contract, including, without excluding others, those stated in Article 3, this Article 6, and Articles 10, 11, and 12.

§ 6.2 Mutual Responsibility

§ 6.2.1 The Contractor shall afford the Owner's own forces, Separate Contractors, Construction Manager and other ~~Multiple Prime~~ Contractors reasonable opportunity for introduction and storage of their materials and equipment and performance of their activities, and shall connect and coordinate the Contractor's construction and operations with theirs as required by the Contract Documents.

§ 6.2.2 If part of the Contractor's Work depends for proper execution or results upon construction or operations by the Owner's own forces ~~or other Multiple Prime~~, Separate Contractors or other Contractors, the Contractor shall, prior to proceeding with that portion of the Work, promptly ~~report to~~notify the Construction Manager and Architect of apparent discrepancies or defects in ~~such other~~the construction or operations by the Owner or Separate Contractor or other Contractors that would render it unsuitable for ~~such~~ proper execution and results~~.~~ of the Contractor's Work. Failure of the Contractor ~~so~~to notify the Construction Manager and the Architect of apparent discrepancies or defects prior to ~~report~~proceeding with the Work shall constitute an acknowledgment that the Owner's ~~own forces~~or Separate Contractor's or other ~~Multiple Prime~~ Contractors' completed or partially completed construction is fit and proper to receive the Contractor's Work~~, except as to defects not then reasonably discoverable~~. The Contractor shall not be responsible for discrepancies or defects in the construction or operations by the Owner or Separate Contractors or other Contractors that are not apparent.

§ 6.2.3 The Contractor shall reimburse the Owner for costs the Owner incurs, including costs that are payable to a ~~separate contractor~~Separate Contractors or to other ~~Multiple Prime~~ Contractors, because of the Contractor's delays, improperly timed activities or defective construction. The Owner shall be responsible to the Contractor for costs the Contractor incurs because of delays, improperly timed activities, damage to the Work or defective construction by the Owner's own forces, Separate Contractors, or other ~~Multiple Prime~~ Contractors.

§ 6.2.4 The Contractor shall promptly remedy damage that the Contractor wrongfully causes to completed or partially completed construction, or to property of the Owner, ~~separate contractors, or other Multiple Prime~~Separate Contractors, or other Contractors as provided in Section 10.2.5.

§ 6.2.5 The Owner, Separate Contractors, and other ~~Multiple Prime~~ Contractors shall have the same responsibilities for cutting and patching as are described for the Contractor in Section 3.14.

§ 6.3 Owner's Right to Clean Up

If a dispute arises among the Contractor, ~~other Multiple Prime~~Separate Contractors, other Contractors, and the Owner as to the responsibility under their respective contracts for maintaining the premises and surrounding area free from waste materials and rubbish, the Owner may clean up and the Construction Manager, with notice to the Architect, will allocate the cost among those responsible.

Article 7 Changes in the Work

§ 7.1 General

§ 7.1.1 Changes in the Work may be accomplished after execution of the Contract, and without invalidating the Contract, by Change Order, Construction Change Directive or order for a minor change in the Work, subject to the limitations stated in this Article 7 and elsewhere in the Contract Documents.

§ 7.1.2 A Change Order shall be based upon agreement among the Owner, Construction Manager, Architect and Contractor~~; a~~. A Construction Change Directive requires agreement by the Owner, Construction Manager and Architect and may or may not be agreed to by the Contractor~~; an~~. An order for a minor change in the Work may be issued by the Architect alone.

§ 7.1.3 Changes in the Work shall be performed under applicable provisions of the Contract Documents~~, and the~~. The Contractor shall proceed promptly with changes in the Work, unless otherwise provided in the Change Order, Construction Change Directive, or order for a minor change in the Work.

§ 7.2 Change Orders
A Change Order is a written instrument prepared by the Construction Manager and signed by the Owner, Construction Manager, Architect, and Contractor, stating their agreement upon all of the following:

.1 The change in the Work;
.2 The amount of the adjustment, if any, in the Contract Sum; and
.3 The extent of the adjustment, if any, in the Contract Time.

§ 7.3 Construction Change Directives
§ 7.3.1 A Construction Change Directive is a written order prepared by the Construction Manager and signed by the Owner, Construction Manager and Architect, directing a change in the Work prior to agreement on adjustment, if any, in the Contract Sum or Contract Time, or both. The Owner may by Construction Change Directive, without invalidating the Contract, order changes in the Work within the general scope of the Contract consisting of additions, deletions, or other revisions, the Contract Sum and Contract Time being adjusted accordingly.

§ 7.3.2 A Construction Change Directive shall be used in the absence of total agreement on the terms of a Change Order.

§ 7.3.3 If the Construction Change Directive provides for an adjustment to the Contract Sum, the adjustment shall be based on one of the following methods:

.1 Mutual acceptance of a lump sum properly itemized and supported by sufficient substantiating data to permit evaluation;
.2 Unit prices stated in the Contract Documents or subsequently agreed upon;
.3 Cost to be determined in a manner agreed upon by the parties and a mutually acceptable fixed or percentage fee; or
.4 As provided in Section 7.3.~~7~~4.

Note: Former Section 7.4.3 is now Section 9.1.2.

~~**§ 7.3.4** If unit prices are stated in the Contract Documents or subsequently agreed upon, and if quantities originally contemplated are materially changed in a proposed Change Order or Construction Change Directive so that application of such unit prices to quantities of Work proposed will cause substantial inequity to the Owner or Contractor, the applicable unit prices shall be equitably adjusted.~~

§ 7.3.4 If the Contractor does not respond promptly or disagrees with the method for adjustment in the Contract Sum, the Construction Manager shall determine the adjustment on the basis of reasonable expenditures and savings of those performing the Work attributable to the change, including, in case of an increase in the Contract Sum, an amount for overhead and profit as set forth in the Agreement, or if no such amount is set forth in the Agreement, a reasonable amount. In such case, and also under Section 7.3.3.3, the Contractor shall keep and present, in such form as the Construction Manager may prescribe, an itemized accounting together with appropriate supporting data. Unless otherwise provided in the Contract Documents, costs for the purposes of this Section 7.3.4 shall be limited to the following:

.1 Costs of labor, including applicable payroll taxes, fringe benefits required by agreement or custom, workers' compensation insurance, and other employee costs approved by the Construction Manager and Architect;
.2 Costs of materials, supplies, and equipment, including cost of transportation, whether incorporated or consumed;
.3 Rental costs of machinery and equipment, exclusive of hand tools, whether rented from the Contractor or others;
.4 Costs of premiums for all bonds and insurance, permit fees, and sales, use, or similar taxes, directly related to the change; and
.5 Costs of supervision and field office personnel directly attributable to the change.

§ 7.3.5 If the Contractor disagrees with the adjustment in the Contract Time, the Contractor may make a Claim in accordance with applicable provisions of Article 15.

§ 7.3.56 Upon receipt of a Construction Change Directive, the Contractor shall promptly proceed with the change in the Work involved and advise the Construction Manager ~~and Architect~~ of the Contractor's agreement or disagreement with the method, if any, provided in the Construction Change Directive for determining the proposed adjustment in the Contract Sum or Contract Time.

§ 7.3.67 A Construction Change Directive signed by the Contractor indicates the Contractor's agreement therewith, including adjustment in Contract Sum and Contract Time or the method for determining them. Such agreement shall be effective immediately and shall be recorded as a Change Order.

> ***Note:*** *Former Section 7.3.7 is now Section 7.3.4*

~~**§ 7.3.7** If the Contractor does not respond promptly or disagrees with the method for adjustment in the Contract Sum, the Construction Manager shall determine the method and the adjustment on the basis of reasonable expenditures and savings of those performing the Work attributable to the change, including, in case of an increase in the Contract Sum, an amount for overhead and profit as set forth in the Agreement, or if no such amount is set forth in the Agreement, a reasonable amount. In such case, and also under Section 7.3.3.3, the Contractor shall keep and present, in such form as the Construction Manager may prescribe, an itemized accounting together with appropriate supporting data. Unless otherwise provided in the Contract Documents, costs for the purposes of this Section 7.3.7 shall be limited to the following:~~

- ~~**.1** Costs of labor, including social security, old age and unemployment insurance, fringe benefits required by agreement or custom, and workers compensation insurance;~~
- ~~**.2** Costs of materials, supplies and equipment, including cost of transportation, whether incorporated or consumed;~~
- ~~**.3** Rental costs of machinery and equipment, exclusive of hand tools, whether rented from the Contractor or others;~~
- ~~**.4** Costs of premiums for all bonds and insurance, permit fees, and sales, use or similar taxes related to the Work; and~~
- ~~**.5** Additional costs of supervision and field office personnel directly attributable to the change.~~

§ 7.3.8 The amount of credit to be allowed by the Contractor to the Owner for a deletion or change that results in a net decrease in the Contract Sum shall be actual net cost as confirmed by the Construction Manager and Architect. When both additions and credits covering related Work or substitutions are involved in a change, the allowance for overhead and profit shall be figured on the basis of net increase, if any, with respect to that change.

§ 7.3.9 Pending final determination of the total cost of a Construction Change Directive to the Owner, the Contractor may request payment for Work completed under the Construction Change Directive in Applications for Payment. The Construction Manager and Architect will make an interim determination for purposes of monthly certification for payment for those costs and certify for payment the amount that the Construction Manager and Architect determine to be reasonably justified. The interim determination of cost shall adjust the Contract Sum on the same basis as a Change Order, subject to the right of either party to disagree and assert a Claim in accordance with Article 15.

§ 7.3.10 When the Owner and Contractor agree with a determination made by the Construction Manager and Architect concerning the adjustments in the Contract Sum and Contract Time, or otherwise reach agreement upon the adjustments, such agreement shall be effective immediately and the Construction Manager shall prepare a Change Order. Change Orders may be issued for all or any part of a Construction Change Directive.

§ 7.4 Minor Changes in the Work

The Architect ~~has authority to~~ may order minor changes in the Work that are consistent with the intent of the Contract Documents and do not ~~involving~~involve an adjustment in the Contract Sum or an extension of the Contract Time ~~and not inconsistent with the intent of the Contract Documents. Such~~. The Architect's order for minor changes shall be in writing. If the Contractor believes that the proposed minor change in the Work will ~~be effected by written order issued through~~affect the Contract Sum or Contract Time, the Contractor shall notify the Construction Manager and shall ~~be binding on the Owner and Contractor.~~ not proceed to implement the change in the Work. If the Contractor performs the Work set forth in the Architect's order for a minor change without prior notice to the Construction Manager that such change will affect the Contract Sum or Contract Time, the Contractor waives any adjustment to the Contract Sum or extension of the Contract Time.

Article 8 Time

§ 8.1 Definitions
§ 8.1.1 Unless otherwise provided, Contract Time is the period of time, including authorized adjustments, allotted in the Contract Documents for Substantial Completion of the Work.

§ 8.1.2 The date of commencement of the Work is the date established in the Agreement.

§ 8.1.3 The date of Substantial Completion is the date certified by the Architect in accordance with Section 9.8.

§ 8.1.4 The term "day" as used in the Contract Documents shall mean calendar day unless otherwise specifically defined.

§ 8.2 Progress and Completion
§ 8.2.1 Time limits stated in the Contract Documents are of the essence of the Contract. By executing the Agreement, the Contractor confirms that the Contract Time is a reasonable period for performing the Work.

§ 8.2.2 The Contractor shall not knowingly, except by agreement or instruction of the Owner in writing, ~~prematurely~~ commence ~~operations on~~ the ~~site or elsewhere~~Work prior to the effective date of insurance required ~~by Article 11~~ to be furnished by the Contractor and Owner. ~~The date of commencement of the Work shall not be changed by the effective date of such insurance.~~

§ 8.2.3 The Contractor shall proceed expeditiously with adequate forces and shall achieve Substantial Completion within the Contract Time.

§ 8.3 Delays and Extensions of Time
§ 8.3.1 If the Contractor is delayed at any time in the commencement or progress of the Work by (1) an act or neglect of the Owner, ~~Owner's own forces,~~ Architect, Construction Manager, ~~Architect, any of the other Multiple Prime Contractors~~ or an employee of any of them, or of the Owner's own forces, Separate Contractors, or other Contractors; (2) by changes ordered in the Work~~, or~~; (3) by labor disputes, fire, unusual delay in deliveries, unavoidable casualties, adverse weather conditions documented in accordance with Section 15.1.6.2, or other causes beyond the Contractor's control; ~~or~~(4) by delay authorized by the Owner pending mediation and ~~arbitration, or~~binding dispute resolution; or (5) by other causes that the Contractor asserts and the Architect, based on the recommendation of the Construction Manager, determines ~~may~~ justify delay, then the Contract Time shall be extended ~~by Change Order~~ for such reasonable time as the Architect may determine.

§ 8.3.2 Claims relating to time shall be made in accordance with applicable provisions of Article 15.

§ 8.3.3 This Section 8.3 does not preclude recovery of damages for delay by either party under other provisions of the Contract Documents.

Article 9 Payments and Completion

§ 9.1 Contract Sum
§ 9.1.1 The Contract Sum is stated in the Agreement and, including authorized adjustments, is the total amount payable by the Owner to the Contractor for performance of the Work under the Contract Documents.

§ 9.1.2 If unit prices are stated in the Contract Documents or subsequently agreed upon, and if quantities originally contemplated are materially changed so that application of such unit prices to the actual quantities causes substantial inequity to the Owner or Contractor, the applicable unit prices shall be equitably adjusted.

§ 9.2 Schedule of Values
Where the Contract is based on a ~~Stipulated Sum~~stipulated sum or Guaranteed Maximum Price, the Contractor shall submit a schedule of values to the Construction Manager, before the first Application for Payment, ~~a schedule of values~~ allocating the entire Contract Sum to the various portions of the Work ~~and~~. The schedule of values shall be prepared in ~~such~~the form, and supported by ~~such~~the data to substantiate its accuracy ~~as~~, required by the Construction Manager and the Architect ~~may require~~. This schedule, unless objected to by the Construction Manager or Architect, shall be used as a basis for reviewing the Contractor's Applications for Payment. ~~In the event there is one~~

~~Contractor, the~~The Construction Manager shall forward to the Architect the Contractor's schedule of values. ~~If there are Multiple Prime Contractors responsible for performing different portions of the Project,~~Any changes to the schedule of values shall be submitted to the Construction Manager ~~shall forward the Multiple Prime Contractors' schedules of values only if requested~~and supported by such data to substantiate its accuracy as the Construction Manager and the Architect may require, and unless objected to by the Construction Manager or the Architect, shall be used as a basis for reviewing the Contractor's subsequent Applications for Payment.

§ 9.3 Applications for Payment

§ 9.3.1 At least fifteen days before the date established for each progress payment, the Contractor shall submit to the Construction Manager an itemized Application for Payment prepared in accordance with the schedule of values, if required under Section 9.2, for completed portions of the Work. ~~Such~~The application shall be notarized, if required, and supported by ~~such~~all data substantiating the Contractor's right to payment ~~as~~that the Owner, Construction Manager or Architect ~~may~~ require, such as copies of requisitions, and releases of waivers of lien from Subcontractors and ~~material~~ suppliers, and shall reflect retainage if provided for in the Contract Documents.

§ 9.3.1.1 As provided in Section 7.3.9, such applications may include requests for payment on account of changes in the Work that have been properly authorized by Construction Change Directives, or by interim determinations of the Construction Manager and Architect, but not yet included in Change Orders.

§ 9.3.1.2 Applications for Payment shall not include requests for payment for portions of the Work for which the Contractor does not intend to pay a Subcontractor or ~~material~~ supplier, unless such Work has been performed by others whom the Contractor intends to pay.

§ 9.3.2 Unless otherwise provided in the Contract Documents, payments shall be made on account of materials and equipment delivered and suitably stored at the site for subsequent incorporation in the Work. If approved in advance by the Owner, payment may similarly be made for materials and equipment suitably stored off the site at a location agreed upon in writing. Payment for materials and equipment stored on or off the site shall be conditioned upon compliance by the Contractor with procedures satisfactory to the Owner to establish the Owner's title to such materials and equipment or otherwise protect the Owner's interest, and shall include the costs of applicable insurance, storage, and transportation to the site, for such materials and equipment stored off the site.

§ 9.3.3 The Contractor warrants that title to all Work covered by an Application for Payment will pass to the Owner no later than the time of payment. The Contractor further warrants that upon submittal of an Application for Payment all Work for which Certificates for Payment have been previously issued and payments received from the Owner shall, to the best of the Contractor's knowledge, information, and belief, be free and clear of liens, claims, security interests, or encumbrances, in favor of the Contractor, Subcontractors, ~~material~~ suppliers, or other persons or entities ~~making a claim by reason of having~~that provided labor, materials and equipment relating to the Work.

§ 9.4 Certificates for Payment

§ 9.4.1 Where there is only one Contractor, the Construction Manager will, within seven days after the Construction Manager's receipt of the Contractor's Application for Payment, review the Application, certify the amount the Construction Manager determines is due the Contractor, and forward the Contractor's Application and Certificate for Payment to the Architect. Within seven days after the Architect receives the Contractor's Application for Payment from the Construction Manager, the Architect will either (1) issue to the Owner a Certificate for Payment, in the full amount of the Application for Payment, with a copy to the Construction Manager~~,~~; or (2) issue to the Owner a Certificate for Payment for such amount as the Architect determines is properly due, ~~or~~and notify the Construction Manager and Owner ~~in writing~~ of the Architect's reasons for withholding certification in ~~whole or in~~ part as provided in Section 9.5.1; or (3) withhold certification of the entire Application for Payment, and notify the Construction Manager and Owner of the Architect's reason for withholding certification in whole as provided in Section 9.5.1. The Construction Manager will promptly forward to the Contractor the Architect's notice of withholding certification.

§ 9.4.2 Where there ~~are Multiple Prime Contractors~~ is more than one Contractor performing- portions of the Project, the Construction Manager will, within seven days after the Construction Manager receives all of the ~~Multiple Prime~~ Contractors' Applications for Payment: (1) review the Applications and certify the amount the Construction Manager determines is due each of the ~~Multiple Prime~~ Contractors; (2) prepare a Summary of Contractors' Applications for Payment by combining information from each ~~Multiple Prime Contractors'~~Contractor's application with information from similar applications for progress payments from the other ~~Multiple Prime~~ Contractors; (3) prepare a Project Application and Certificate for Payment; (4) certify the amount the Construction Manager determines is due all ~~Multiple Prime~~ Contractors; and (5) forward the Summary of Contractors' Applications for Payment and Project Application and Certificate for Payment to the Architect.

§ 9.4.32.1 Within seven days after the Architect receives the Project Application and Project Certificate for Payment and the Summary of Contractors' Applications for Payment from the Construction Manager, the Architect will either (1) issue to the Owner a Project Certificate for Payment, with a copy to the Construction Manager,; or (2) issue to the Owner a Project Certificate for Payment for such amount as the Architect determines is properly due, ~~or~~and notify the Construction Manager and Owner ~~in writing~~ of the Architect's reasons for withholding certification in ~~whole or in~~ part as provided in Section 9.5.1; or (3) withhold certification of the entire Project Application for Payment, and notify the Construction Manager and Owner of the Architect's reason for withholding certification in whole as provided in Section 9.5.1. The Construction Manager will promptly forward the Architect's notice of withholding certification to the Contractors.

§ 9.4.43 The Construction Manager's certification of an -Application for Payment or, in the case of ~~Multiple Prime Contractors~~more than one Contractor, a Project Application and Certificate for Payment, shall be based upon the Construction Manager's evaluation of the Work and the ~~information provided as part of~~data in the Application or Applications for Payment. The Construction Manager's certification will constitute a representation that, to the best of the Construction Manager's knowledge, information, and belief, the Work has progressed to the point indicated ~~and~~, the quality of the Work is in accordance with the Contract Documents~~. The certification will also constitute a recommendation to the Architect and Owner~~, and that the Contractor ~~be paid~~is, or Contractors are, entitled to payment in the amount certified.

§ 9.4.54 The Architect's issuance of a Certificate for Payment or, in the case of ~~Multiple Prime Contractors~~more than one Contractor, Project Application and Certificate for Payment, shall be based upon the Architect's evaluation of the Work, the recommendation of the Construction Manager, and ~~information provided as part of~~data in the Application for Payment or Project Application for Payment. The Architect's certification will constitute a representation that, to the best of the Architect's knowledge, information, and belief, the Work has progressed to the point indicated, ~~that~~ the quality of the Work is in accordance with the Contract Documents, and that the Contractor is, or Contractors are, entitled to payment in the amount certified.

§ 9.4.65 The representations made pursuant to Sections 9.4.43 and 9.4.54 are subject to an evaluation of the Work for conformance with the Contract Documents upon Substantial Completion, to results of subsequent tests and inspections, to correction of minor deviations from the Contract Documents prior to completion, and to specific qualifications expressed by the Construction Manager or Architect.

§ 9.4.76 The issuance of a ~~separate~~ Certificate for Payment or a Project Certificate for Payment will not be a representation that the Construction Manager or Architect has (1) made exhaustive or continuous on-site inspections to check the quality or quantity of the Work,; (2) reviewed ~~the Contractor's~~ construction means, methods, techniques, sequences, or procedures,; (3) reviewed copies of requisitions received from Subcontractors and ~~material~~ suppliers and other data requested by the Owner to substantiate the Contractor's right to payment; or (4) made examination to ascertain how or for what purpose the Contractor has used money previously paid on account of the Contract Sum.

§ 9.5 Decisions to Withhold Certification

§ 9.5.1 The Construction Manager or Architect may withhold a Certificate for Payment or Project Certificate for Payment in whole or in part, to the extent reasonably necessary to protect the Owner, if in the Construction Manager's or Architect's opinion the representations to the Owner required by Section 9.4.43 and 9.4.54 cannot be made. If the Construction Manager or Architect is unable to certify payment in the amount of the Application, the Construction Manager will notify the Contractor and Owner as provided in Section 9.4.1 and 9.4.32. If the Contractor, Construction Manager and Architect cannot agree on a revised amount, the Architect will promptly issue a Certificate for Payment or a Project Certificate for Payment for the amount for which the Architect is able to make such representations to the Owner. The Construction Manager or Architect may also withhold a Certificate for Payment or, because of subsequently discovered evidence ~~or subsequent observations~~, may nullify the whole or a part of a Certificate for Payment or Project Certificate for Payment previously issued, to such extent as may be necessary in the Construction Manager's or Architect's opinion to protect the Owner from loss for which the Contractor is responsible, including loss resulting from the acts and omissions described in Section 3.3.2 because of

.1 defective Work not remedied;

.2 third party claims filed or reasonable evidence indicating probable filing of such claims, unless security acceptable to the Owner is provided by the Contractor;

.3 failure of the Contractor to make payments properly to Subcontractors or suppliers for labor, materials or equipment;
.4 reasonable evidence that the Work cannot be completed for the unpaid balance of the Contract Sum;
.5 damage to the Owner or a ~~separate contractor~~Separate Contractor or other Contractor;
.6 reasonable evidence that the Work will not be completed within the Contract Time, and that the unpaid balance would not be adequate to cover actual or liquidated damages for the anticipated delay; or
.7 repeated failure to carry out the Work in accordance with the Contract Documents.

§ 9.5.2 When ~~the above~~either party disputes the Architect's decision regarding a Certificate for Payment under Section 9.5.1, in whole or in part, that party may submit a Claim in accordance with Article 15.

§ 9.5.3 When the reasons for withholding certification are removed, certification will be made for amounts previously withheld.

§ 9.5.3~~4~~ If the Architect or Construction Manager withholds certification for payment under Section 9.5.1, the Owner may, at its sole option, issue joint checks to the Contractor and to any Subcontractor or ~~material or equipment suppliers~~supplier to whom the Contractor failed to make payment for Work properly performed or material or equipment suitably delivered. If the Owner makes payments by joint check, the Owner shall notify the Architect and the Construction Manager, and both will reflect such payment on the next Certificate for Payment.

§ 9.6 Progress Payments

§ 9.6.1 After the Architect has issued a Certificate for Payment or Project Certificate for Payment, the Owner shall make payment in the manner and within the time provided in the Contract Documents, and shall so notify the Construction Manager and Architect.

§ 9.6.2 The Contractor shall pay each Subcontractor, no later than seven days after receipt of payment from the Owner, the amount to which the Subcontractor is entitled, reflecting percentages actually retained from payments to the Contractor on account of the Subcontractor's portion of the Work. The Contractor shall, by appropriate agreement with each Subcontractor, require each Subcontractor to make payments to Sub-subcontractors in a similar manner.

§ 9.6.3 The Construction Manager will, on request, furnish to a Subcontractor, if practicable, information regarding percentages of completion or amounts applied for by the Contractor and action taken thereon by the Owner, Construction Manager and Architect on account of portions of the Work done by such Subcontractor.

§ 9.6.4 The Owner has the right to request written evidence from the Contractor that the Contractor has properly paid Subcontractors and ~~material and equipment~~ suppliers amounts paid by the Owner to the Contractor for subcontracted Work. If the Contractor fails to furnish such evidence within seven days, the Owner shall have the right to contact Subcontractors and suppliers to ascertain whether they have been properly paid. Neither the Owner, Construction Manager nor Architect shall have an obligation to pay, or to see to the payment of money to, a Subcontractor or supplier, except as may otherwise be required by law.

§ 9.6.5 ~~Contractor~~The Contractor's payments to ~~material and equipment~~ suppliers shall be treated in a manner similar to that provided in Sections 9.6.2, 9.6.3 and 9.6.4.

§ 9.6.6 A Certificate for Payment, a progress payment, or partial or entire use or occupancy of the Project by the Owner shall not constitute acceptance of Work not in accordance with the Contract Documents.

§ 9.6.7 Unless the Contractor provides the Owner with a payment bond in the full penal sum of the Contract Sum, payments received by the Contractor for Work properly performed by Subcontractors ~~and~~or provided by suppliers shall be held by the Contractor for those Subcontractors or suppliers who performed Work or furnished materials, or both, under contract with the Contractor for which payment was made by the Owner. Nothing contained herein shall require money to be placed in a separate account and not commingled with money of the Contractor, ~~shall~~ create any fiduciary liability or tort liability on the part of the Contractor for breach of trust, or ~~shall~~ entitle any person or entity to an award of punitive damages against the Contractor for breach of the requirements of this provision.

§ 9.6.8 Provided the Owner has fulfilled its payment obligations under the Contract Documents, the Contractor shall defend and indemnify the Owner from all loss, liability, damage or expense, including reasonable attorney's fees and litigation expenses, arising out of any lien claim or other claim for payment by any Subcontractor or supplier of any tier. Upon receipt of notice of a lien claim or other claim for payment, the Owner shall notify the Contractor. If approved by the applicable court, when required, the Contractor may substitute a surety bond for the property against which the lien or other claim for payment has been asserted.

§ 9.7 Failure of Payment
If the Construction Manager and Architect do not issue a Certificate for Payment or a Project Certificate for Payment, through no fault of the Contractor, within fourteen days after the Construction Manager's receipt of the Contractor's Application for Payment, or if the Owner does not pay the Contractor within seven days after the date established in the Contract Documents, the amount certified by the Construction Manager and Architect or awarded by binding dispute resolution, then the Contractor may, upon seven additional days' ~~written~~ notice to the Owner, Construction Manager and Architect, stop the Work until payment of the amount owing has been received. The Contract Time shall be extended appropriately and the Contract Sum shall be increased by the amount of the Contractor's reasonable costs of ~~shut-down~~shutdown, delay and start-up, plus interest as provided for in the Contract Documents.

§ 9.8 Substantial Completion
§ 9.8.1 Substantial Completion is the stage in the progress of the Work when the Work or designated portion thereof is sufficiently complete in accordance with the Contract Documents so the Owner can occupy or utilize the Work for its intended use.

§ 9.8.2 When the Contractor considers that the Work, or a portion thereof which the Owner agrees to accept separately, is substantially complete, the Contractor shall notify the Construction Manager, and the Contractor and Construction Manager shall jointly prepare and submit to the Architect a comprehensive list of items to be completed or corrected prior to final payment. Failure to include an item on such list does not alter the responsibility of the Contractor to complete all Work in accordance with the Contract Documents.

§ 9.8.3 Upon receipt of the list, the Architect, assisted by the Construction Manager, will make an inspection to determine whether the Work or designated portion thereof is substantially complete. If the Architect's inspection discloses any item, whether or not included on the list, which is not sufficiently complete in accordance with the ~~requirements of the~~ Contract Documents so that the Owner can occupy or utilize the Work or designated portion thereof for its intended use, the Contractor shall, before issuance of the Certificate of Substantial Completion, complete or correct such item upon notification by the Architect. In such case, the Contractor shall then submit a request for another inspection by the Architect, assisted by the Construction Manager, to determine Substantial Completion.

§ 9.8.4 When the Architect, assisted by the Construction Manager, determines that the Work of all of the Contractors, or designated portion thereof, is substantially complete, the Construction Manager will prepare, and the Construction Manager and Architect shall execute, a Certificate of Substantial Completion that shall establish the date of Substantial Completion~~, shall~~; establish responsibilities of the Owner and Contractor for security, maintenance, heat, utilities, damage to the Work and insurance~~,~~; and ~~shall~~ fix the time within which the Contractor shall finish all items on the list accompanying the Certificate. Warranties required by the Contract Documents shall commence on the date of Substantial Completion of the Work or designated portion thereof unless otherwise provided in the Certificate of Substantial Completion.

§ 9.8.5 The Certificate of Substantial Completion shall be submitted to the Owner and Contractor for their written acceptance of responsibilities assigned to them in ~~such~~the Certificate. Upon such acceptance, and consent of surety~~,~~ if any, the Owner shall make payment of retainage applying to ~~such~~the Work or designated portion thereof. Such payment shall be adjusted for Work that is incomplete or not in accordance with the requirements of the Contract Documents.

§ 9.9 Partial Occupancy or Use
§ 9.9.1 The Owner may occupy or use any completed or partially completed portion of the Work at any stage when such portion is designated by separate agreement with the Contractor, provided such occupancy or use is consented to by the insurer ~~as required under Section 11.3.1.5~~ and authorized by public authorities having jurisdiction over the Project. Such partial occupancy or use may commence whether or not the portion is substantially complete, provided the Owner and Contractor have accepted in writing the responsibilities assigned to each of them for payments, retainage if any, security, maintenance, heat, utilities, damage to the Work and insurance, and have agreed in writing concerning the period for correction of the Work and commencement of warranties required by the Contract

Documents. When the Contractor considers a portion substantially complete, the Contractor and Construction Manager shall jointly prepare and submit a list to the Architect as provided under Section 9.8.2. Consent of the Contractor to partial occupancy or use shall not be unreasonably withheld. The stage of the progress of the Work shall be determined by written agreement between the Owner and Contractor or, if no agreement is reached, by decision of the Architect after consultation with the Construction Manager.

§ 9.9.2 Immediately prior to such partial occupancy or use, the Owner, Construction Manager, Contractor, and Architect shall jointly inspect the area to be occupied or portion of the Work to be used in order to determine and record the condition of the Work.

§ 9.9.3 Unless otherwise agreed upon, partial occupancy or use of a portion or portions of the Work shall not constitute acceptance of Work not complying with the requirements of the Contract Documents.

§ 9.10 Final Completion and Final Payment

§ 9.10.1 Upon completion of the Work, the Contractor shall forward to the Construction Manager a ~~written~~ notice that the Work is ready for final inspection and acceptance, and shall also forward to the Construction Manager a final Contractor's Application for Payment. Upon receipt, the Construction Manager ~~will evaluate~~shall perform an inspection to confirm the completion of Work of the Contractor~~ and then forward the notice and Application, with the~~. The Construction ~~Manager's~~ Manager shall make recommendations~~,~~ to the Architect when the Work of all of the Contractors is ready for final inspection, and shall then forward the Contractors' notices and Application for Payment or Project Application for Payment, to the Architect, who will promptly make such inspection. When the Architect~~,~~ finds the Work acceptable under the Contract Documents and the Contract fully performed, the Construction Manager and Architect will promptly issue a final Certificate for Payment or Project Certificate for Payment stating that to the best of their knowledge, information and belief, and on the basis of their on-site visits and inspections, the Work has been completed in accordance with ~~terms and conditions of~~ the Contract Documents and that the entire balance found to be due the Contractor and noted in the final Certificate is due and payable. The Construction Manager's and Architect's final Certificate for Payment or Project Certificate for Payment will constitute a further representation that conditions listed in Section 9.10.2 as precedent to the Contractor's being entitled to final payment have been fulfilled.

§ 9.10.2 Neither final payment nor any remaining retained percentage shall become due until the Contractor submits to the Architect through the Construction Manager (1) an affidavit that payrolls, bills for materials and equipment, and other indebtedness connected with the Work for which the Owner or the Owner's property might be responsible or encumbered (less amounts withheld by Owner) have been paid or otherwise satisfied, (2) a certificate evidencing that insurance required by the Contract Documents to remain in force after final payment is currently in effect~~ and will not be canceled or allowed to expire until at least 30 days' prior written notice has been given to the Owner~~, (3) a written statement that the Contractor knows of no~~ substantial~~ reason that the insurance will not be renewable to cover the period required by the Contract Documents, (4) consent of surety, if any, to final payment ~~and (5~~(5) documentation of any special warranties, such as manufacturers' warranties or specific Subcontractor warranties, and (6), if required by the Owner, other data establishing payment or satisfaction of obligations, such as receipts~~,~~ and releases and waivers of liens, claims, security interests, or encumbrances arising out of the Contract, to the extent and in such form as may be designated by the Owner. If a Subcontractor refuses to furnish a release or waiver required by the Owner, the Contractor may furnish a bond satisfactory to the Owner to indemnify the Owner against such lien~~. If such lien~~, claim, security interest, or encumbrance. If a lien, claim, security interest, or encumbrance remains unsatisfied after payments are made, the Contractor shall refund to the Owner all money that the Owner may be compelled to pay in discharging ~~such lien~~the lien, claim, security interest, or encumbrance, including all costs and reasonable attorneys' fees.

§ 9.10.3 If, after Substantial Completion of the Work, final completion thereof is materially delayed through no fault of the Contractor or by issuance of Change Orders affecting final completion, and the Construction Manager and Architect so confirm, the Owner shall, upon application by the Contractor and certification by the Construction Manager and Architect, and without terminating the Contract, make payment of the balance due for that portion of the Work fully completed, corrected, and accepted. If the remaining balance for Work not fully completed or corrected is less than retainage stipulated in the Contract Documents, and if bonds have been furnished, the written consent of the surety to payment of the balance due for that portion of the Work fully completed and accepted shall be submitted by the Contractor to the Architect through the Construction Manager prior to certification of such payment. Such payment shall be made under terms and conditions governing final payment, except that it shall not constitute a waiver of Claims.

§ 9.10.4 The making of final payment shall constitute a waiver of Claims by the Owner except those arising from

- **.1** liens, Claims, security interests, or encumbrances arising out of the Contract and unsettled;
- **.2** failure of the Work to comply with the requirements of the Contract Documents; ~~or~~
- **.3** terms of special warranties required by the Contract Documents~~.~~; or
- **.4** audits performed by the Owner, if permitted by the Contract Documents, after final payment.

§ 9.10.5 Acceptance of final payment by the Contractor, a Subcontractor, or ~~material~~a supplier, shall constitute a waiver of claims by that payee except those previously made in writing and identified by that payee as unsettled at the time of final Application for Payment.

Article 10 Protection of Persons and Property

§ 10.1 Safety Precautions and Programs

The Contractor shall be responsible for initiating, maintaining, and supervising all safety precautions and programs in connection with the performance of the Contract. The Contractor shall submit the Contractor's safety program to the Construction Manager for review and coordination with the safety programs of other Contractors. The Construction Manager's responsibilities for review and coordination of safety programs shall not extend to direct control over or charge of the acts or omissions of the Contractors, Subcontractors, agents or employees of the Contractors or Subcontractors, or any other persons performing portions of the Work and not directly employed by the Construction Manager.

§ 10.2 Safety of Persons and Property

§ 10.2.1 The Contractor shall take reasonable precautions for safety of, and shall provide reasonable protection to prevent damage, injury, or loss to

- **.1** employees on the Work and other persons who may be affected thereby;
- **.2** the Work and materials and equipment to be incorporated therein, whether in storage on or off the site, under care, custody, or control of the Contractor, a Subcontractor, or ~~the Contractor's Subcontractors or~~a Sub-~~subcontractors;~~ subcontractor;
- **.3** other property at the site or adjacent thereto, such as trees, shrubs, lawns, walks, pavements, roadways, structures, and utilities not designated for removal, relocation, or replacement in the course of construction; and
- **.4** construction or operations by the Owner, Separate Contractors, or other Contractors.

§ 10.2.2 The Contractor shall comply with, and give notices required by applicable laws, statutes, ordinances, codes, rules and regulations, and lawful orders of public authorities, bearing on safety of persons or property or their protection from damage, injury, or loss.

§ 10.2.3 The Contractor shall implement, erect, and maintain, as required by existing conditions and performance of the Contract, reasonable safeguards for safety and protection, including posting danger signs and other warnings against hazards~~,~~; promulgating safety regulations; and notifying the owners and users of adjacent sites and utilities of the safeguards.

§ 10.2.4 When use or storage of explosives or other hazardous materials or equipment or unusual methods are necessary for execution of the Work, the Contractor shall exercise utmost care and carry on such activities under supervision of properly qualified personnel.

§ 10.2.5 The Contractor shall promptly remedy damage and loss (other than damage or loss insured under property insurance required by the Contract Documents) to property referred to in Sections 10.2.1.2, 10.2.1.3 and 10.2.1.4 caused in whole or in part by the Contractor, a Subcontractor, a Sub-subcontractor, or anyone directly or indirectly employed by any of them, or by anyone for whose acts they may be liable and for which the Contractor is responsible under Sections 10.2.1.2, 10.2.1.3 and 10.2.1.4~~, except damage or loss~~. The Contractor may make a Claim for the cost to remedy the damage or loss to the extent such damage or loss is attributable to acts or omissions of the Owner, Construction Manager or Architect or anyone directly or indirectly employed by any of them, or by anyone for whose acts any of them may be liable, and not attributable to the fault or negligence of the Contractor. The foregoing obligations of the Contractor are in addition to the Contractor's obligations under Section 3.18.

§ 10.2.6 The Contractor shall designate a responsible member of the Contractor's organization at the site whose duty shall be the prevention of accidents. This person shall be the Contractor's superintendent unless otherwise designated by the Contractor in writing to the Owner, Construction Manager and Architect.

§ 10.2.7 The Contractor shall not permit any part of the construction or site to be loaded so as to cause damage or create an unsafe condition.

§ 10.2.8 Injury or Damage to Person or Property
If either party suffers injury or damage to person or property because of an act or omission of the other party, or of others for whose acts such party is legally responsible, ~~written~~ notice of ~~such~~the injury or damage, whether or not insured, shall be given to the other party within a reasonable time not exceeding 21 days after discovery. The notice shall provide sufficient detail to enable the other party to investigate the matter.

§ 10.3 Hazardous Materials
§ 10.3.1 The Contractor is responsible for compliance with any requirements included in the Contract Documents regarding hazardous materials~~.~~ or substances. If the Contractor encounters a hazardous material or substance not addressed in the Contract Documents and if reasonable precautions will be inadequate to prevent foreseeable bodily injury or death to persons resulting from a material or substance, including but not limited to~~,~~ asbestos or polychlorinated biphenyl (PCB), encountered on the site by the Contractor, the Contractor shall, upon recognizing the condition, immediately stop Work in the affected area and ~~report the condition to~~notify the Owner, Construction Manager and Architect ~~in writing.~~ of the condition.

§ 10.3.2 Upon receipt of the Contractor's ~~written~~ notice, the Owner shall obtain the services of a licensed laboratory to verify ~~a~~the presence or absence of the material or substance reported by the Contractor and, in the event such material or substance is found to be present, to cause it to be rendered harmless. Unless otherwise required by the Contract Documents, the Owner shall furnish in writing to the Contractor, Construction Manager and Architect the names and qualifications of persons or entities who are to perform tests verifying the presence or absence of ~~such~~the material or substance or who are to perform the task of removal or safe containment of ~~such~~the material or substance. The Contractor, the Construction Manager and the Architect will promptly reply to the Owner in writing stating whether or not any of them has reasonable objection to the persons or entities proposed by the Owner. If the Contractor, Construction Manager or Architect has an objection to a person or entity proposed by the Owner, the Owner shall propose another to whom the Contractor, the Construction Manager and the Architect have no reasonable objection. When the material or substance has been rendered harmless, Work in the affected area shall ~~resumed~~resume upon written agreement of the Owner and Contractor. By Change Order, the Contract Time shall be extended appropriately and the Contract Sum shall be increased ~~in~~by the amount of the Contractor's reasonable additional costs of ~~shut-down~~shutdown, delay, and start-up.

§ 10.3.3 To the fullest extent permitted by law, the Owner shall indemnify and hold harmless the Contractor, Subcontractors, Construction Manager, Architect, their consultants, and agents and employees of any of them from and against claims, damages, losses, and expenses, including but not limited to attorneys' fees, arising out of or resulting from performance of the Work in the affected area if in fact the material or substance presents the risk of bodily injury or death as described in Section 10.3.1 and has not been rendered harmless, provided that such claim, damage, loss, or expense is attributable to bodily injury, sickness, disease or death, or to injury to or destruction of tangible property (other than the Work itself), except to the extent that such damage, loss, or expense is due to the fault or negligence of the party seeking indemnity.

§ 10.3.4 The Owner shall not be responsible under this Section 10.3 for hazardous materials or substances the Contractor brings to the site unless such materials or substances are required by the Contract Documents. The Owner shall be responsible for hazardous materials or substances required by the Contract Documents, except to the extent of the Contractor's fault or negligence in the use and handling of such materials or substances.

§ 10.3.5 The Contractor shall ~~indemnify~~reimburse the Owner for the cost and expense the Owner incurs (1) for remediation of ~~a material~~hazardous materials or ~~substance~~substances the Contractor brings to the site and negligently handles, or (2) where the Contractor fails to perform its obligations under Section 10.3.1, except to the extent that the cost and expense are due to the Owner's fault or negligence.

§ 10.3.6 If, without negligence on the part of the Contractor, the Contractor is held liable by a government agency for the cost of remediation of a hazardous material or substance solely by reason of performing Work as required by the Contract Documents, the Owner shall ~~indemnify~~reimburse the Contractor for all cost and expense thereby incurred.

§ 10.4 Emergencies
In an emergency affecting safety of persons or property, the Contractor shall act, at the Contractor's discretion, to prevent threatened damage, injury, or loss. Additional compensation or extension of time claimed by the Contractor on account of an emergency shall be determined as provided in Article 15 and Article 7.

Article 11 Insurance and Bonds

> ***Note:*** *Many of the terms and provisions previously located in Article 11 are relocated to a new Insurance and Bonds Exhibit, which is Exhibit A to AIA Document A132™–2019.*

§ 11.1 Contractor's ~~Liability~~ Insurance and Bonds
§ 11.1.1 The Contractor shall purchase and maintain insurance of the types and limits of liability, containing the endorsements, and subject to the terms and conditions, as described in the Agreement or elsewhere in the Contract Documents. The Contractor shall purchase and maintain the required insurance from an insurance company or insurance companies lawfully authorized to issue insurance in the jurisdiction where the Project is located. The Owner, Construction Manager and Construction Manager's consultants, and the Architect and Architect's consultants, shall be named as additional insureds under the Contractor's commercial general liability policy or as otherwise described in the Contract Documents.

~~**§ 11.1.1** The Contractor shall purchase from and maintain in a company or companies lawfully authorized to do business in the jurisdiction in which the Project is located such insurance as will protect the Contractor from claims set forth below which may arise out of or result from the Contractor's operations and completed operations under the Contract and for which the Contractor may be legally liable, whether such operations be by the Contractor or by a Subcontractor or by anyone directly or indirectly employed by any of them, or by anyone for whose acts any of them may be liable:~~

~~**.1** Claims under workers' compensation, disability benefit and other similar employee benefit acts which are applicable to the Work to be performed;~~

~~**.2** Claims for damages because of bodily injury, occupational sickness or disease, or death of the Contractor's employees;~~

~~**.3** Claims for damages because of bodily injury, sickness or disease, or death of any person other than the Contractor's employees;~~

~~**.4** Claims for damages insured by usual personal injury liability coverage;~~

~~**.5** Claims for damages, other than to the Work itself, because of injury to or destruction of tangible property, including loss of use resulting therefrom;~~

~~**.6** Claims for damages because of bodily injury, death of a person or property damage arising out of ownership, maintenance or use of a motor vehicle; and~~

~~**.7** Claims for bodily injury or property damage arising out of completed operations; and~~

~~**.8** Claims involving contractual liability insurance applicable to the Contractor's obligations under Section 3.18.~~

~~**§ 11.1.2** The insurance required by Section 11.1.1 shall be written for not less than limits of liability specified in the Contract Documents or required by law, whichever coverage is greater. Coverages, whether written on an occurrence or claims-made basis, shall be maintained without interruption from the date of commencement of the Work until the date of final payment and termination of any coverage required to be maintained after final payment and, with respect to the Contractor's completed operations coverage, until the expiration of the period for correction of Work or for such other period for maintenance of completed operations coverage as specified in the Contract Documents.~~

~~**§ 11.1.3** Certificates of insurance acceptable to the Owner shall be submitted to the Construction Manager for transmittal to the Owner with a copy to the Architect prior to commencement of the Work and thereafter upon renewal or replacement of each required policy of insurance. These certificates and the insurance policies required by this Section 11.1 shall contain a provision that coverages afforded under the policies will not be canceled or allowed to expire until at least 30 days' prior written notice has been given to the Owner. An additional certificate evidencing continuation of liability coverage, including coverage for completed operations, shall be submitted with~~

~~the final Application for Payment as required by Section 9.10.2 and thereafter upon renewal or replacement of such coverage until the expiration of the time required by Section 11.1.2. Information concerning reduction of coverage shall be furnished by the Contractor with reasonable promptness.~~

~~**§ 11.1.4** The Contractor shall cause the commercial liability coverage required by the Contract Documents to include (1) the Construction Manager, the Construction Manager's consultants, the Owner, the Architect, and the Architect's consultants as additional insureds for claims caused in whole or in part by the Contractor's negligent acts or omissions during the Contractor's operations; and (2) the Owner as an additional insured for claims caused in whole or in part by the Contractor's negligent acts or omissions during the Contractor's completed operations.~~

~~**§ 11.2 Owner's Liability Insurance**~~
~~The Owner shall be responsible for purchasing and maintaining the Owner's usual liability insurance.~~

~~**§ 11.3 Property Insurance**~~
~~**§ 11.3.1** Unless otherwise provided, the Owner shall purchase and maintain, in a company or companies lawfully authorized to do business in the jurisdiction in which the Project is located, property insurance written on a builder's risk "all risk" or equivalent policy form in the amount of the initial Contract Sum, plus value of subsequent Contract modifications and cost of materials supplied or installed by others, comprising total value for the entire Project at the site on a replacement cost basis without optional deductibles. Such property insurance shall be maintained, unless otherwise provided in the Contract Documents or otherwise agreed in writing by all persons and entities who are beneficiaries of such insurance, until final payment has been made as provided in Section 9.10 or until no person or entity other than the Owner has an insurable interest in the property required by this Section 11.3 to be covered, whichever is later. This insurance shall include interests of the Owner, the Contractor, Subcontractors and Sub-subcontractors in the Project.~~

~~**§ 11.3.1.1** Property insurance shall be on an "all-risk" or equivalent policy form and shall include, without limitation, insurance against the perils of fire (with extended coverage) and physical loss or damage including, without duplication of coverage, theft, vandalism, malicious mischief, collapse, earthquake, flood, windstorm, falsework, testing and startup, temporary buildings and debris removal including demolition occasioned by enforcement of any applicable legal requirements, and shall cover reasonable compensation for the Architect's, Contractor's, and Construction Manager's services and expenses required as a result of such insured loss.~~

~~**§ 11.3.1.2** If the Owner does not intend to purchase such property~~
§ 11.1.2 The Contractor shall provide surety bonds of the types, for such penal sums, and subject to such terms and conditions as required by the Contract Documents. The Contractor shall purchase and maintain the required bonds from a company or companies lawfully authorized to issue surety bonds in the jurisdiction where the Project is located.

§ 11.1.3 Upon the request of any person or entity appearing to be a potential beneficiary of bonds covering payment of obligations arising under the Contract, the Contractor shall promptly furnish a copy of the bonds or shall authorize a copy to be furnished.

§ 11.1.4 Notice of Cancellation or Expiration of Contractor's Required Insurance. Within three (3) business days of the date the Contractor becomes aware of an impending or actual cancellation or expiration of any insurance required by the Contract Documents, the Contractor shall provide notice directly to the Owner, and separately to the Construction Manager, of such impending or actual cancellation or expiration. Upon receipt of notice from the Contractor, the Owner shall, unless the lapse in coverage arises from an act or omission of the Owner, have the right to stop the Work until the lapse in coverage has been cured by the procurement of replacement coverage by the Contractor. The furnishing of notice by the Contractor shall not relieve the Contractor of any contractual obligation to provide any required coverage.

§ 11.2 Owner's Insurance
§ 11.2.1 The Owner shall purchase and maintain insurance of the types and limits of liability, containing the endorsements, and subject to the terms and conditions, as described in the Agreement or elsewhere in the Contract Documents. The Owner shall purchase and maintain the required insurance ~~required by the Contract and~~ from an insurance company or insurance companies lawfully authorized to issue insurance in the jurisdiction where the Project is located.

§ 11.2.2 Failure to Purchase Required Property Insurance. If the Owner fails to purchase and maintain the required property insurance, with all of the coverages and in the ~~amount~~amounts described ~~above~~in the Agreement or elsewhere in the Contract Documents, the Owner shall ~~so~~ inform both the Contractor and the Construction Manager, separately and in writing, prior to commencement of the Work. ~~The~~Upon receipt of notice from the Owner, the Contractor may ~~then effect~~delay commencement of the Work and may obtain insurance that will protect the interests of the Contractor, Subcontractors, and Sub-Subcontractors in the Work. When the failure to provide coverage has been cured or resolved, the Contract Sum and Contract Time shall be equitably adjusted. In the event the Owner fails to procure coverage, the Owner waives all rights against the Contractor, Subcontractors, and Sub-subcontractors ~~in the Work, and by appropriate Change Order the~~to the extent the loss to the Owner would have been covered by the insurance to have been procured by the Owner. The cost ~~thereof~~ of the insurance shall be charged to the Owner~~. If~~ by a Change Order. If the Owner does not provide written notice, and the Contractor is damaged by the failure or neglect of the Owner to purchase or maintain the required insurance ~~as described above, without so notifying the Contractor in writing, then~~, the Owner shall ~~bear~~reimburse the Contractor for all reasonable costs ~~properly~~and damages attributable thereto.

§ 11.2.3~~.1.3~~ ~~If the~~ **Notice of Cancellation or Expiration of Owner's Required Property Insurance.** Within three (3) business days of the date the Owner becomes aware of an impending or actual cancellation or expiration of any property insurance required by the Contract Documents, the Owner shall provide notice directly to the Contractor, and separately to the Construction Manager, of such impending or actual cancellation or expiration. Unless the lapse in coverage arises from an act or omission of the Contractor: (1) the Contractor, upon receipt of notice from the Owner, shall have the right to stop the Work until the lapse in coverage has been cured by the procurement of replacement coverage by either the Owner or the Contractor; (2) the Contract Time and Contract Sum shall be equitably adjusted; and (3) the Owner waives all rights against the Contractor, Subcontractors, and Sub-subcontractors to the extent any loss to the Owner would have been covered by the insurance had it not expired or been cancelled. If the Contractor purchases replacement coverage, the cost of the insurance shall be charged to the Owner by an appropriate Change Order. The furnishing of notice by the Owner shall not relieve the Owner of any contractual obligation to provide required insurance.

~~Within three (3) business days of the date the Owner becomes aware of an impending or actual cancellation or expiration of any property insurance requires deductibles, the Owner shall pay costs not covered because of such deductibles.~~

§ ~~11.3.1.4~~ ~~This property insurance shall cover portions of the Work stored off the site, and also portions of the Work in transit.~~

§ ~~11.3.1.5~~ ~~Partial occupancy or use in accordance with Section 9.9 shall not commence until the insurance company or companies providing property insurance have consented to such partial occupancy or use by endorsement or otherwise. The Owner and the Contractor shall take reasonable steps to obtain consent of the insurance company or companies and shall, without mutual written consent, take no action with respect to partial occupancy or use that would cause cancellation, lapse or reduction of insurance.~~

~~§ 11.3.2 Boiler and Machinery Insurance.~~ ~~The Owner shall purchase and maintain boiler and machinery insurance required by the Contract Documents or by law, which shall specifically cover such insured objects during installation and until final acceptance by the Owner; this insurance shall include interests of the Owner, Construction Manager, Contractor, Subcontractors and Sub-subcontractors in the Work, and the Owner and Contractor shall be named insureds.~~

~~§ 11.3.3 Loss of Use Insurance.~~ ~~The Owner, at the Owner's option, may purchase and maintain such insurance as will insure the Owner against loss of use of the Owner's property due to fire or other hazards, however caused. The Owner waives all rights of action against the Contractor for loss of use of the Owner's property, including consequential losses due to fire or other hazards however caused.~~

~~§ 11.3.4~~ ~~If the Contractor requests in writing that insurance for risks other than those described herein or other special causes of loss be included in the property insurance policy, the Owner shall, if possible, include such insurance, and the cost thereof shall be charged to the Contractor by appropriate Change Order.~~

§ 11.3 Waivers of Subrogation

§ 11.3.1 The Owner and Contractor waive all rights against (1) each other and any of their subcontractors, sub-

subcontractors, agents, and employees, each of the other; (2) the Construction Manager and Construction Manager's consultants; (3) the Architect and Architect's consultants; (4) other Contractors and any of their subcontractors, sub-subcontractors, agents, and employees; and (5) Separate Contractors, if any, and any of their subcontractors, sub-subcontractors, agents, and employees, for damages caused by fire, or other causes of loss, to the extent those losses are covered by property insurance required by the Agreement or other property insurance applicable to the Project, except such rights as they have to proceeds of such insurance. The Owner or Contractor, as appropriate, shall require similar written waivers in favor of the individuals and entities identified above from the Construction Manager, Construction Manager's consultants, Architect, Architect's consultants, other Contractors, Separate Contractors, subcontractors, and sub-subcontractors. The policies of insurance purchased and maintained by each person or entity agreeing to waive claims pursuant to this Section 11.3.1 shall not prohibit this waiver of subrogation. This waiver of subrogation shall be effective as to a person or entity (1) even though that person or entity would otherwise have a duty of indemnification, contractual or otherwise, (2) even though that person or entity did not pay the insurance premium directly or indirectly, or (3) whether or not the person or entity had an insurable interest in the damaged property.

§ 11.3.52 If during the Project construction period the Owner insures properties, real or personal or both, adjoiningat or adjacent to the site by property insurance under policies separate from those insuring the Project, or if after final payment property insurance is to be provided on the completed Project through a policy or policies other than those insuring the Project during the construction period, to the extent permissible by such policies, the Owner shall waivewaives all rights in accordance with the terms of Section- 11.3.71 for damages caused by fire or other causes of loss covered by this separate property insurance. All separate policies shall provide this waiver of subrogation by endorsement or otherwise.

§ 11.3.6 Before an exposure to loss may occur, the Owner shall file with the Contractor a copy of each policy that includes insurance coverages required by this Section 11.3. Each policy shall contain all generally applicable conditions, definitions, exclusions and endorsements related to this Project. Each policy shall contain a provision that the policy will not be canceled or allowed to expire, and that its limits will not be reduced, until at least 30 days' prior written notice has been given to the Contractor.

§ 11.3.7 Waivers of Subrogation. The Owner and Contractor waive all rights against (1) each other and any of their subcontractors, sub-subcontractors, agents and employees each of the other, and (2) the Construction Manager, Architect, Architect's consultants, separate contractors described in Article 6, if any, and any of their subcontractors, sub-subcontractors, agents and employees, for damages caused by fire or other causes of loss to the extent covered by property insurance obtained pursuant to this Section 11.3 or other property insurance applicable to the Work, except such rights as the Owner and Contractor may have to the proceeds of such insurance held by the Owner as fiduciary. The Owner or Contractor, as appropriate, shall require of the Construction Manager, Construction Manager's consultants, Architect, Architect's consultants, Owner's separate contractors described in Article 6, if any, and the subcontractors, sub-subcontractors, agents and employees of any of them, by appropriate agreements, written where legally required for validity, similar waivers each in favor of other parties enumerated herein. The policies shall provide such waivers of subrogation by endorsement or otherwise. A waiver of subrogation shall be effective as to a person or entity even though that person or entity would otherwise have a duty of indemnification, contractual or otherwise, did not pay the insurance premium directly or indirectly, and whether or not the person or entity had an insurable interest in the property damaged.

§ 11.3.8

§ 11.4 Loss of Use, Business Interruption, and Delay in Completion Insurance

The Owner, at the Owner's option, may purchase and maintain insurance that will protect the Owner against loss of use of the Owner's property, or the inability to conduct normal operations, due to fire or other causes of loss. The Owner waives all rights of action against the Contractor, Architect, and Construction Manager for loss of use of the Owner's property, due to fire or other hazards however caused.

§ 11.5 Adjustment and Settlement of Insured Loss

§ 11.5.1 A loss insured under the Owner's property insurance required by the Agreement shall be adjusted by the Owner as fiduciary and made payable to the Owner as fiduciary for the insureds, as their interests may appear, subject to requirements of any applicable mortgagee clause and of Section- 11.3.105.2. The Owner shall pay the Construction Manager, Architect and Contractor shall pay Subcontractors their just shares of insurance proceeds received by the ContractorOwner, and by appropriate agreements, written where legally required for validity, the Construction Manager, Architect and Contractor shall require Subcontractors to make payments to their Sub-subcontractorsconsultants and Subcontractors in similar manner.

~~§ 11.3.9~~ ~~If required in writing by a party in interest, the Owner as fiduciary shall, upon occurrence of an insured loss, give bond for proper performance of the Owner's duties. The cost of required bonds shall be charged against proceeds received as fiduciary. The Owner shall deposit in a separate account proceeds so received, which the Owner shall distribute in accordance with such agreement as the parties in interest may reach, or as determined in accordance with the method of binding dispute resolution selected in the Agreement between the Owner and Contractor. If after such loss no other special agreement is made and unless the Owner terminates the Contract for convenience, replacement of damaged property shall be performed by the Contractor after notification of a Change in the Work in accordance with Article 7.~~

~~§ 11.3.10~~ ~~The Owner as fiduciary shall have power to adjust and settle a loss with insurers unless one of the parties in interest shall object in writing within five days after occurrence of loss to the Owner's exercise of this power; if such objection is made, the dispute shall be resolved in the manner selected by the Owner and Contractor as the method of binding dispute resolution in the Agreement. If the Owner and Contractor have selected arbitration as the method of binding dispute resolution, the Owner as fiduciary shall make settlement with insurers or distribution of insurance proceeds in accordance with the direction of the arbitrators.~~

~~§ 11.4 Performance Bond and Payment Bond~~
~~§ 11.4.1~~ ~~The Owner shall have the right to require the Contractor to furnish bonds covering faithful performance of the Contract and payment of obligations arising thereunder as stipulated in bidding requirements or specifically required in the Contract Documents on the date of execution of the Contract.~~

~~§ 11.4.2~~ ~~Upon the request of any person or entity appearing to be a potential beneficiary of bonds covering payment of obligations arising under the Contract, the Contractor shall promptly furnish a copy of the bonds or shall authorize a copy to be furnished.~~

§ 11.5.2 Prior to settlement of an insured loss, the Owner shall notify the Contractor of the terms of the proposed settlement as well as the proposed allocation of the insurance proceeds. The Contractor shall have 14 days from receipt of notice to object to the proposed settlement or allocation of the proceeds. If the Contractor does not object, the Owner shall settle the loss and the Contractor shall be bound by the settlement and allocation. Upon receipt, the Owner shall deposit the insurance proceeds in a separate account and make the appropriate distributions. Thereafter, if no other agreement is made or the Owner does not terminate the Contract for convenience, the Owner and Contractor shall execute a Change Order for reconstruction of the damaged or destroyed Work in the amount allocated for that purpose. If the Contractor timely objects to either the terms of the proposed settlement or the allocation of the proceeds, the Owner may proceed to settle the insured loss, and any dispute between the Owner and Contractor arising out of the settlement or allocation of the proceeds shall be resolved pursuant to Article 15. Pending resolution of any dispute, the Owner may issue a Construction Change Directive for the reconstruction of the damaged or destroyed Work.

Article 12 Uncovering and Correction of Work

§ 12.1 Uncovering of Work
§ 12.1.1 If a portion of the Work is covered contrary to the Construction Manager's or Architect's request or to requirements specifically expressed in the Contract Documents, it must, if requested in writing by either, be uncovered for their ~~observation~~examination and be replaced at the Contractor's expense without change in the Contract Time.

§ 12.1.2 If a portion of the Work has been covered ~~which~~that the Construction Manager or Architect has not specifically requested to ~~observe~~examine prior to its being covered, the Construction Manager or Architect may request to see such Work and it shall be uncovered by the Contractor. If such Work is in accordance with the Contract Documents, ~~costs of uncovering and replacement~~the Contractor shall~~, by~~ be entitled to an equitable adjustment to the Contract Sum and Contract Time as may be appropriate~~ Change Order, be at the Owner's expense.~~. If such Work is not in accordance with the Contract Documents, ~~such~~the costs of uncovering the Work, and the cost of correction, shall be at the Contractor's expense~~ unless the condition was caused by the Owner or one of the other Contractors in which event the Owner shall be responsible for payment of such costs~~.

§ 12.2 Correction of Work
§ 12.2.1 Before ~~or After~~ Substantial Completion

The Contractor shall promptly correct Work rejected by the Construction Manager or Architect or failing to conform to the requirements of the Contract Documents, ~~whether~~ discovered before ~~or after~~ Substantial Completion, and whether or not fabricated, installed or completed. Costs of correcting such rejected Work, including additional testing and inspections, the cost of uncovering and replacement, and compensation for the Construction Manager's and Architect's services and expenses made necessary thereby, shall be at the Contractor's expense.

§ 12.2.2 After Substantial Completion

§ 12.2.2.1 In addition to the Contractor's obligations under Section 3.5, if, within one year after the date of Substantial Completion of the Work or designated portion thereof, or after the date for commencement of warranties established under Section 9.9.1, or by terms of ~~an~~any applicable special warranty required by the Contract Documents, any of the Work is found to be not in accordance with the requirements of the Contract Documents, the Contractor shall correct it promptly after receipt of ~~written~~ notice from the Owner to do so, unless the Owner has previously given the Contractor a written acceptance of such condition. The Owner shall give such notice promptly after discovery of the condition. During the one-year period for correction of Work, if the Owner fails to notify the Contractor and give the Contractor an opportunity to make the correction, the Owner waives the rights to require correction by the Contractor and to make a claim for breach of warranty. If the Contractor fails to correct nonconforming Work within a reasonable time during that period after receipt of notice from the Owner, Construction Manager or Architect, the Owner may correct it in accordance with Section 2.4~~5~~5.

§ 12.2.2.2 The one-year period for correction of Work shall be extended with respect to portions of Work first performed after Substantial Completion by the period of time between Substantial Completion and the actual completion of that portion of the Work.

§ 12.2.2.3 The one-year period for correction of Work shall not be extended by corrective Work performed by the Contractor pursuant to this Section 12.2.

§ 12.2.3 The Contractor shall remove from the site portions of the Work that are not in accordance with the requirements of the Contract Documents and are neither corrected by the Contractor nor accepted by the Owner.

§ 12.2.4 The Contractor shall bear the cost of correcting destroyed or damaged construction of the Owner, Separate Contractors, or other Contractors, whether completed or partially completed, ~~of the Owner or separate contractors or other Multiple Prime Contractors~~ caused by the Contractor's correction or removal of Work that is not in accordance with the requirements of the Contract Documents.

§ 12.2.5 Nothing contained in this Section 12.2 shall be construed to establish a period of limitation with respect to other obligations the Contractor has under the Contract Documents. Establishment of the one-year period for correction of Work as described in Section 12.2.2 relates only to the specific obligation of the Contractor to correct the Work, and has no relationship to the time within which the obligation to comply with the Contract Documents may be sought to be enforced, nor to the time within which proceedings may be commenced to establish the Contractor's liability with respect to the Contractor's obligations other than specifically to correct the Work.

§ 12.3 Acceptance of Nonconforming Work

If the Owner prefers to accept Work that is not in accordance with the requirements of the Contract Documents, the Owner may do so instead of requiring its removal and correction, in which case the Contract Sum will be reduced as appropriate and equitable. Such adjustment shall be effected whether or not final payment has been made.

Article 13 Miscellaneous Provisions

§ 13.1 Governing Law

The Contract shall be governed by the law of the place where the Project is located ~~except that, if~~excluding that jurisdiction's choice of law rules. If the parties have selected arbitration as the method of binding dispute resolution, the Federal Arbitration Act shall govern Section~~-~~ 15.4.

§ 13.2 Successors and Assigns

§ 13.2.1 The Owner and Contractor respectively bind themselves, their partners, successors, assigns, and legal representatives to covenants, agreements, and obligations contained in the Contract Documents. Except as provided in Section 13.2.2, neither party to the Contract shall assign the Contract as a whole without written consent of the other. If either party attempts to make ~~such~~ an assignment without such consent, that party shall nevertheless remain legally responsible for all obligations under the Contract.

§ 13.2.2 The Owner may, without consent of the Contractor, assign the Contract to a lender providing construction financing for the Project, if the lender assumes the Owner's rights and obligations under the Contract Documents. The Contractor shall execute all consents reasonably required to facilitate ~~such~~the assignment.

***Note:** Former Section 13.3 now appears at Section 1.6.*

~~§ 13.3 Written Notice~~
~~Written notice shall be deemed to have been duly served if delivered in person to the individual, to a member of the firm or entity or to an officer of the corporation for which it was intended; or if delivered at or sent by registered or certified mail or by courier service providing proof of delivery to, the last business address known to the party giving notice.~~

~~§ 13.4~~ § 13.3 Rights and Remedies
§ 13.43.1 Duties and obligations imposed by the Contract Documents and rights and remedies available thereunder shall be in addition to and not a limitation of duties, obligations, rights, and remedies otherwise imposed or available by law.

§ 13.43.2 No action or failure to act by the Owner, Construction Manager, Architect, or Contractor shall constitute a waiver of a right or duty afforded them under the Contract, nor shall such action or failure to act constitute approval of or acquiescence in a breach thereunder, except as may be specifically agreed upon in writing.

§ 13.54 Tests and Inspections
§ 13.54.1 Tests, inspections, and approvals of portions of the Work shall be made as required by the Contract Documents and by applicable laws, statutes, ordinances, codes, rules, and regulations or lawful orders of public authorities. Unless otherwise provided, the Contractor shall make arrangements for such tests, inspections, and approvals with an independent testing laboratory or entity acceptable to the Owner, or with the appropriate public authority, and shall bear all related costs of tests, inspections, and approvals. The Contractor shall give the Construction Manager and Architect timely notice of when and where tests and inspections are to be made so that the Construction Manager and Architect may be present for such procedures. The Owner shall bear costs of ~~(1)~~ tests, inspections, or approvals that do not become requirements until after bids are received or negotiations concluded~~;~~. The Owner shall directly arrange and ~~(2)~~pay for tests, inspections, or approvals where building codes or applicable laws or regulations ~~prohibit the Owner from delegating their cost to the Contractor~~so require.

§ 13.54.2 If the Construction Manager, Architect, Owner, or public authorities having jurisdiction determine that portions of the Work require additional testing, inspection, or approval not included under Section 13.54.1, the Construction Manager and Architect will, upon written authorization from the Owner, instruct the Contractor to make arrangements for such additional testing, inspection, or approval, by an entity acceptable to the Owner, and the Contractor shall give timely notice to the Construction Manager and Architect of when and where tests and inspections are to be made so that the Construction Manager and Architect may be present for such procedures. Such costs, except as provided in Section 13.54.3, shall be at the Owner's expense.

§ 13.54.3 If ~~such~~ procedures for testing, inspection, or approval under Sections 13.54.1 and 13.54.2 reveal failure of the portions of the Work to comply with requirements established by the Contract Documents, all costs made necessary by such failure, including those of repeated procedures and compensation for the Construction Manager's and Architect's services and expenses, shall be at the Contractor's expense.

§ 13.54.4 Required certificates of testing, inspection, or approval shall, unless otherwise required by the Contract Documents, be secured by the Contractor and promptly delivered to the Construction Manager for transmittal to the Architect.

§ 13.54.5 If the Construction Manager or Architect is to observe tests, inspections, or approvals required by the Contract Documents, the Construction Manager or Architect will do so promptly and, where practicable, at the normal place of testing.

§ 13.54.6 Tests or inspections conducted pursuant to the Contract Documents shall be made promptly to avoid unreasonable delay in the Work.

§ 13.65 Interest
Payments due and unpaid under the Contract Documents shall bear interest from the date payment is due at suchthe rate as the parties may agree upon in writing or, in the absence thereof, at the legal rate prevailing from time to time at the place where the Project is located.

***Note:** Former Section 13.7 is now Section 15.1.2.*

~~§ 13.7 Time Limits on Claims~~
~~The Owner and the Contractor shall commence all claims and causes of action, whether in contract, tort, breach of warranty or otherwise, against the other arising out of or related to the Contract in accordance with the requirements of the final dispute resolution method selected in the Agreement within the time period specified by applicable law, but in any case not more than 10 years after the date of Substantial Completion of the Work. The Owner and the Contractor waive all claims and causes of action not commenced in accordance with this Section 13.7~~

Article 14 Termination or Suspension of the Contract

§ 14.1 Termination by the Contractor
§ 14.1.1 The Contractor may terminate the Contract if the Work is stopped for a period of 30 consecutive days through no act or fault of the Contractor ~~or~~, a Subcontractor, a Sub-subcontractor ~~or~~, their agents or employees, or any other persons or entities performing portions of the Work ~~under direct or indirect contract with the Contractor~~, for any of the following reasons:

- **.1** Issuance of an order of a court or other public authority having jurisdiction that requires all Work to be stopped;
- **.2** An act of government, such as a declaration of national emergency, that requires all Work to be stopped;
- **.3** Because the Construction Manager has not certified or the Architect has not issued a Certificate for Payment and has not notified the Contractor of the reason for withholding certification as provided in Section 9.4, or because the Owner has not made payment on a Certificate for Payment within the time stated in the Contract Documents; or
- **.4** The Owner has failed to furnish to the Contractor ~~promptly, upon the Contractor's request,~~ reasonable evidence as required by Section 2.2~~.1~~.

§ 14.1.2 The Contractor may terminate the Contract if, through no act or fault of the Contractor ~~or~~, a Subcontractor, a Sub-subcontractor ~~or~~, their agents or employees, or any other persons or entities performing portions of the Work ~~under direct or indirect contract with the Contractor~~, repeated suspensions, delays, or interruptions of the entire Work by the Owner as described in Section 14.3, constitute in the aggregate more than 100 percent of the total number of days scheduled for completion, or 120 days in any 365-day period, whichever is less.

§ 14.1.3 If one of the reasons described in Section 14.1.1 or 14.1.2 exists, the Contractor may, upon seven days' ~~written~~ notice to the Owner, Construction Manager and Architect, terminate the Contract and recover from the Owner payment for Work executed ~~including~~, as well as reasonable overhead and profit~~,~~ on Work not executed, and costs incurred by reason of such termination~~, and damages~~.

§ 14.1.4 If the Work is stopped for a period of 60 consecutive days through no act or fault of the Contractor ~~or~~, a Subcontractor, a Sub-subcontractor, or their agents or employees, or any other persons performing portions of the Work ~~under contract with the Contractor~~ because the Owner has repeatedly failed to fulfill the Owner's obligations under the Contract Documents with respect to matters important to the progress of the Work, the Contractor may, upon seven additional days' ~~written~~ notice to the Owner, Construction Manager and Architect, terminate the Contract and recover from the Owner as provided in Section 14.1.3.

§ 14.2 Termination by the Owner for Cause
§ 14.2.1 The Owner may terminate the Contract if the Contractor

- **.1** repeatedly refuses or fails to supply enough properly skilled workers or proper materials;
- **.2** fails to make payment to Subcontractors ~~for materials~~ or ~~labor~~suppliers in accordance with the respective agreements between the Contractor and the Subcontractors or suppliers;
- **.3** repeatedly disregards applicable laws, statutes, ordinances, codes, rules and regulations, or lawful orders of a public authority; or
- **.4** otherwise is guilty of substantial breach of a provision of the Contract Documents.

§ 14.2.2 When any of the ~~above~~ reasons described in Section 14.2.1 exist~~, the Owner~~, after consultation with the Construction Manager, and upon certification by the ~~Initial Decision Maker~~Architect that sufficient cause exists to justify such action, the Owner may, without prejudice to any other rights or remedies of the Owner and after giving the Contractor and the Contractor's surety, if any, seven days' ~~written~~ notice, terminate employment of the Contractor and may, subject to any prior rights of the surety:

- **.1** Exclude the Contractor from the site and take possession of all materials, equipment, tools, and construction equipment and machinery thereon owned by the Contractor;
- **.2** Accept assignment of subcontracts pursuant to Section 5.4; and
- **.3** Finish the Work by whatever reasonable method the Owner may deem expedient. Upon written request of the Contractor, the Owner shall furnish to the Contractor a detailed accounting of the costs incurred by the Owner in finishing the Work.

§ 14.2.3 When the Owner terminates the Contract for one of the reasons stated in Section 14.2.1, the Contractor shall not be entitled to receive further payment until the Work is finished.

§ 14.2.4 If the unpaid balance of the Contract Sum exceeds costs of finishing the Work, including compensation for the Construction Manager's and Architect's services and expenses made necessary thereby, and other damages incurred by the Owner and not expressly waived, such excess shall be paid to the Contractor. If such costs and damages exceed the unpaid balance, the Contractor shall pay the difference to the Owner. The amount to be paid to the Contractor or Owner, as the case may be, shall, upon application, be certified by the Initial Decision Maker after consultation with the Construction Manager, and this obligation for payment shall survive termination of the Contract.

§ 14.3 Suspension by the Owner for Convenience

§ 14.3.1 The Owner may, without cause, order the Contractor in writing to suspend, delay or interrupt the Work, in whole or in part for such period of time as the Owner may determine.

§ 14.3.2 The Contract Sum and the Contract Time shall be adjusted for increases in the cost and time caused by suspension, delay, or interruption ~~as described in~~under Section 14.3.1. Adjustment of the Contract Sum shall include profit. No adjustment shall be made to the extent:

- **.1** that performance is, was, or would have been, so suspended, delayed, or interrupted, by another cause for which the Contractor is responsible; or
- **.2** that an equitable adjustment is made or denied under another provision of this Contract.

§ 14.4 Termination by the Owner for Convenience

§ 14.4.1 The Owner may, at any time, terminate the Contract for the Owner's convenience and without cause.

§ 14.4.2 Upon receipt of ~~written~~ notice from the Owner of such termination for the Owner's convenience, the Contractor shall

- **.1** cease operations as directed by the Owner in the notice;
- **.2** take actions necessary, or that the Owner may direct, for the protection and preservation of the Work; and
- **.3** except for Work directed to be performed prior to the effective date of termination stated in the notice, terminate all existing subcontracts and purchase orders and enter into no further subcontracts and purchase orders.

§ 14.4.3 In case of such termination for the Owner's convenience, the Owner shall pay the Contractor ~~shall be entitled to receive payment~~ for Work properly executed~~, and~~; costs incurred by reason of ~~such~~the termination, ~~along with reasonable overhead and profit on the Work not executed~~including costs attributable to termination of Subcontracts; and the termination fee, if any, set forth in the Agreement.

Article 15 Claims and Disputes

§ 15.1 Claims

§ 15.1.1 Definition

A Claim is a demand or assertion by one of the parties seeking, as a matter of right, payment of money, a change in the Contract Time, or other relief with respect to the terms of the Contract. The term "Claim" also includes other disputes and matters in question between the Owner and Contractor arising out of or relating to the Contract. The responsibility to substantiate Claims shall rest with the party making the Claim. This Section 15.1.1 does not require the Owner to file a Claim in order to impose liquidated damages in accordance with the Contract Documents.

§ 15.1.2 ~~Notice of~~ Time Limits on Claims~~.~~
The Owner and Contractor shall commence all Claims and causes of action against the other and arising out of or related to the Contract, whether in contract, tort, breach of warranty or otherwise, in accordance with the requirements of the binding dispute resolution method selected in the Agreement and within the period specified by applicable law, but in any case not more than 10 years after the date of Substantial Completion of the Work. The Owner and Contractor waive all Claims and causes of action not commenced in accordance with this Section 15.1.2.

§ 15.1.3 Notice of Claims
§ 15.1.3.1 Claims by either the Owner or Contractor ~~must~~, where the condition giving rise to the Claim is first discovered prior to expiration of the period for correction of the Work set forth in Section 12.2.2, shall be initiated by ~~written~~ notice to the other party and to the Initial Decision Maker with a copy sent to the Construction Manager and Architect, if the ~~Construction Manager and or~~ Architect is not serving as the Initial Decision Maker. Claims by either party ~~must~~under this Section 15.1.3.1 shall be initiated within 21 days after occurrence of the event giving rise to such Claim or within 21 days after the claimant first recognizes the condition giving rise to the Claim, whichever is later.

§ 15.1.3.2 Claims by either the Owner or Contractor, where the condition giving rise to the Claim is first discovered after expiration of the period for correction of the Work set forth in Section 12.2.2, shall be initiated by notice to the other party. In such event, no decision by the Initial Decision Maker is required.

~~§ 15.1.3 Continuing Contract Performance.~~
§ 15.1.4 Continuing Contract Performance
§ 15.1.4.1 Pending final resolution of a Claim, except as otherwise agreed in writing or as provided in Section 9.7 and Article 14, the Contractor shall proceed diligently with performance of the Contract and the Owner shall continue to make payments in accordance with the Contract Documents. ~~The Construction Manager will prepare Change Orders and the Architect will issue a Certificate for Payment or Project Certificate for Payment in accordance with the decisions of the Initial Decision Maker.~~

§ 15.1.4.2 The Contract Sum and Contract Time shall be adjusted in accordance with the Initial Decision Maker's decision, subject to the right of either party to proceed in accordance with this Article 15. The Architect will issue Certificates for Payment in accordance with the decision of the Initial Decision Maker.

§ 15.1.5 Claims for Additional Cost. If the Contractor wishes to make a Claim for an increase in the Contract Sum, ~~written~~ notice as provided ~~herein~~in Section 15.1.3 shall be given before proceeding to execute the portion of the Work that is the subject of the Claim. Prior notice is not required for Claims relating to an emergency endangering life or property arising under Section 10.~~3.~~4.

§ 15.1.~~5~~6 Claims for Additional Time
§ 15.1.~~5~~6.1 If the Contractor wishes to make a Claim for an increase in the Contract Time, ~~written~~ notice as provided ~~herein~~in Section 15.1.3 shall be given. The Contractor's Claim shall include an estimate of cost and of probable effect of delay on progress of the Work. In the case of a continuing delay only one Claim is necessary.

§ 15.1.~~5~~6.2 If adverse weather conditions are the basis for a Claim for additional time, such Claim shall be documented by data substantiating that weather conditions were abnormal for the period of time, could not have been reasonably anticipated and had an adverse effect on the scheduled construction.

§ 15.1.~~6~~7 Waiver of Claims for Consequential Damages. The Contractor and Owner waive Claims against each other for consequential damages arising out of or relating to this Contract. This mutual waiver includes

- **.1** damages incurred by the Owner for rental expenses, for losses of use, income, profit, financing, business and reputation, and for loss of management or employee productivity or of the services of such persons; and
- **.2** damages incurred by the Contractor for principal office expenses including the compensation of personnel stationed there, for losses of financing, business and reputation, and for loss of profit except anticipated profit arising directly from the Work.

This mutual waiver is applicable, without limitation, to all consequential damages due to either party's termination in accordance with Article 14. Nothing contained in this Section 15.1.~~6~~7 shall be deemed to preclude ~~an award~~assessment of liquidated damages, when applicable, in accordance with the requirements of the Contract Documents.

§ 15.2 Initial Decision

§ 15.2.1 Claims, excluding those where the condition giving rise to the Claim is first discovered after expiration of the period for correction of the Work set forth in Section 12.2.2 or arising under Sections 10.3, 10.4, ~~11.3.9,~~ and 11.~~3.10~~5, shall be referred to the Initial Decision Maker for initial decision. The Architect will serve as the Initial Decision Maker, unless otherwise indicated in the Agreement. Except for those Claims excluded by this Section 15.2.1, an initial decision shall be required as a condition precedent to mediation of any Claim~~ arising prior to the date final payment is due, unless~~. If an initial decision has not been rendered within 30 days ~~have passed~~ after the Claim has been referred to the Initial Decision Maker~~ with no~~, the party asserting the Claim may demand mediation and binding dispute resolution without a decision having been rendered. Unless the Initial Decision Maker and all affected parties agree, the Initial Decision Maker will not decide disputes between the Contractor and persons or entities other than the Owner.

§ 15.2.2 The Initial Decision Maker will review Claims and within ten days of the receipt of a Claim take one or more of the following actions: (1) request additional supporting data from the claimant or a response with supporting data from the other party, (2) reject the Claim in whole or in part, (3) approve the Claim, (4) suggest a compromise, or (5) advise the parties that the Initial Decision Maker is unable to resolve the Claim if the Initial Decision Maker lacks sufficient information to evaluate the merits of the Claim or if the Initial Decision Maker concludes that, in the Initial Decision Maker's sole discretion, it would be inappropriate for the Initial Decision Maker to resolve the Claim.

§ 15.2.3 In evaluating Claims, the Initial Decision Maker may, but shall not be obligated to, consult with or seek information from either party or from persons with special knowledge or expertise who may assist the Initial Decision Maker in rendering a decision. The Initial Decision Maker may request the Owner to authorize retention of such persons at the Owner's expense.

§ 15.2.4 If the Initial Decision Maker requests a party to provide a response to a Claim or to furnish additional supporting data, such party shall respond, within ten days after receipt of ~~such~~the request, and shall either (1) provide a response on the requested supporting data, (2) advise the Initial Decision Maker when the response or supporting data will be furnished, or (3) advise the Initial Decision Maker that no supporting data will be furnished. Upon receipt of the response or supporting data, if any, the Initial Decision Maker will either reject or approve the Claim in whole or in part.

§ 15.2.5 The Initial Decision Maker will render an initial decision approving or rejecting the Claim, or indicating that the Initial Decision Maker is unable to resolve the Claim. This initial decision shall (1) be in writing; (2) state the reasons therefor; and (3) notify the parties~~ and~~, the ~~Architect and~~ Construction Manager, and the Architect, if the Architect~~ or Construction Manager~~ is not serving as the Initial Decision Maker, of any change in the Contract Sum or Contract Time or both. The initial decision shall be final and binding on the parties but subject to mediation and, if the parties fail to resolve their dispute through mediation, to binding dispute resolution.

§ 15.2.6 Either party may file for mediation of an initial decision at any time, subject to the terms of Section 15.2.6.1.

§ 15.2.6.1 Either party may, within 30 days from the date of receipt of an initial decision, demand in writing that the other party file for mediation~~ within 60 days of the initial decision.~~. If such a demand is made and the party receiving the demand fails to file for mediation within ~~the time required~~30 days of receipt thereof, then both parties waive their rights to mediate or pursue binding dispute resolution proceedings with respect to the initial decision.

§ 15.2.7 In the event of a Claim against the Contractor, the Owner may, but is not obligated to, notify the surety, if any, of the nature and amount of the Claim. If the Claim relates to a possibility of a Contractor's default, the Owner may, but is not obligated to, notify the surety and request the surety's assistance in resolving the controversy.

§ 15.2.8 If a Claim relates to or is the subject of a mechanic's lien, the party asserting such Claim may proceed in accordance with applicable law to comply with the lien notice or filing deadlines.

§ 15.3 Mediation
§ 15.3.1 Claims, disputes, or other matters in controversy arising out of or related to the Contract, except those waived as provided for in Sections 9.10.4, 9.10.5, and 15.1.~~6~~7, shall be subject to mediation as a condition precedent to binding dispute resolution.

§ 15.3.2 The parties shall endeavor to resolve their Claims by mediation which, unless the parties mutually agree otherwise, shall be administered by the American Arbitration Association in accordance with its Construction Industry Mediation Procedures in effect on the date of the Agreement. A request for mediation shall be made in writing, delivered to the other party to the Contract, and filed with the person or entity administering the mediation. The request may be made concurrently with the filing of binding dispute resolution proceedings but, in such event, mediation shall proceed in advance of binding dispute resolution proceedings, which shall be stayed pending mediation for a period of 60 days from the date of filing, unless stayed for a longer period by agreement of the parties or court order. If an arbitration is stayed pursuant to this Section 15.3.2, the parties may nonetheless proceed to the selection of the arbitrator(s) and agree upon a schedule for later proceedings.

§ 15.3.3 Either party may, within 30 days from the date that mediation has been concluded without resolution of the dispute or 60 days after mediation has been demanded without resolution of the dispute, demand in writing that the other party file for binding dispute resolution. If such a demand is made and the party receiving the demand fails to file for binding dispute resolution within 60 days after receipt thereof, then both parties waive their rights to binding dispute resolution proceedings with respect to the initial decision.

§ 15.3.4 The parties shall share the mediator's fee and any filing fees equally. The mediation shall be held in the place where the Project is located, unless another location is mutually agreed upon. Agreements reached in mediation shall be enforceable as settlement agreements in any court having jurisdiction thereof.

§ 15.4 Arbitration
§ 15.4.1 If the parties have selected arbitration as the method for binding dispute resolution in the Agreement, any Claim subject to, but not resolved by, mediation shall be subject to arbitration which, unless the parties mutually agree otherwise, shall be administered by the American Arbitration Association in accordance with its Construction Industry Arbitration Rules in effect on the date of the Agreement. The Arbitration shall be conducted in the place where the Project is located, unless another location is mutually agreed upon. A demand for arbitration shall be made in writing, delivered to the other party to the Contract, and filed with the person or entity administering the arbitration. The party filing a notice of demand for arbitration must assert in the demand all Claims then known to that party on which arbitration is permitted to be demanded.

§ 15.4.1.1 A demand for arbitration shall be made no earlier than concurrently with the filing of a request for mediation, but in no event shall it be made after the date when the institution of legal or equitable proceedings based on the Claim would be barred by the applicable statute of limitations. For statute of limitations purposes, receipt of a written demand for arbitration by the person or entity administering the arbitration shall constitute the institution of legal or equitable proceedings based on the Claim.

§ 15.4.2 The award rendered by the arbitrator or arbitrators shall be final, and judgment may be entered upon it in accordance with applicable law in any court having jurisdiction thereof.

§ 15.4.3 The foregoing agreement to arbitrate and other agreements to arbitrate with an additional person or entity duly consented to by parties to the Agreement, shall be specifically enforceable under applicable law in any court having jurisdiction thereof.

§ 15.4.4 Consolidation or Joinder
~~§ 15.4.4.1 Either party, at its sole discretion,~~
§ 15.4.4.1 Subject to the rules of the American Arbitration Association or other applicable arbitration rules, either party may consolidate an arbitration conducted under this Agreement with any other arbitration to which it is a party provided that (1) the arbitration agreement governing the other arbitration permits consolidation, (2) the arbitrations to be consolidated substantially involve common questions of law or fact, and (3) the arbitrations employ materially similar procedural rules and methods for selecting arbitrator(s).

~~§ 15.4.4.2 Either party, at its sole discretion,~~
§ 15.4.4.2 Subject to the rules of the American Arbitration Association or other applicable arbitration rules, either party may include by joinder persons or entities substantially involved in a common question of law or fact whose

presence is required if complete relief is to be accorded in arbitration, provided that the party sought to be joined consents in writing to such joinder. Consent to arbitration involving an additional person or entity shall not constitute consent to arbitration of any claim, dispute or other matter in question not described in the written consent.

§ 15.4.4.3 The Owner and Contractor grant to any person or entity made a party to an arbitration conducted under this Section 15.4, whether by joinder or consolidation, the same rights of joinder and consolidation as <u>those of</u> the Owner and Contractor under this Agreement.